# SEWING SEAMS for
# TECH PACKS

A Visual Guide To Produce Clothing

# Sewing Seams for Tech Packs
A Visual Guide to Produce Clothing.

copyright © 2020 by ABC Seams® Pty. Ltd.

All rights reserved. No parts of this book may be reproduced, stored in a retrieval system or transmitted, in any format or by any means, electronic, mechanical, photo-copying, recording or otherwise, without the written permission of the author.

Edited and published by Memory Card Publishing.

ABC Seams® is a Trade Mark
P.O. Box 30 (4886), QLD, Australia

ISBN: 978-0-6482734-4-8

Discover more at www.abcseams.com

If you have any feedback,
please do not hesitate to contact us to
*feedback@abcseams.com*

Thank you.

*ABC Seams® Team*

To all those *Teachers* who open up the doors of creativity and push us to make our dreams a reality.

... thank you!

# CONTENTS

### Part One
## INTRODUCTION

Preface . . . . . . . 12
Introduction . . . . . . . 14
How to Read This Book . . . . . . . 18
Icons & Abbreviations . . . . . . . 23

### Part Two
## TECHNICAL SPECIFICATIONS

Tops . . . . . . . 26
Dress . . . . . . . 66
Bottoms . . . . . . . 72
Outerwear . . . . . . . 120
Underwear . . . . . . . 166
Swimwear . . . . . . . 174

### Part Three
## REFERENCE MATERIAL

Sample Tech Pack . . . . . . . 185
Thread Selection Guide . . . . . . . 200
Seams Anatomy . . . . . . . 201
Stitch Types . . . . . . . 202
Topstitch Types . . . . . . . 204
Index . . . . . . . 206

## CREDITS

Selected Bibliography . . . . . . . 218
Acknowledgments . . . . . . . 221

Sewing Seams for Tech Packs

# TECHNICAL
# SPECIFICATIONS
### Part Two

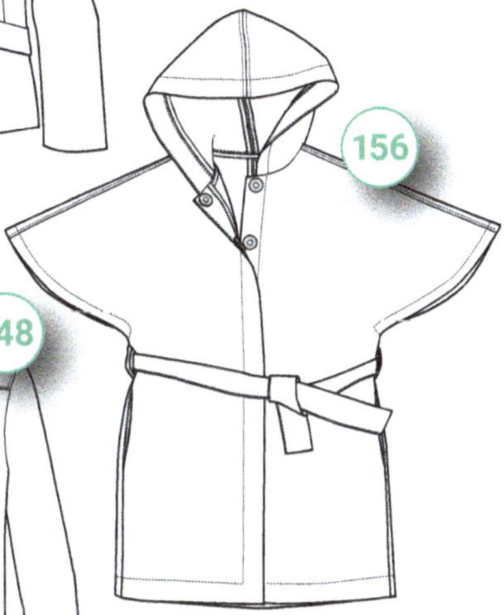

## Part One

# INTRODUCTION

# PREFACE

*The hall is quiet and the lights are dim. I can hear murmurs in the distance. The models wait in line behind the curtain. The colorful make-up enhances their clothing. Everything is ready.*
*The music starts, anxiety overtake us. The show begins...*

For many fashion designers, this is one of the most desired moments in their life.
After months of hard work, this is the time when all the effort makes sense. All the struggle is worth it. The glory after the battle.
But all that happened before was essential to get to this point.

We, humans, are creative beings. It is part of our nature.
Every meaningful moment of our progress happened after sharing our ideas. So then, we worked together to make them real.

But sometimes, good ideas do not see the light. They die even before being born, and you might wonder -*Why does this happen?*
Many people have asked this question before.
Interesting studies explain there is no one single answer. But one of the most common problems is the lack of communication.

**A brilliant idea is not enough. We must also know how to communicate it.**

## Fashion Design

Developing garments successfully is a big challenge.
Many (most?) fashion designers do not go on to become the sort of designers who write technical specifications properly. They get overwhelmed just with the idea of doing this job, and that is a genuine problem. The information is confusing or unhelpful. Then, issues

that could be avoided from the beginning arise, and this consumes time and energy. Even worse, suppliers do not take them seriously, refusing to work with them.

**Nowadays, giving a clear message is a required skill for any designer that wishes to succeed in the competitive textile industry.**
So then, *how should fashion designers explain their ideas?*

If you are a student or a new designer in the industry, the fear of writing technical information is often seen at an early stage; either during the design process, or at the moment of explaining your designs, the terror appears, and your mind goes blank. Much of that fear arises because your task is unclear.

Writing accurate specifications is a skill with principles and methods that have little to do with fashion and trends. We know it's difficult to find information that deals with this. That's the first reason this book was born.

**There is no single way to make technical specifications.**
The information in this book are not prescriptive rules. This material is much broader than just explaining how to make spec sheets. Instead, take it as a tool that encourages you to develop textile products and to push your creativity.

What you'll find here is our best advice from years of working with tech packs and with factories all around the world.
At ABC Seams we work with designers, technicians, patternmakers, manufacturers and teachers. Thanks to their experience and professionalism, we've learned invaluable insights, helping us to tune communication within the textile industry.

We are delighted to share all this knowledge to help you to get your ideas to the next level. Our goal is to smooth your way to develop your designs successfully. So, let's get to it...

# INTRODUCTION

Creating garments is a complex process that involves several steps. Depending on the size of your brand, the type of clothing, where you produce your garments, and how you sell them, these steps may slightly vary. But in any case, you will communicate your ideas through tech packs.

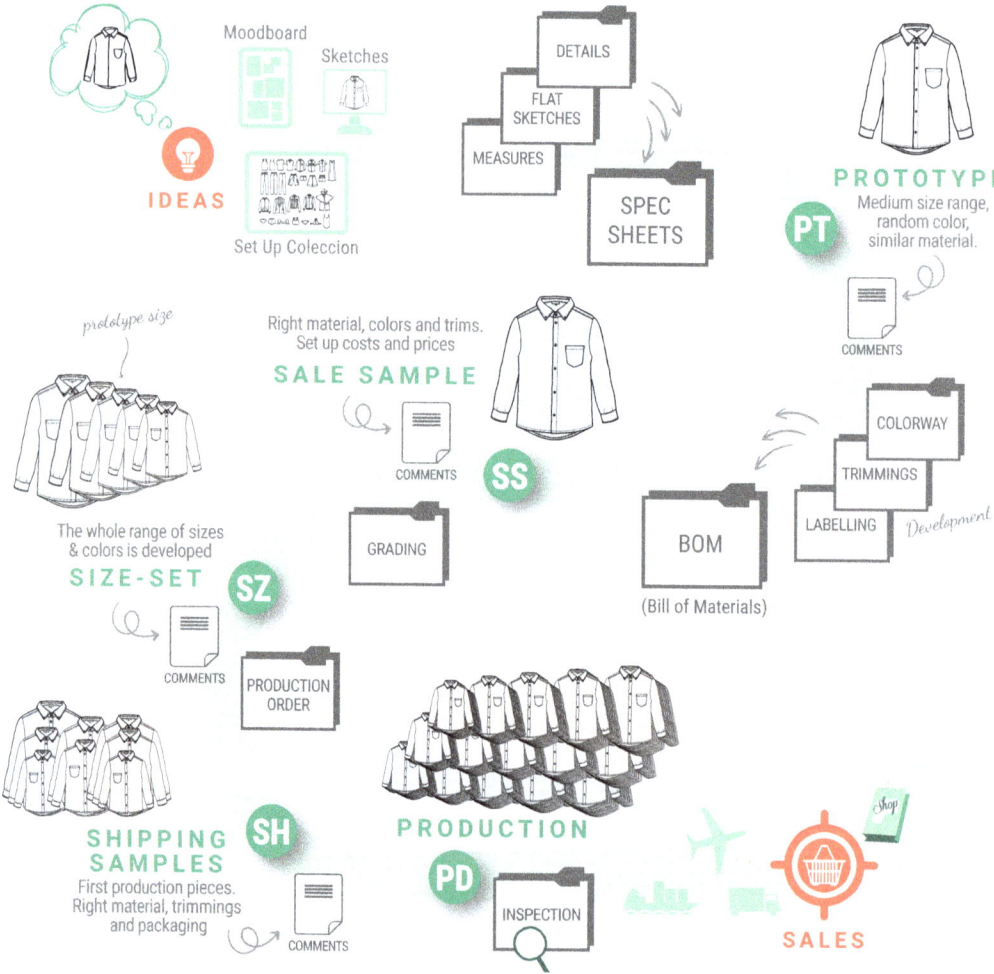

## Tech Packs

Let's start from the beginning... *what is a Tech Pack?*

A *Tech Pack* is a document that provides all the information that a factory needs to develop your product correctly.
This document is made up of several sheets, including construction details, finishes, measurements, materials, colors, trimmings, etc.

The goal of working with tech packs is to minimize mistakes (and time!). This information will help you to keep your design on track and control the quality at all times during the process. You will use it from the prototype to the end of the production.

Another significant benefit is that you keep, not only your work, but the factory work organized as well. This makes the manufacturing process easier. The better you make your tech pack, the better your manufacturer works. Furthermore, you will create a stronger bond with them. They will love working with you.

## Spec Sheets

**The *spec sheets* are those pages where you specify the construction of the garment.** Here you explain those details that require special attention. Also, it is where you set out the type of seams and the required stitches.

These sheets are the files that you deliver to develop the prototype at the very beginning of the process, together with the measurement chart.

**Designing details is not only an aesthetic issue.** The right choice of construction and finishes are fundamental to both good design and commercial success.

This book will support you to make informed construction choices based upon a technical understanding. We encourage you to use it as a reference guide when explaining any design to your internal and external teams.

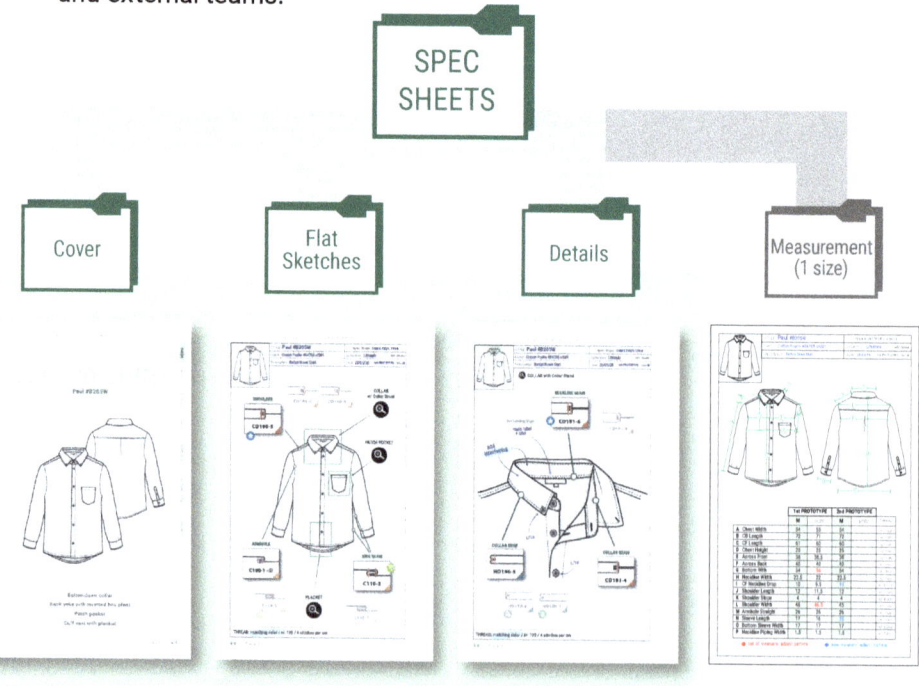

THIS BOOK

These 27 pieces of clothing make up a collection of basic styles. We designed this collection to be used as a starting point when writing your spec sheets.

As a result, you will be more confident. Your colleagues will trust your decisions. You will also improve the quality of your products by making better decisions.

# HOW TO READ

This book has three parts:

- Part One: Introduction
- Part Two: Technical Specifications
- Part Three: Reference Material

In *Part Two* you find the explanation of all the garments covered in the collection. This is the focus and purpose of this book.

Every garment is described from a general perspective to specific details: this includes an inspirational mood, a description, front and back, flat sketches, details, seams, finishes, and some additional notes.

## Sewing Seams

Each part of the garment is pointed out and represented by a seam and its code.

This seam could be a construction, a finish or a detail, depending on its placement and purpose.

We talk in detail about this in our previous book 101 Sewing Seams.

- **Constructions:** those seams that join, at least, two layers of fabric
- **Finishes:** placed at the edge of the fabric
- **Details:** includes seams that give volume, embellish the product or overlap layers of fabrics

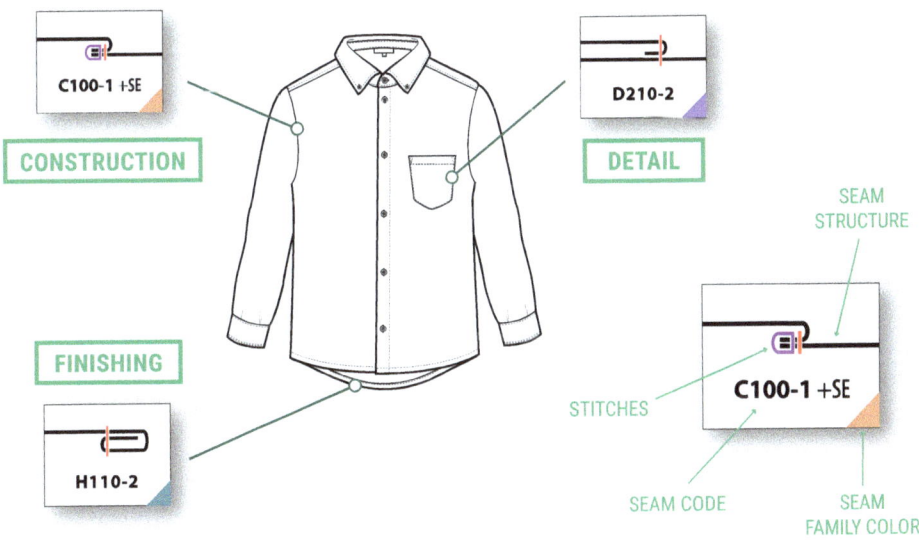

## Seams Options

**There is more than one single way to sew a garment.**

For this reason, in some cases, we have included *options* to the selected seam: these options are either stitching variations or a different type of seam. In any case, the suggested seams are very close alternatives to the selected one.

Also, to help you decide which option better suits your project, you will see icons that refer to the main property of the seam (see page 23).

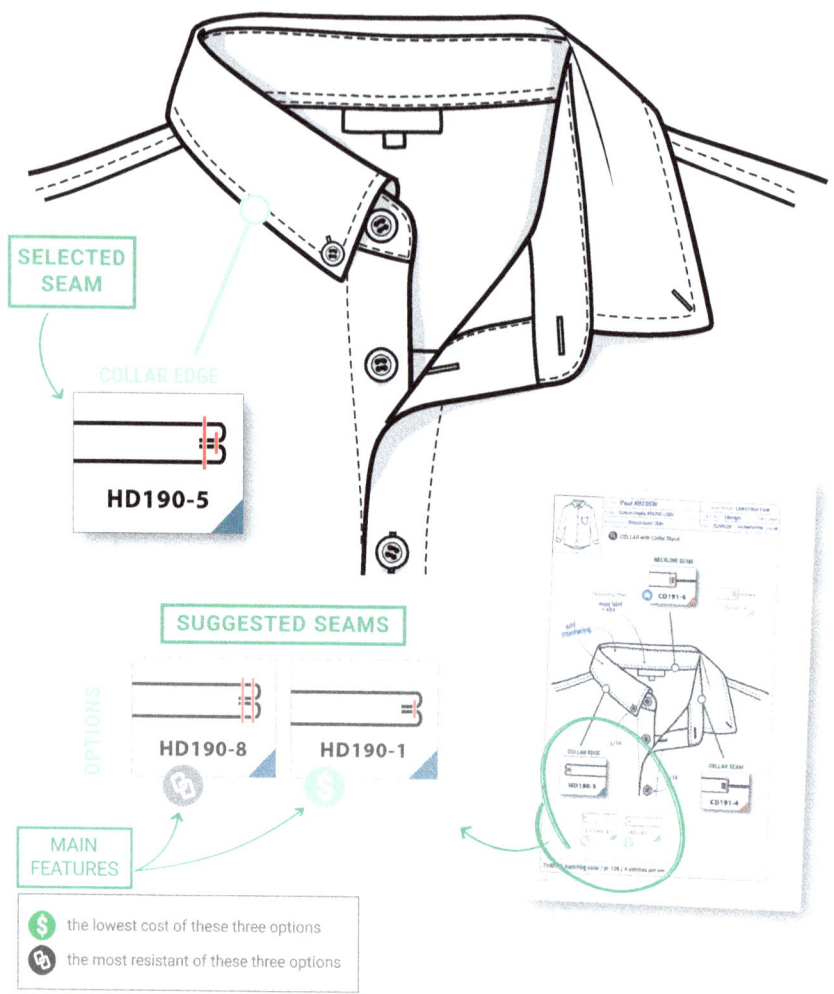

## Additional Notes

Consider adding additional notes that will help the manufacturer to fully understand your ideas:

• *Materials and colors*: if you combine colors and fabrics, or some parts of the garment are lined or need interfacing, please point this out.

• *Measurements*: when the seam width is standard you do not need to add any notes. But wider and narrower seams need to be specified.

• *Trimmings:* naming the trimmings also helps to avoid mistakes. In this sheet you do not usually add information such as codes and materials (that information is going to be on the Colorways and BOM Sheets). But you do need to convey the size of the buttons, the color/quality of the thread and an elastic band width.

• *Quick notes:* as reinforcement of your drawing, you can name some details such as pleats, gathering, bartacks, etc.

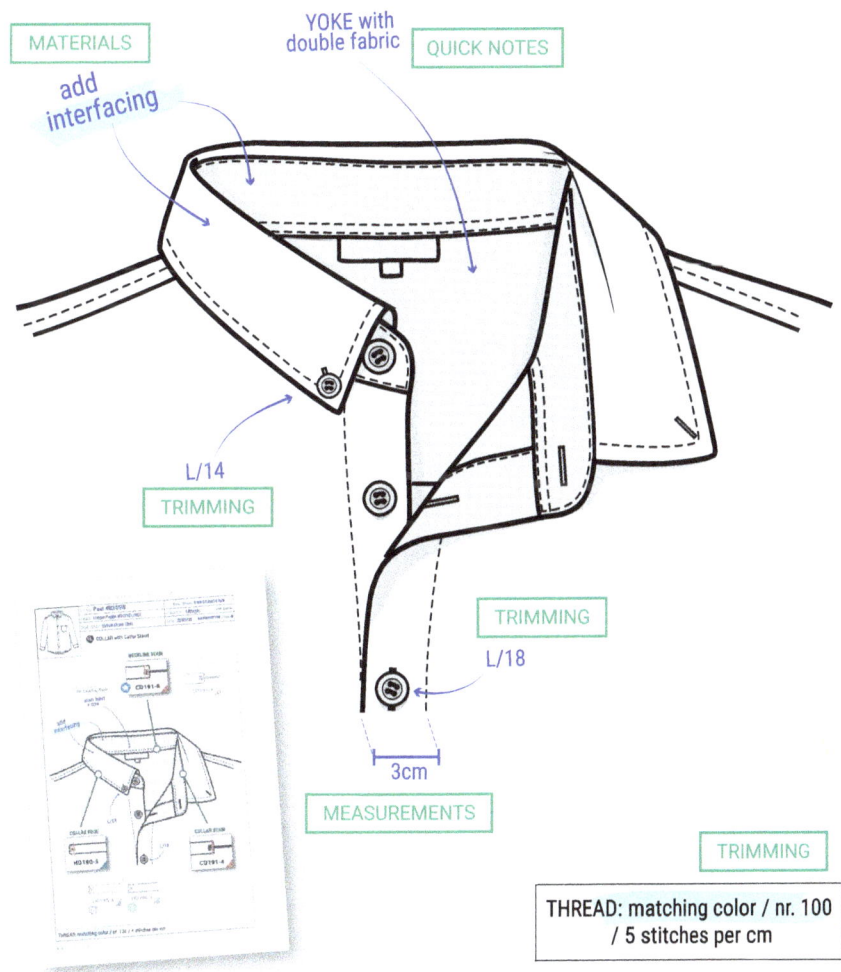

# ICONS

## Seams Properties

- 🔆 knit/stretch
- 💠 denim
- ⭐ the most used
- the most resistant
- ⦿ the most versatile
- 🌿 the most durable
- the thickest

- ✳️ the most flexible
- 💎 the finest
- 💲 the lowest cost
- 💲💲💲 the highest cost
- 💗 the favorite
- 🔍 detail (call out)

# ABBREVIATIONS

## Seams

**BS** Blind Stitch
**CS** Cover Stitch
**FS** Flatlock Stitch
**OS** Overlock Stitch
**RS** Roll Stitch
**SA** Seam Allowance
**SE** Serged Edge

## General

**CB** Center Back
**CF** Center Front
**PD** Production
**PP** Pre-Production
**PT** Prototype
**RS** Right Side
**SS** Sale Sample
**SZ** Size Set
**WS** Wrong Side

Part Two

# TECHNICAL
# SPECIFICATIONS

19-4007 TCX

13-4108 TCX

18-4436 TCX

EVERYDAY

# TANK TOP

Jane #B201K

Scoop neckline

Sleeveless

Jersey fabric

Binded edges

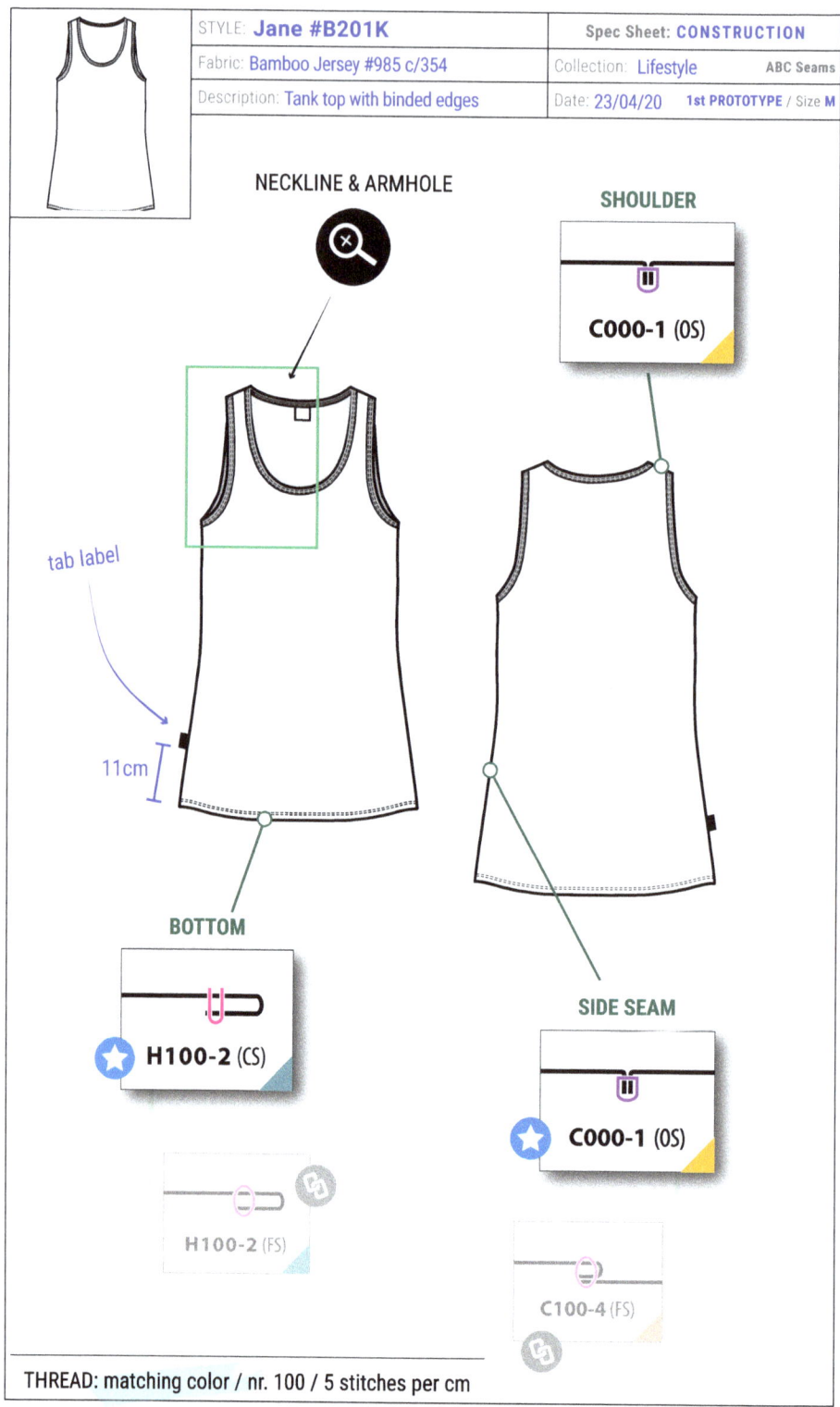

Technical Specifications: Tank Top

| STYLE: **Jane #B201K** | Spec Sheet: **CONSTRUCTION** | |
|---|---|---|
| Fabric: **Bamboo Jersey #985 c/354** | Collection: **Lifestyle** | ABC Seams |
| Description: **Tank top with binded edges** | Date: **23/04/20** **1st PROTOTYPE** / Size **M** | |

**NECKLINE and ARMHOLE** 🔍

(ideal for thick fabrics)
**less bulk**

H201-9 (CS)   H200-1 (CHS)   H200-3 (FS)

★ H200-3 (CS)

fabric 2

CB

main label
See Labelling Sheet

1cm

1cm

THREAD: matching color / nr. 100 / 5 stitches per cm

TOPS · DRESS · PANTS · SKIRTS · OUTERWEAR · UNDERWEAR · SWIMWEAR

second skin

11-0601 TCX
16-1356 TCX
19-4007 TCX

# CAMISOLE
### Mary #B202K

Shoulder straps

V-Neckline

Binded edges

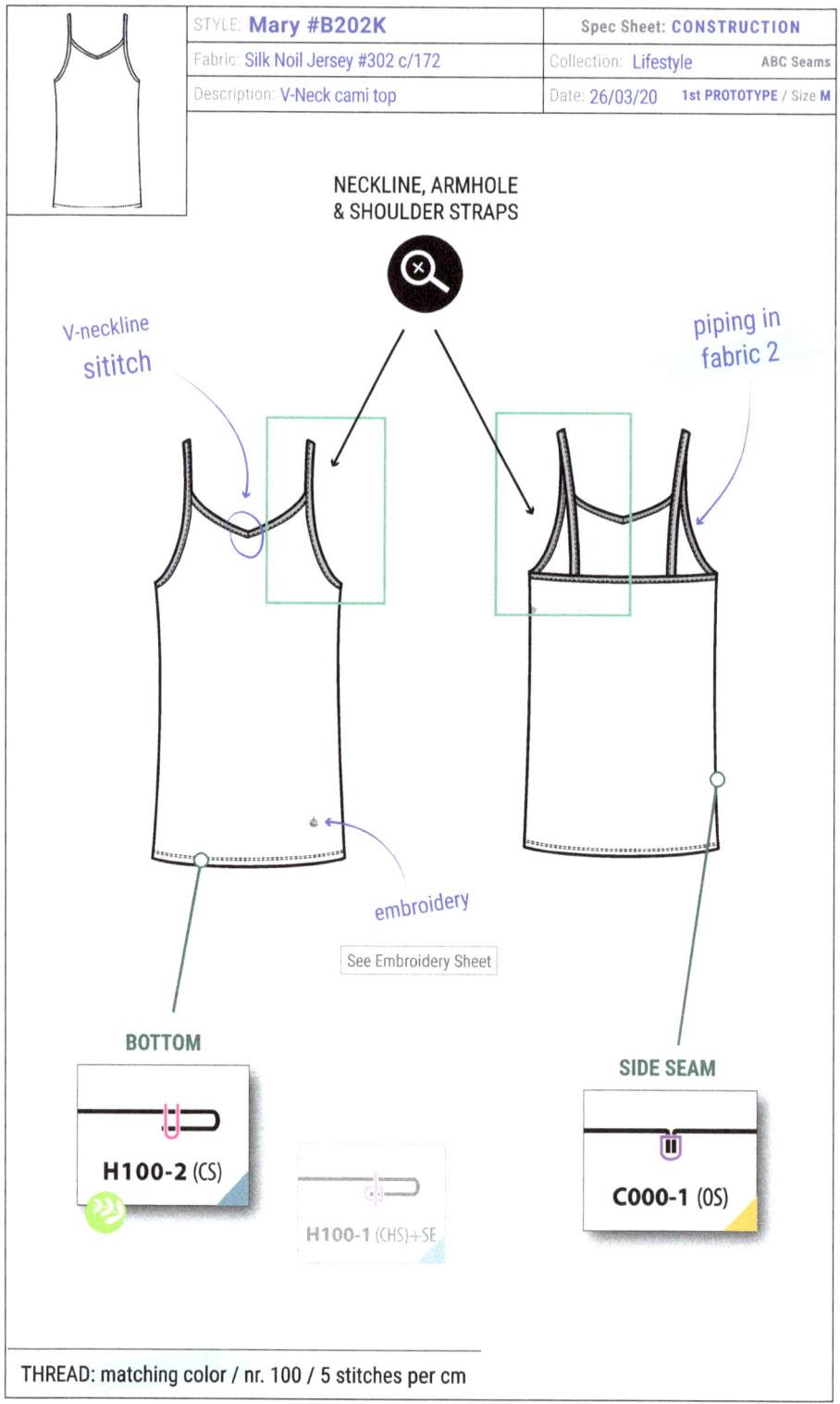

## Technical Specifications: Camisole

| STYLE: **Mary #B202K** | Spec Sheet: **CONSTRUCTION** | |
|---|---|---|
| Fabric: Silk Noil Jersey #302 c/172 | Collection: Lifestyle | ABC Seams |
| Description: V-Neck cami top | Date: 26/03/20 | **1st PROTOTYPE** / Size **M** |

**TOPS** · DRESS · PANTS · SKIRTS · OUTERWEAR · UNDERWEAR · SWIMWEAR

### NECKLINE, ARMHOLE and SHOULDER STRAPS

**SHOULDER STRAP**
T200-1 (CHS)

fabric 2

1cm

1cm

FRONT

BACK

**ARMHOLE & NECKLINE**
H200-1 (CHS)

H300-1 (CHS)　　H201-4 (CHS)

THREAD: matching color / nr. 100 / 5 stitches per cm

REBEL

19-4007 TCX
16-5422 TCX
17-4139 TCX

# T-SHIRT

Nick #B203K

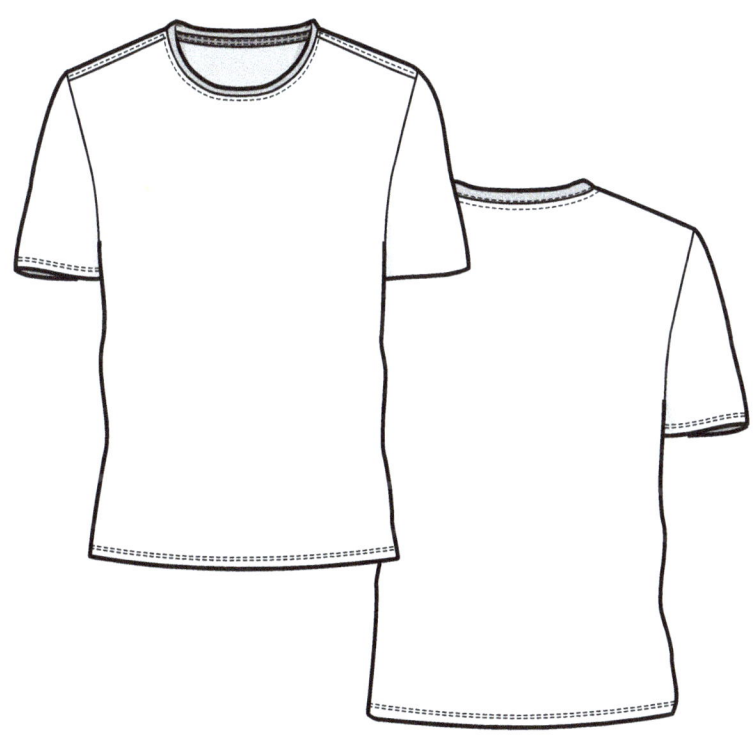

Crew neck
Set-in short sleeve
Back neck tape
Printed back

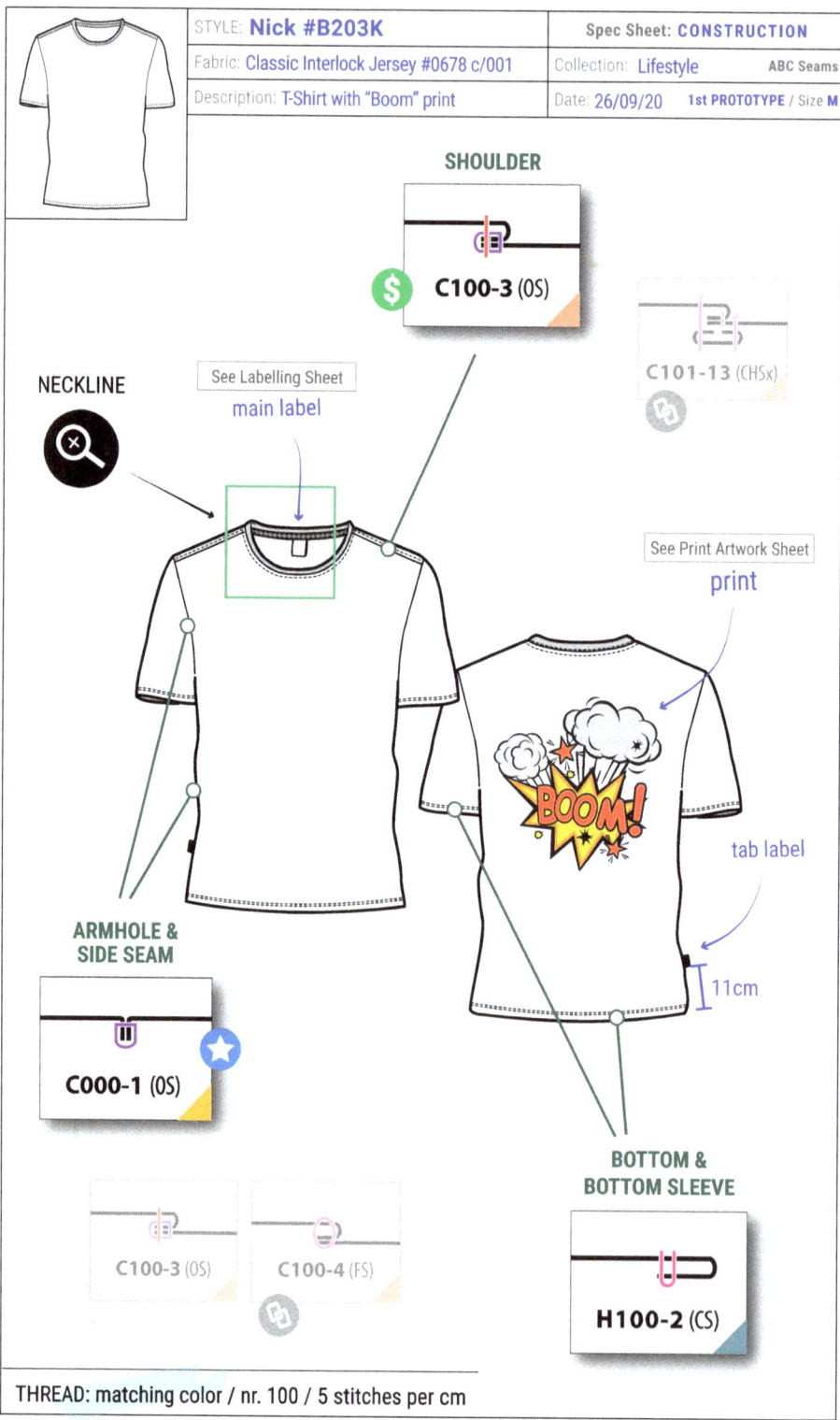

## Technical Specifications: T-Shirt

| STYLE: **Nick #B203K** | Spec Sheet: **CONSTRUCTION** | |
|---|---|---|
| Fabric: Classic Interlock Jersey #0678 c/001 | Collection: **Lifestyle** | ABC Seams |
| Description: T-Shirt with "Boom" print | Date: **26/09/20** | 1st PROTOTYPE / Size **M** |

### NECKLINE 🔍

H210-1 (OS)

**NECKLINE (front)**
H210-3 (OS)

FRONT
1.5cm

back neck tape
binding polishing the inside

SHOULDER SEAM

1cm
BACK

fabric 2

**NECKLINE (back)**
H211-9

H210-1 (OS)   H212-5 (CHSx)   H211-13 (CHSx)

THREAD: matching color / nr. 100 / 5 stitches per cm

TOPS · DRESS · PANTS · SKIRTS · OUTERWEAR · UNDERWEAR · SWIMWEAR

# POLO SHIRT

Richard #B204K

Ribbed collar and cuff
Front button placket
Half-moon back yoke
Side slit

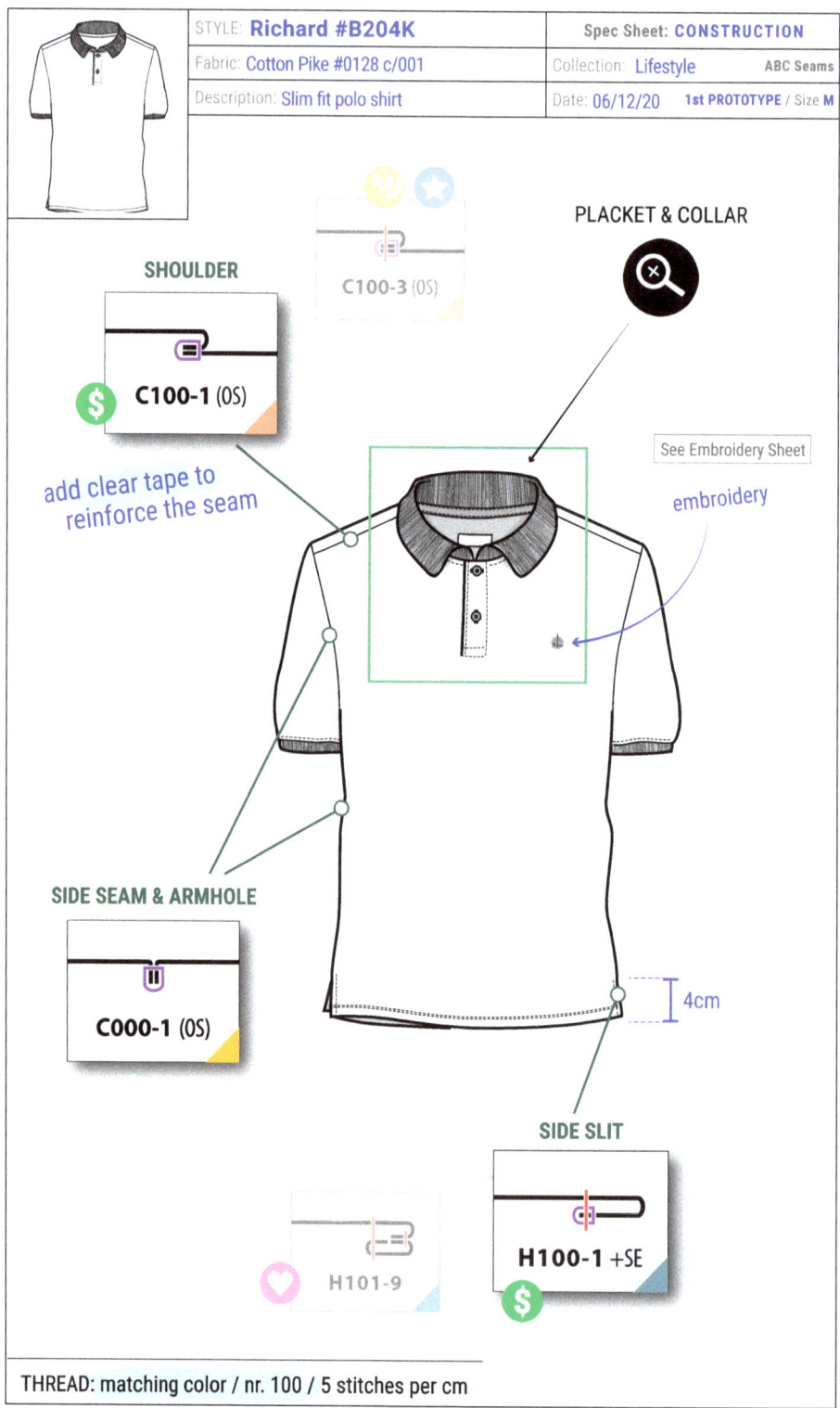

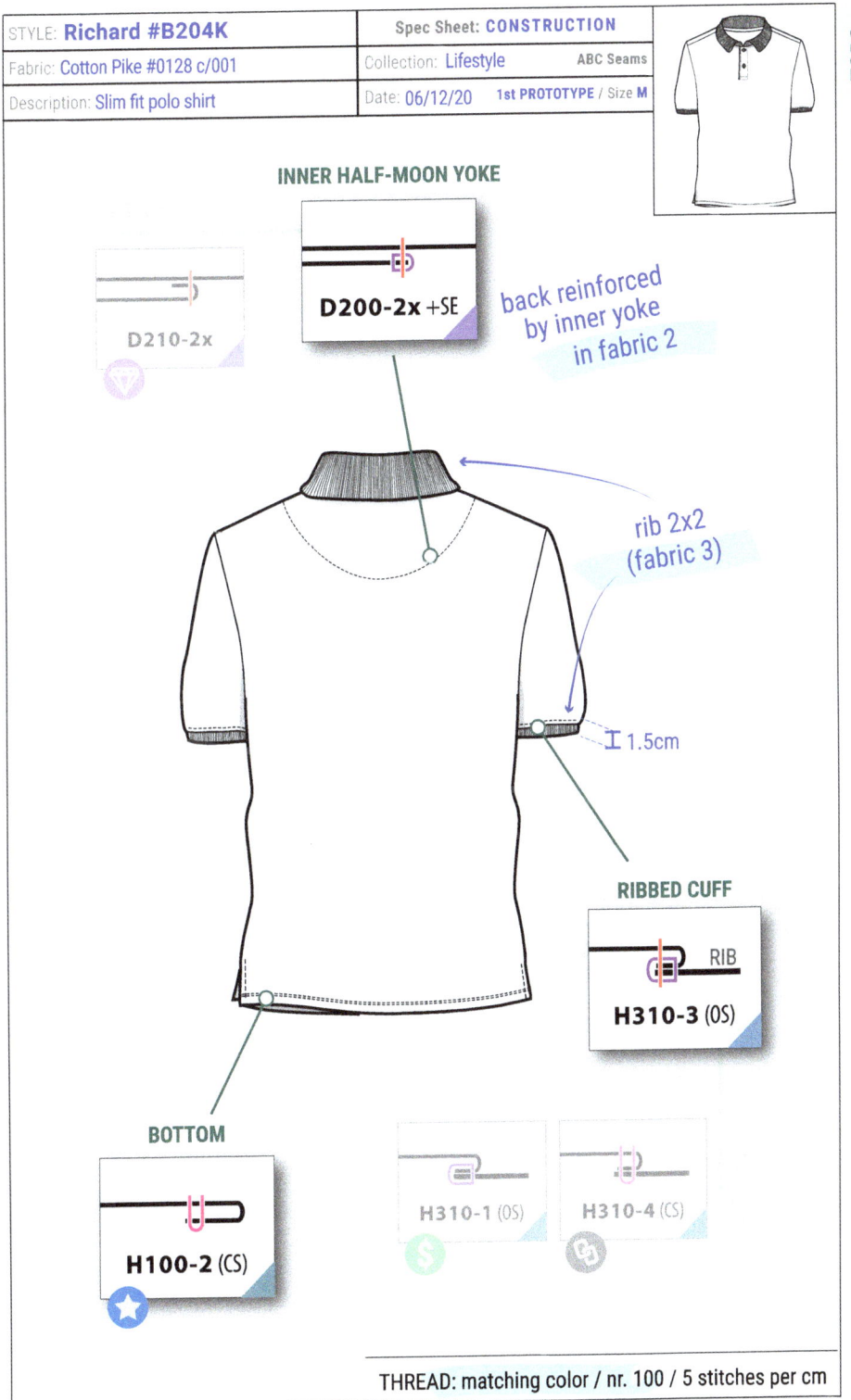

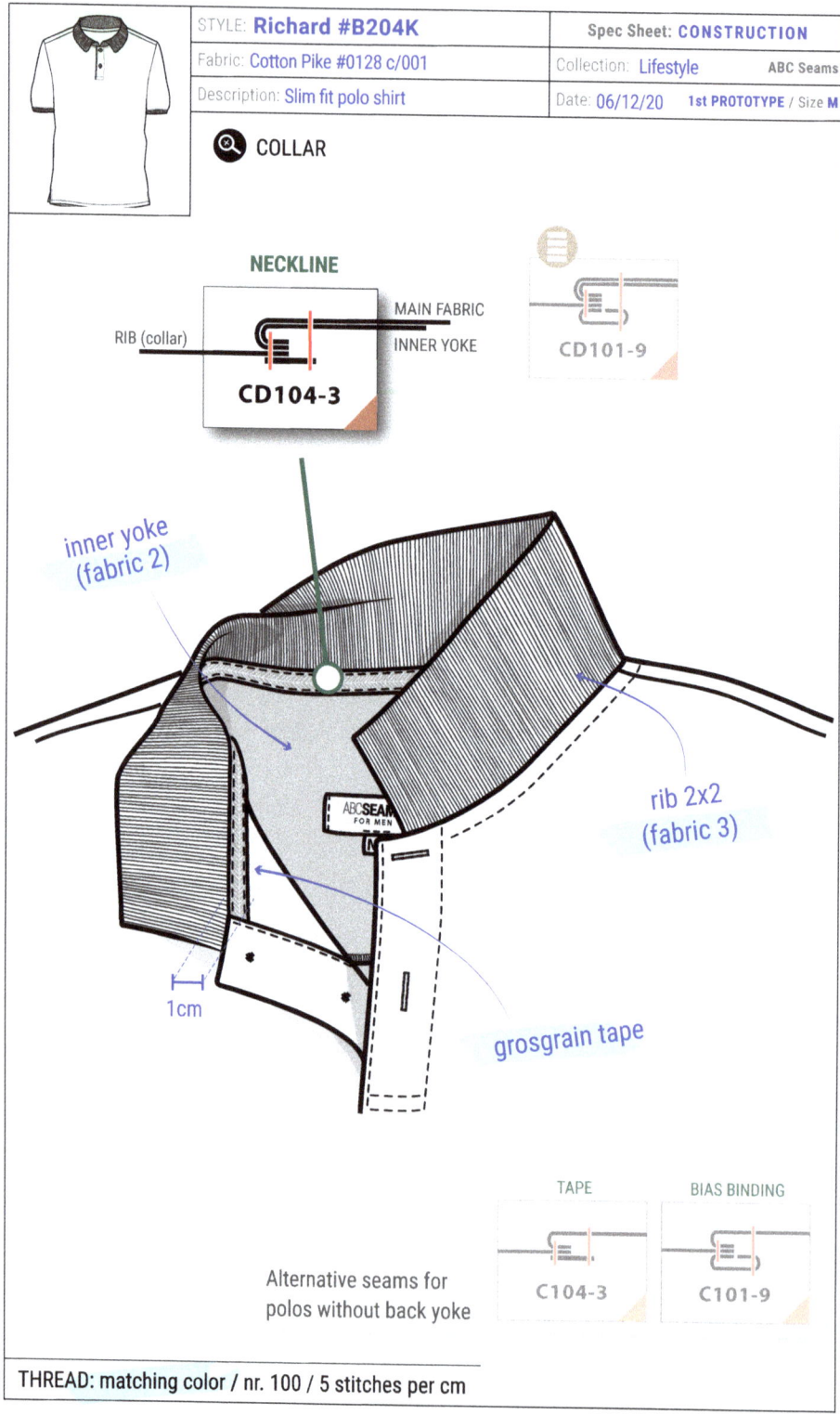

## Technical Specifications: Polo Shirt

| STYLE: **Richard #B204K** | Spec Sheet: **CONSTRUCTION** |
|---|---|
| Fabric: **Cotton Pike #0128 c/001** | Collection: **Lifestyle** — ABC Seams |
| Description: **Slim fit polo shirt** | Date: **06/12/20** — **1st PROTOTYPE** / Size **M** |

**PLACKET**

See Labelling Sheet

main label + size label

L/18

3cm

add interfacing

add interfacing

**UNDER PLACKET**

**H500-2**

double topstitch

**TOP PLACKET**

**H150-34**

H500-12

H150-31

H150-32

THREAD: matching color / nr. 100 / 5 stitches per cm

TOPS • DRESS • PANTS • SKIRTS • OUTERWEAR • UNDERWEAR • SWIMWEAR

# CLEAN

11-0601 TCX
13-4304 TCX
12-0703 TCX

# OXFORD SHIRT

Paul #B205W

Button-down collar

Back yoke with inverted box pleat

Patch pocket

Cuff vent with placket

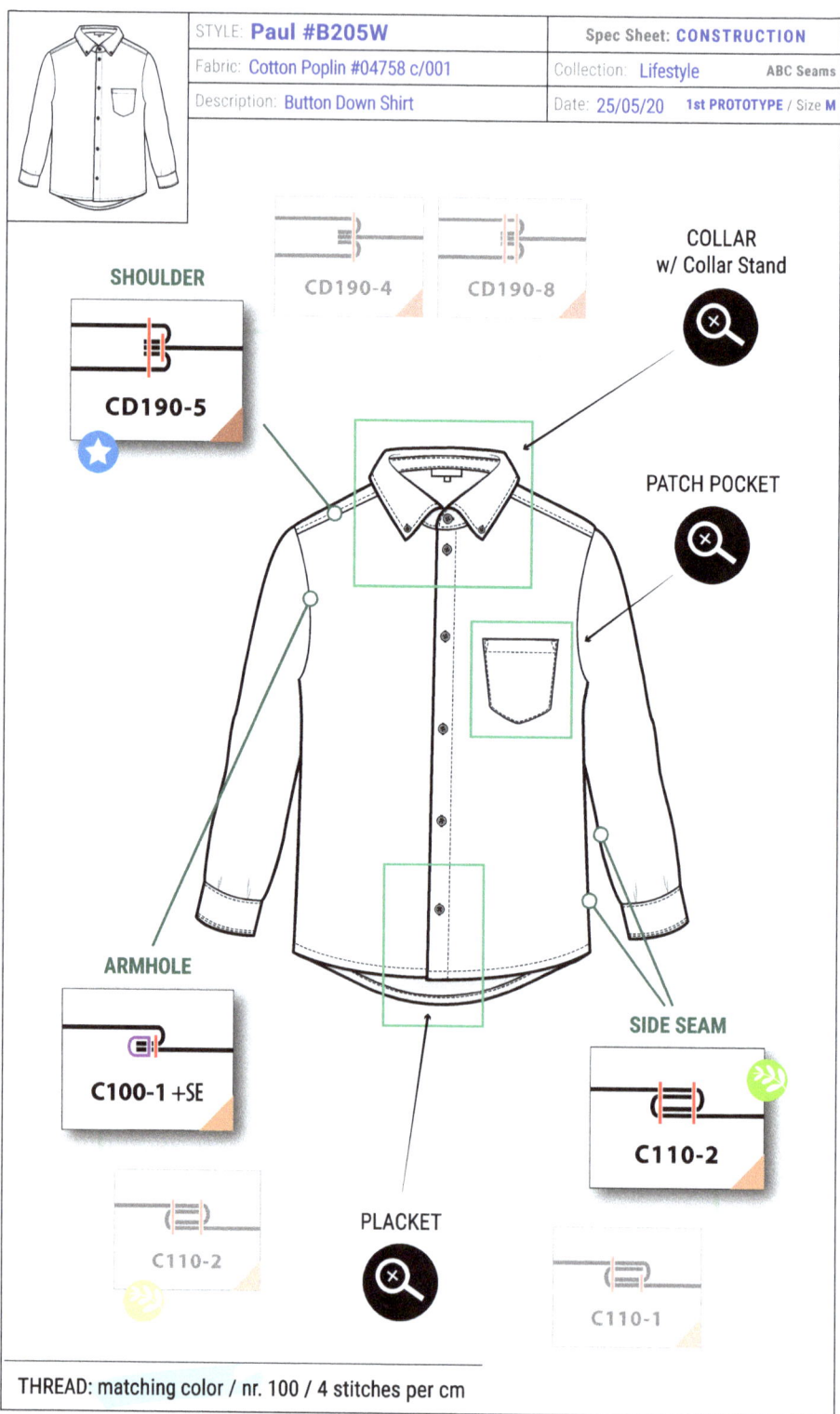

# Technical Specifications: Oxford Shirt

| STYLE: **Paul #B205W** | Spec Sheet: **CONSTRUCTION** | |
|---|---|---|
| Fabric: **Cotton Poplin #04758 c/001** | Collection: **Lifestyle** | ABC Seams |
| Description: **Button Down Shirt** | Date: **25/05/20** | **1st PROTOTYPE** / Size **M** |

**TOPS** · DRESS · PANTS · SKIRTS · OUTERWEAR · UNDERWEAR · SWIMWEAR

## YOKE
2 layers of fabric

**CD190-5**

CD190-1

## INVERTED BOX PLEAT

**D112-0**

4cm

## CUFF VENT

## BOTTOM

**H110-2**

H110-3

H101-9

THREAD: matching color / nr. 100 / 4 stitches per cm

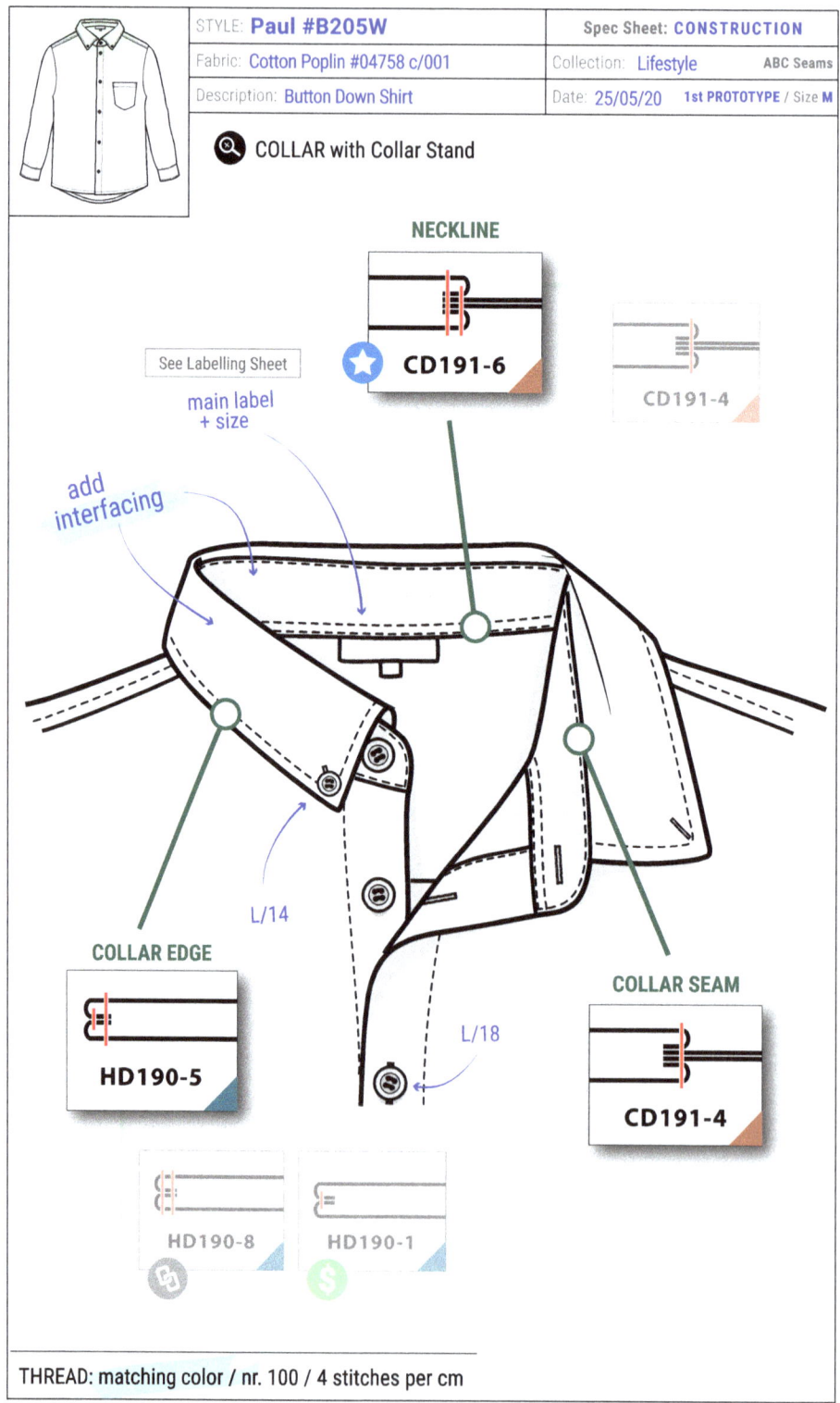

## Technical Specifications: Oxford Shirt

| STYLE: **Paul #B205W** | Spec Sheet: **CONSTRUCTION** | |
|---|---|---|
| Fabric: Cotton Poplin #04758 c/001 | Collection: Lifestyle | ABC Seams |
| Description: Button Down Shirt | Date: 25/05/20 | **1st PROTOTYPE** / Size **M** |

**TOPS** / DRESS / PANTS / SKIRTS / OUTERWEAR / UNDERWEAR / SWIMWEAR

### PLACKET

H120-2 +SE

H130-4

H131-3

**TOP PLACKET**

H150-31

add interfacing

3cm

L/18

**UNDER PLACKET**

H130-19

H130-3

add interfacing

THREAD: matching color / nr. 100 / 4 stitches per cm

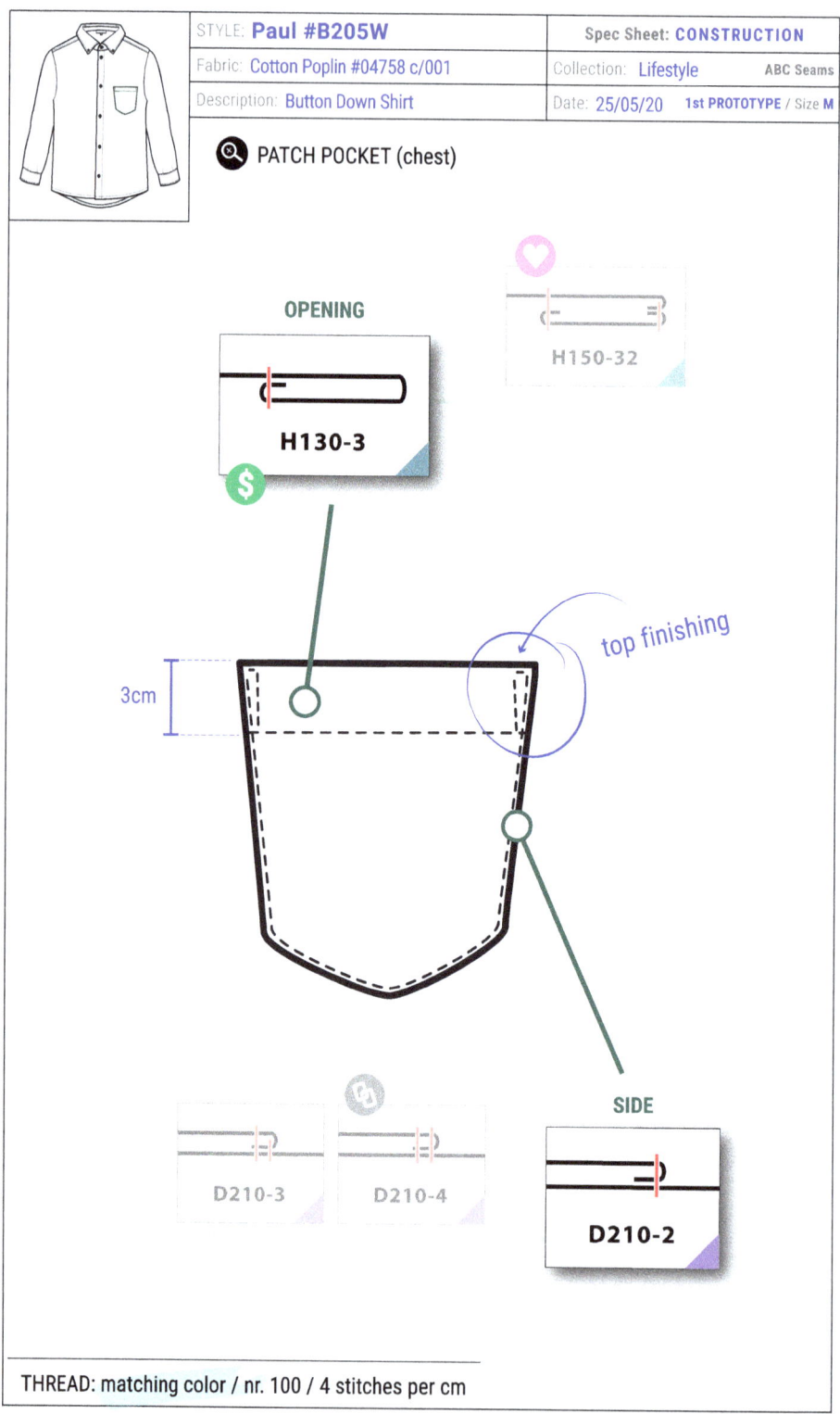

Technical Specifications: Oxford Shirt

| STYLE: **Paul #B205W** | Spec Sheet: **CONSTRUCTION** | |
|---|---|---|
| Fabric: Cotton Poplin #04758 c/001 | Collection: Lifestyle | ABC Seams |
| Description: Button Down Shirt | Date: 25/05/20 | **1st PROTOTYPE** / Size **M** |

CUFF VENT 🔍

**TOP VENT (placket)**

**H500-2**

2.5cm

**UNDER VENT**

narrow hem

**H110-12**

L/14

pleat x3

add interfacing

**CUFF EDGE**

**HD190-5**

L/18

**CUFF SEAM**

**CD190-7**

H160-4

CD190-3

THREAD: matching color / nr. 100 / 4 stitches per cm

TOPS — DRESS — PANTS — SKIRTS — OUTERWEAR — UNDERWEAR — SWIMWEAR

# CHECKED

# WORK SHIRT

John #B206WK

Collar without collar stand

Back yoke with box pleat

Patch pocket with box pleat and flap

Side slit

Short Sleeve

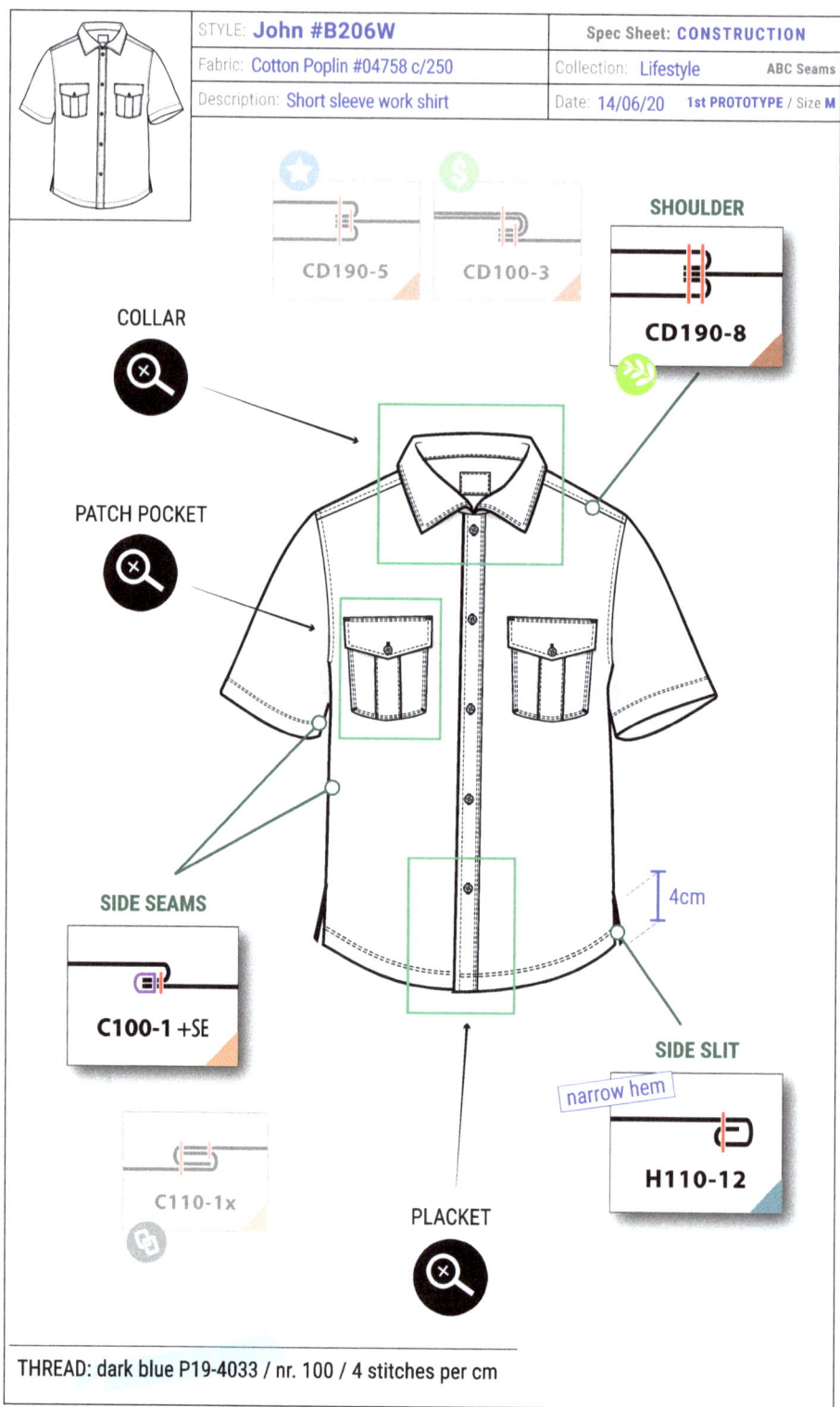

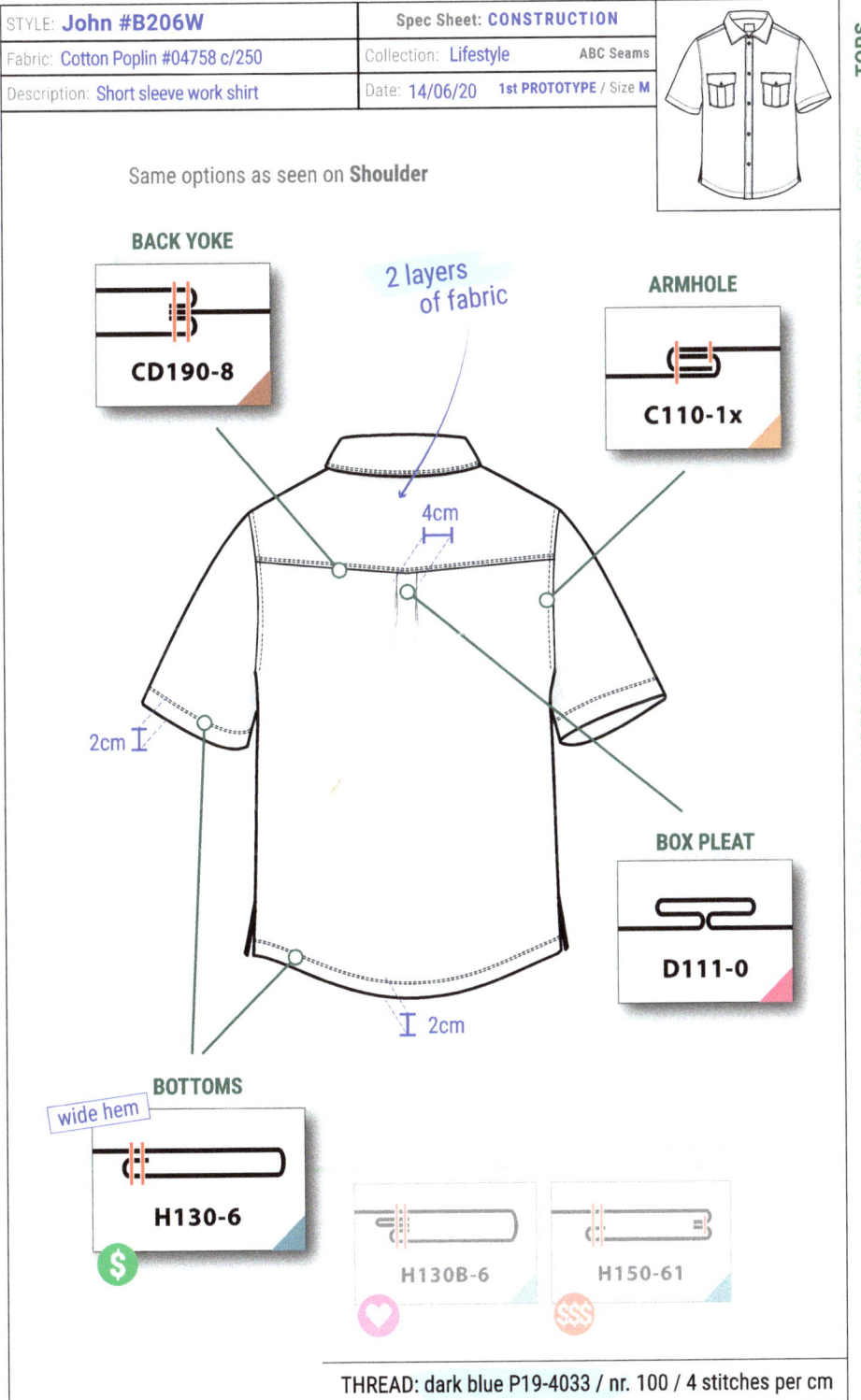

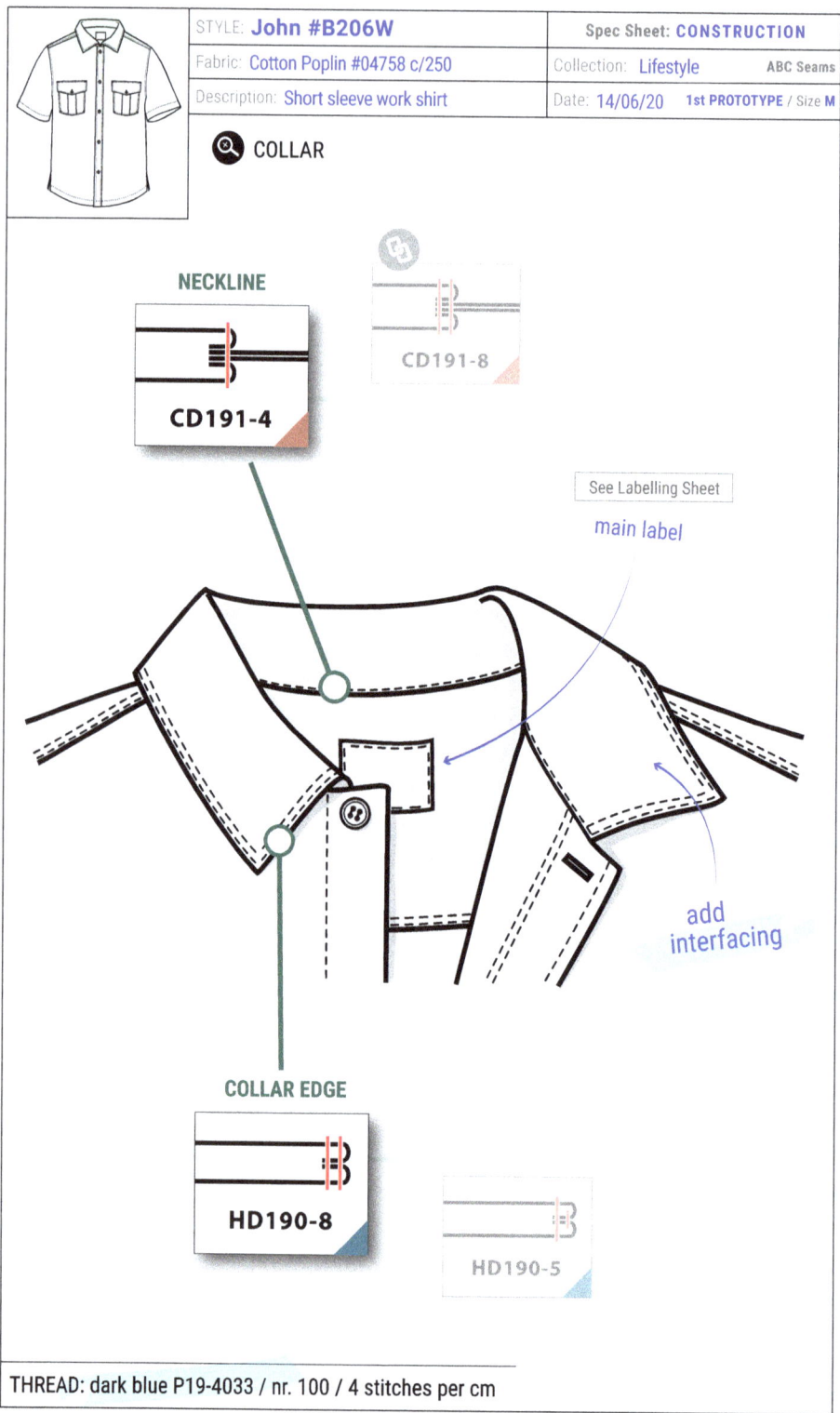

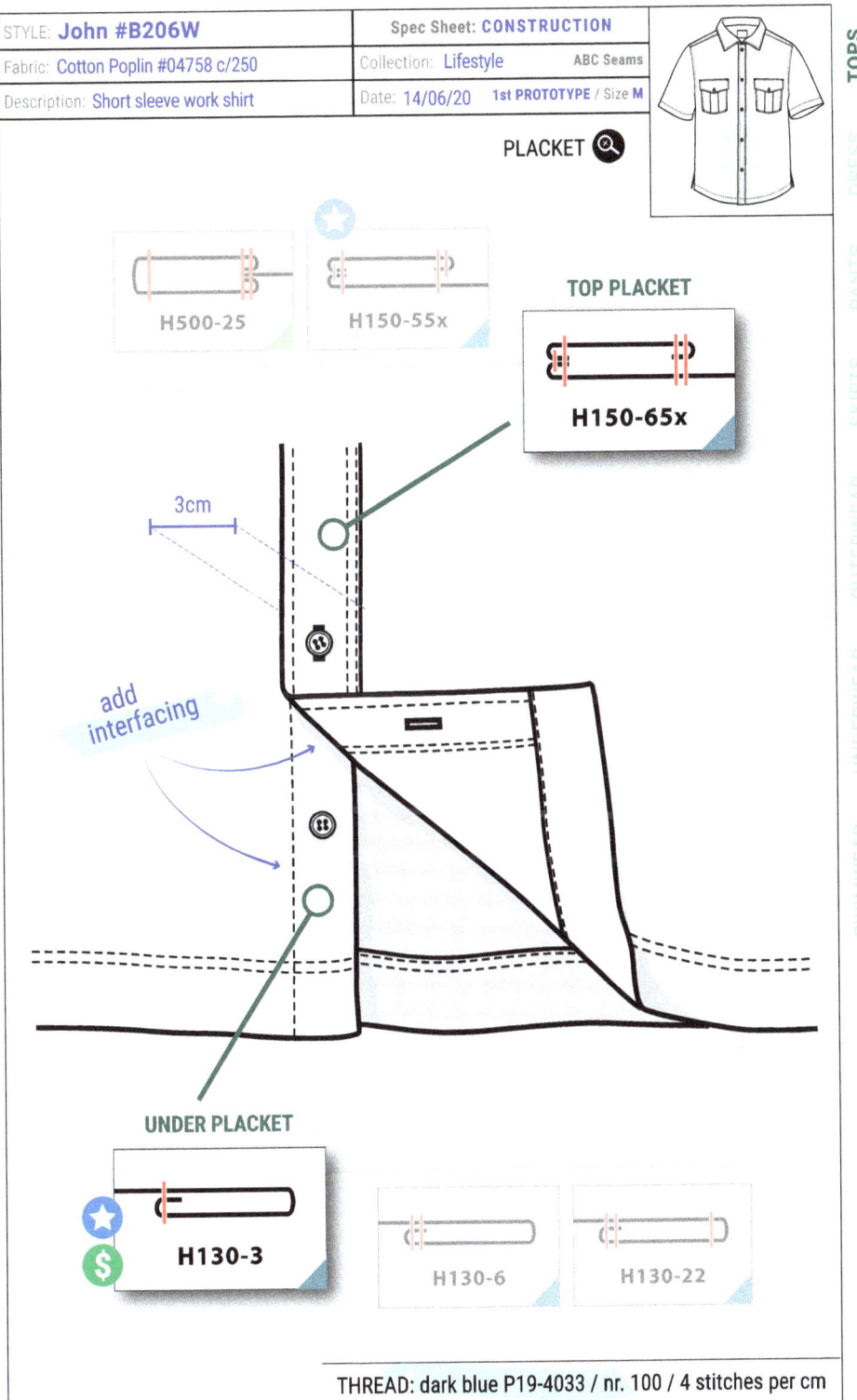

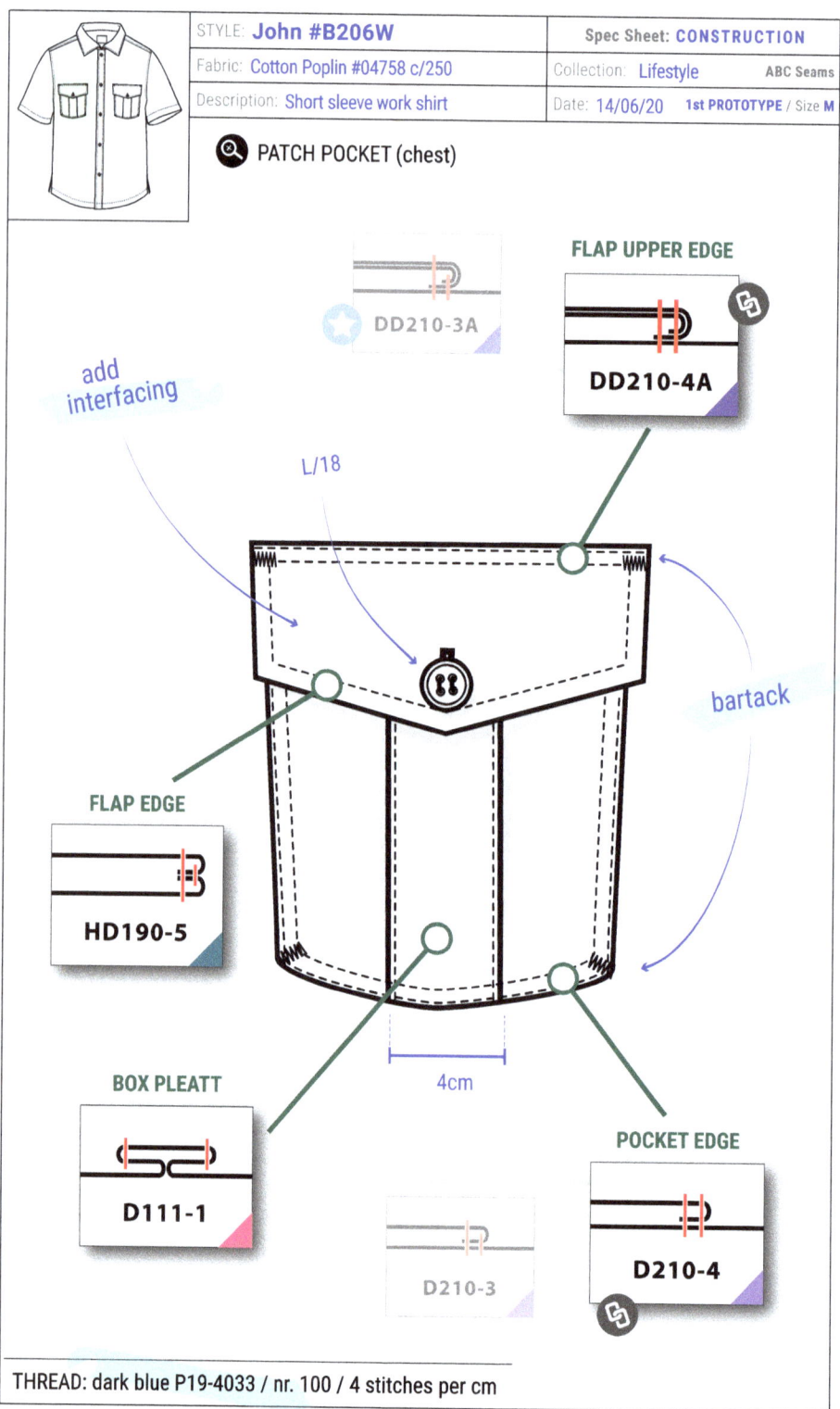

## PATCH POCKETS WITH FLAP

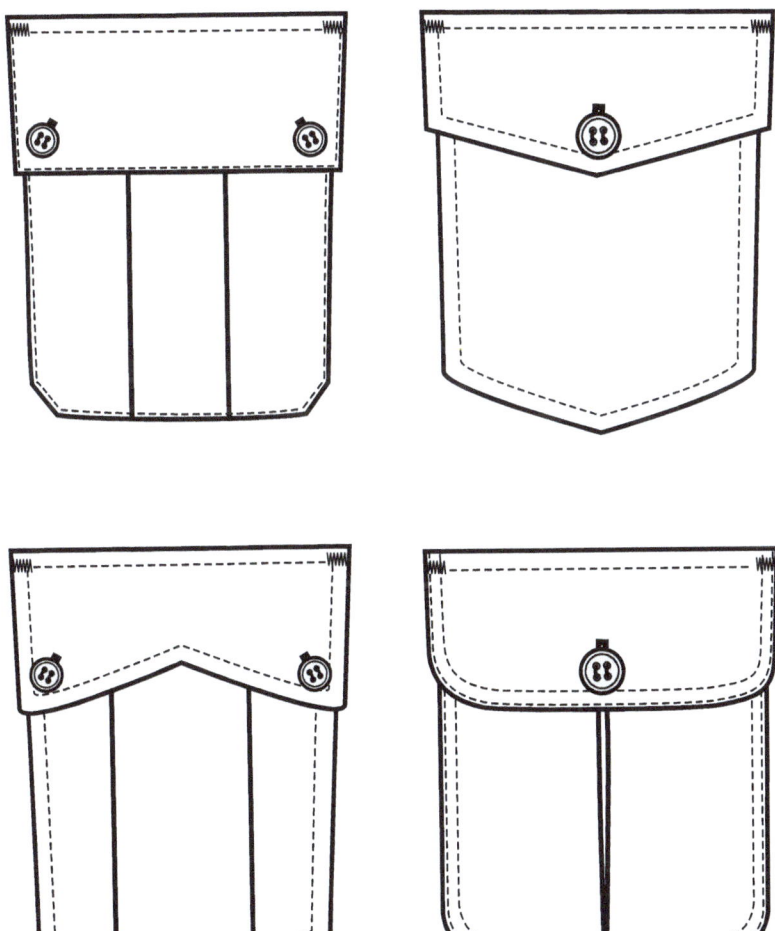

DRESSY

19-4007 TCX
13-1008 TCX
11-0601 TCX

# CLASSIC BLOUSE

Susan #B207W

Mandarin collar

Puff sleeve

Front and back yoke

Cuff with binded vent

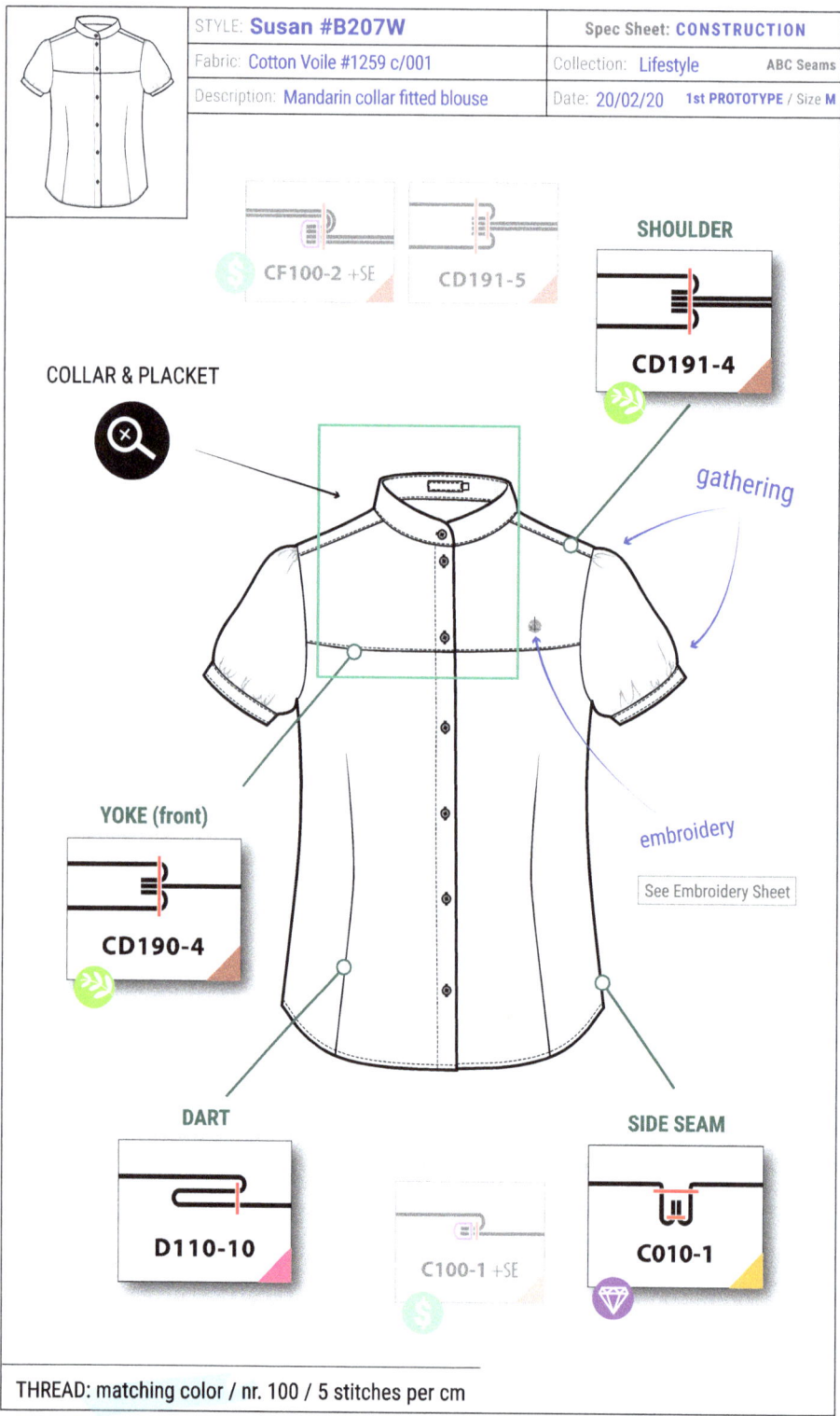

Technical specifications: Classic Blouse

| STYLE: **Susan #B207W** | Spec Sheet: **CONSTRUCTION** | |
|---|---|---|
| Fabric: Cotton Voile #1259 c/001 | Collection: Lifestyle | ABC Seams |
| Description: Mandarin collar fitted blouse | Date: 20/02/20 | **1st PROTOTYPE** / Size **M** |

**TOPS** · DRESS · PANTS · SKIRTS · OUTERWEAR · UNDERWEAR · SWIMWEAR

CD190-5

**YOKE (back)**
CD190-4

*gathering*

**CUFF VENT**

**ARMHOLE**
C100-1 +SE

0.5cm

**DART**
D110-10

**BOTTOM**
narrow hem
H110-12

H101-9

THREAD: matching color / nr. 100 / 5 stitches per cm

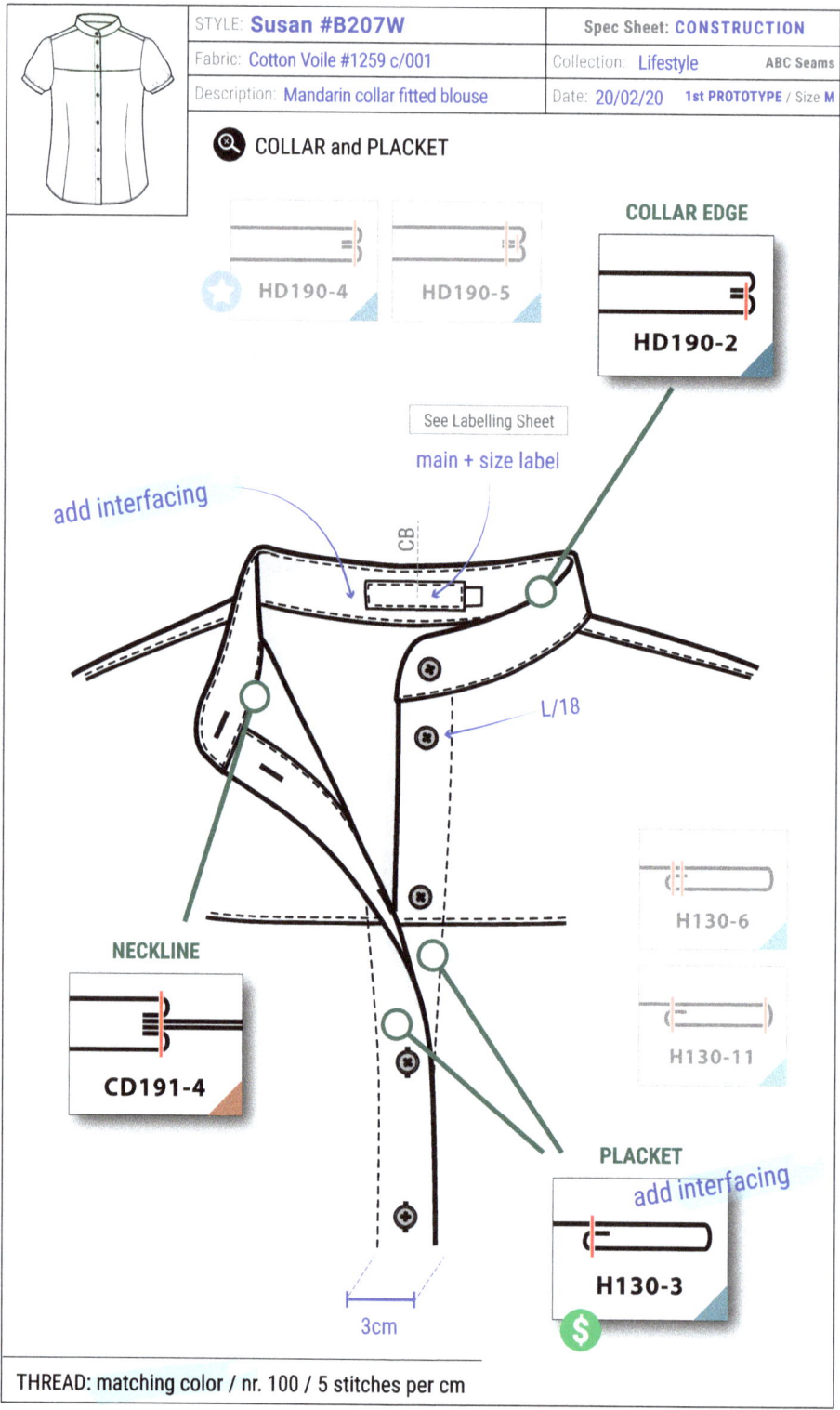

# Technical Specifications - Classic Blouse

| STYLE: **Susan #B207W** | Spec Sheet: **CONSTRUCTION** |
|---|---|
| Fabric: **Cotton Voile #1259 c/001** | Collection: **Lifestyle** — ABC Seams |
| Description: **Mandarin collar fitted blouse** | Date: **20/02/20** — **1st PROTOTYPE** / Size **M** |

**CUFF VENT** 🔍

**TOPS** · **DRESS** · **PANTS** · **SKIRTS** · **OUTERWEAR** · **UNDERWEAR** · **SWIMWEAR**

**TOP VENT**
H200-1

**UNDER VENT**
H103-1

H103-5

gathers all around

0.5cm

1.5cm

L/18

**CUFF SEAM**
CD190-4

H160-0

**CUFF EDGE**
H160-1

THREAD: matching color / nr. 100 / 5 stitches per cm

# PRINCESS LINE DRESS

### Caroline #B208W

Bodycon silhouette

V-Neckline

Sleeveless

Lined and faced

Back Vent

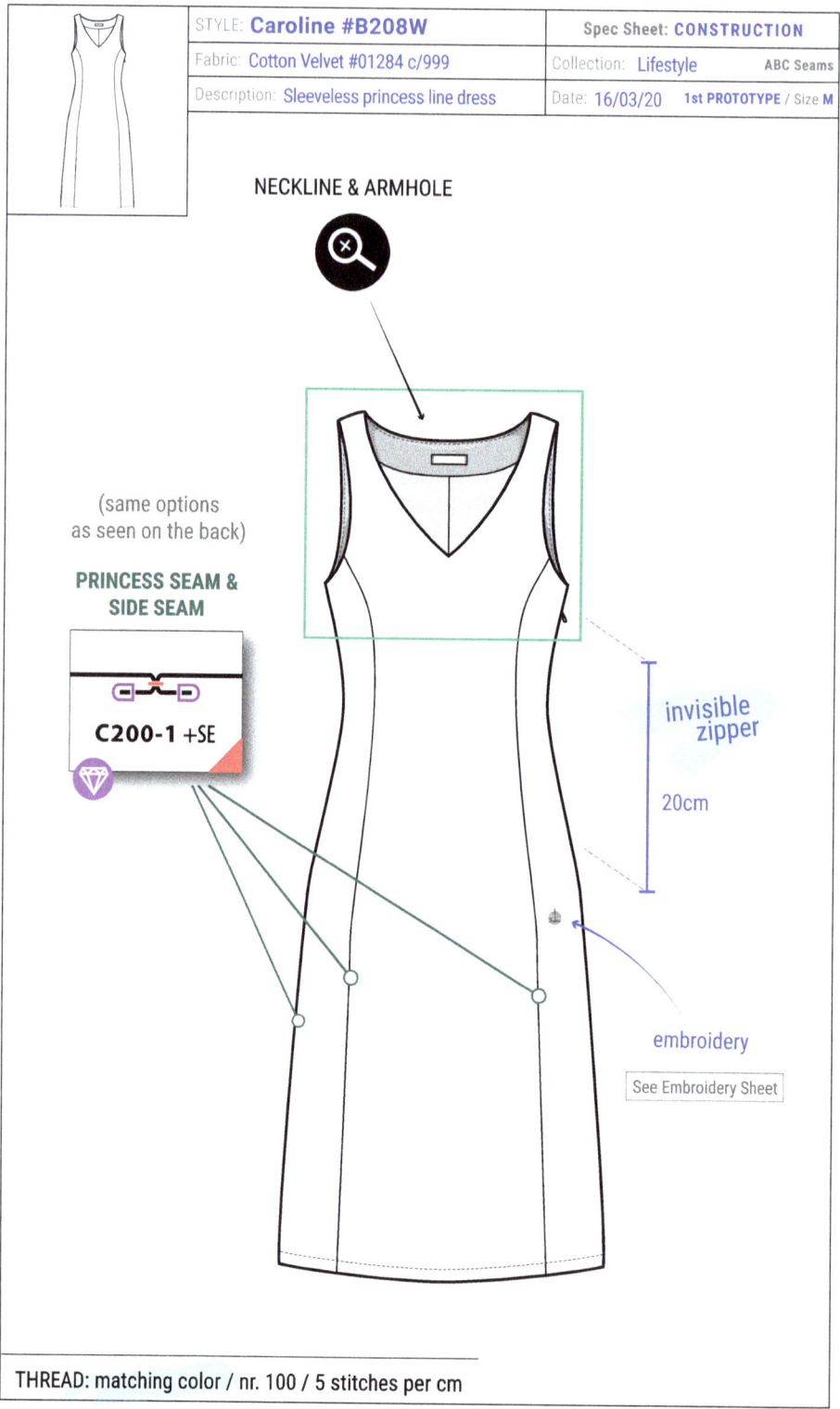

## Technical Specifications: Princess Line Dress

| STYLE: **Caroline #B208W** | Spec Sheet: **CONSTRUCTION** | |
|---|---|---|
| Fabric: Cotton Velvet #01284 c/999 | Collection: **Lifestyle** | ABC Seams |
| Description: Sleeveless princess line dress | Date: 16/03/20 | **1st PROTOTYPE** / Size **M** |

**PRINCESS SEAM & CB**

C200-1 +SE

C200-1

C100-1 +SE

C100-1

**BOTTOM & VENT**

THREAD: matching color / nr. 100 / 5 stitches per cm

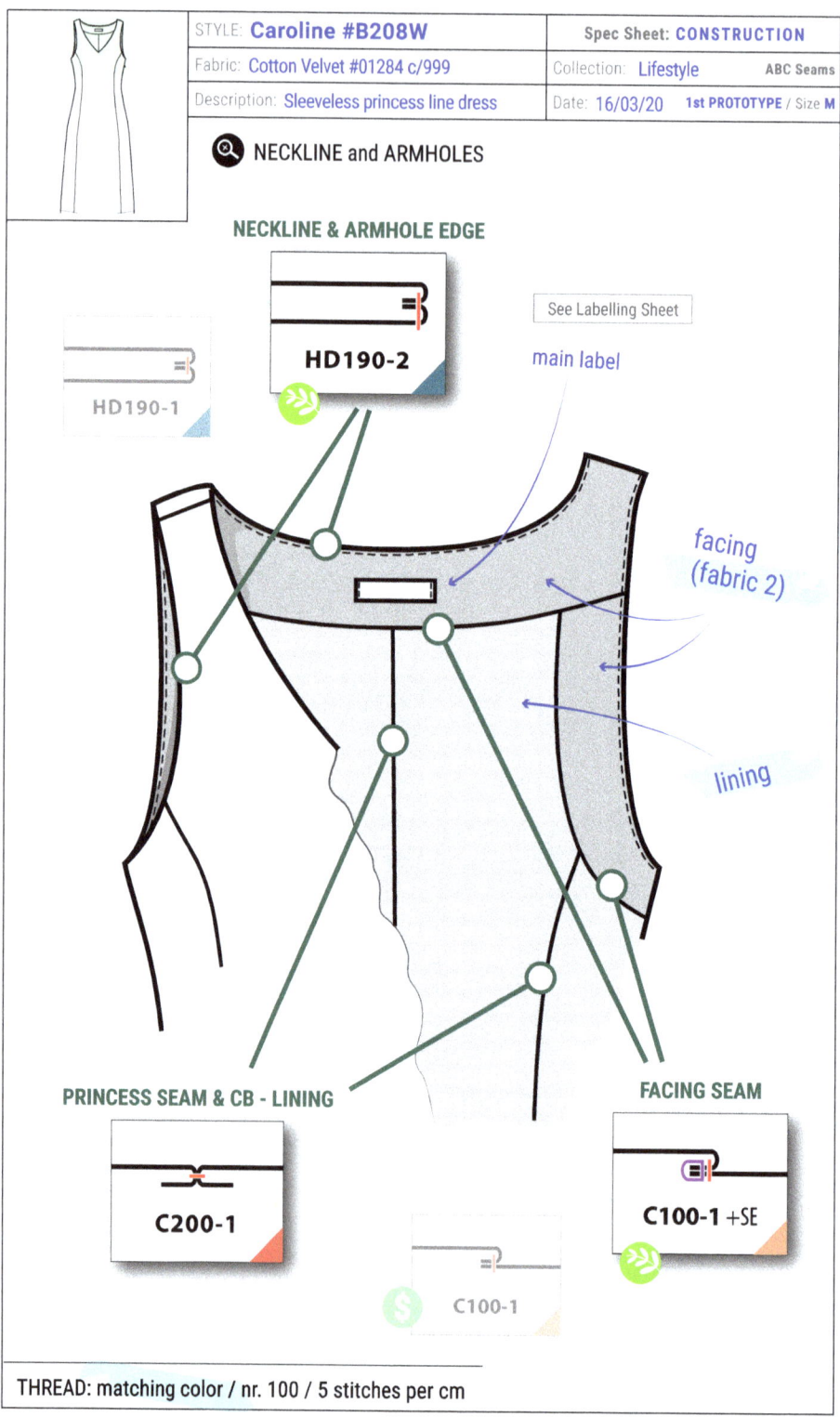

| STYLE: **Caroline #B208W** | Spec Sheet: **CONSTRUCTION** | |
|---|---|---|
| Fabric: Cotton Velvet #01284 c/999 | Collection: Lifestyle | ABC Seams |
| Description: Sleeveless princess line dress | Date: 16/03/20 | **1st PROTOTYPE** / Size **M** |

## BOTTOM and VENT

**TOP VENT**

**HD190-16XL**

**BOTTOM**

**H120-2L** +SE

2cm

2cm

lining

**BOTTOM - LINING**

**H110-2**

HD190-2

**UNDER VENT**

**HD190-4**

THREAD: matching color / nr. 100 / 5 stitches per cm

BLUE ACCENTS

18-4436 TCX
16-3929 TCX
14-4310 TCX

# JEANS
### David #B209J

Regular fit

5 pocket

Zip fly

Double topstitch

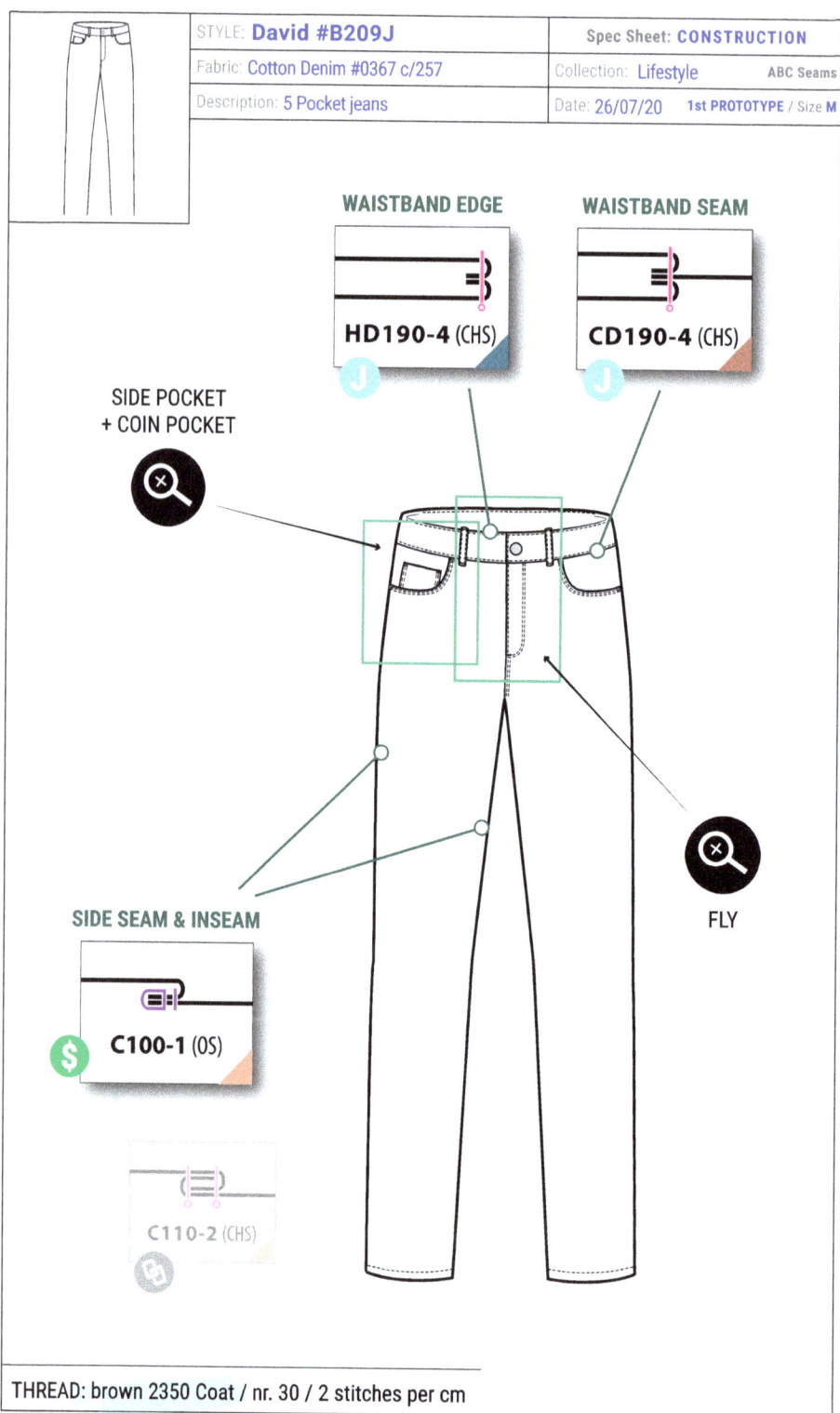

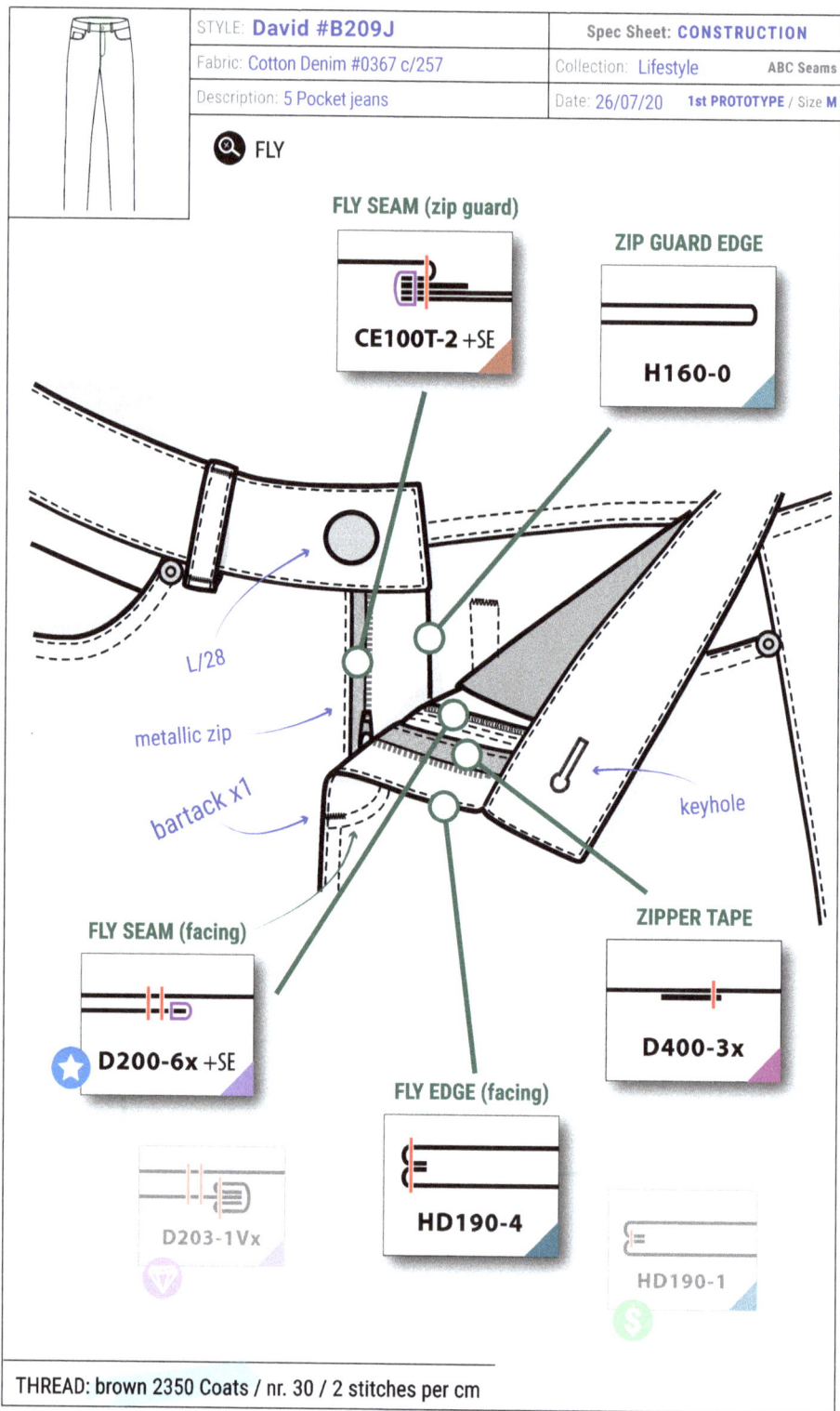

| STYLE: **David #B209J** | Spec Sheet: **CONSTRUCTION** | |
|---|---|---|
| Fabric: Cotton Denim #0367 c/257 | Collection: Lifestyle | ABC Seams |
| Description: 5 Pocket jeans | Date: 26/07/20 | **1st PROTOTYPE** / Size **M** |

## PATCH POCKET (back)

H120-1 +SE

H150-34

**OPENING**

**H120-2 +SE**

2.5cm

bartack

**SIDE**

**D210-4**

D210-2

THREAD: brown 2350 Coats / nr. 30 / 2 stitches per cm

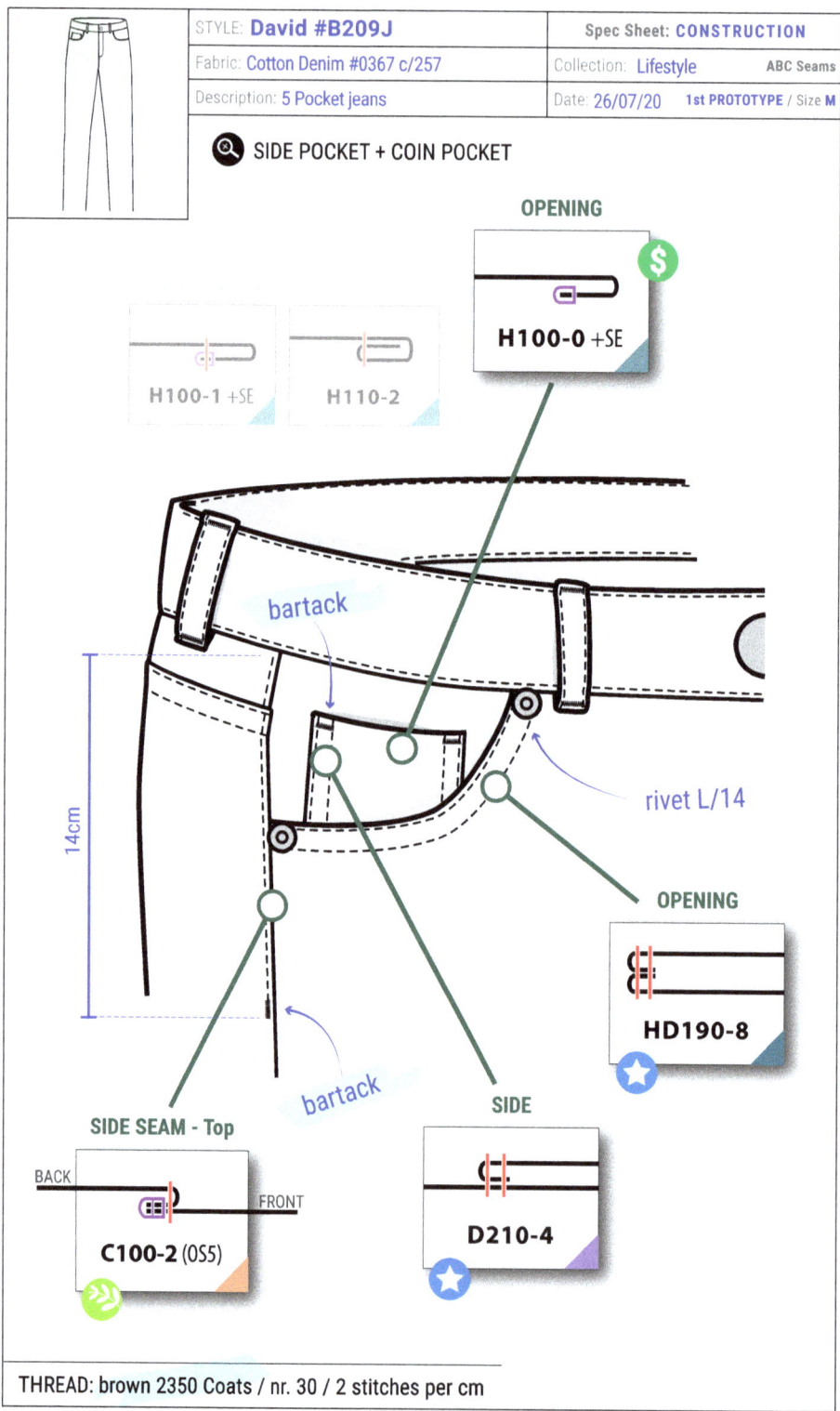

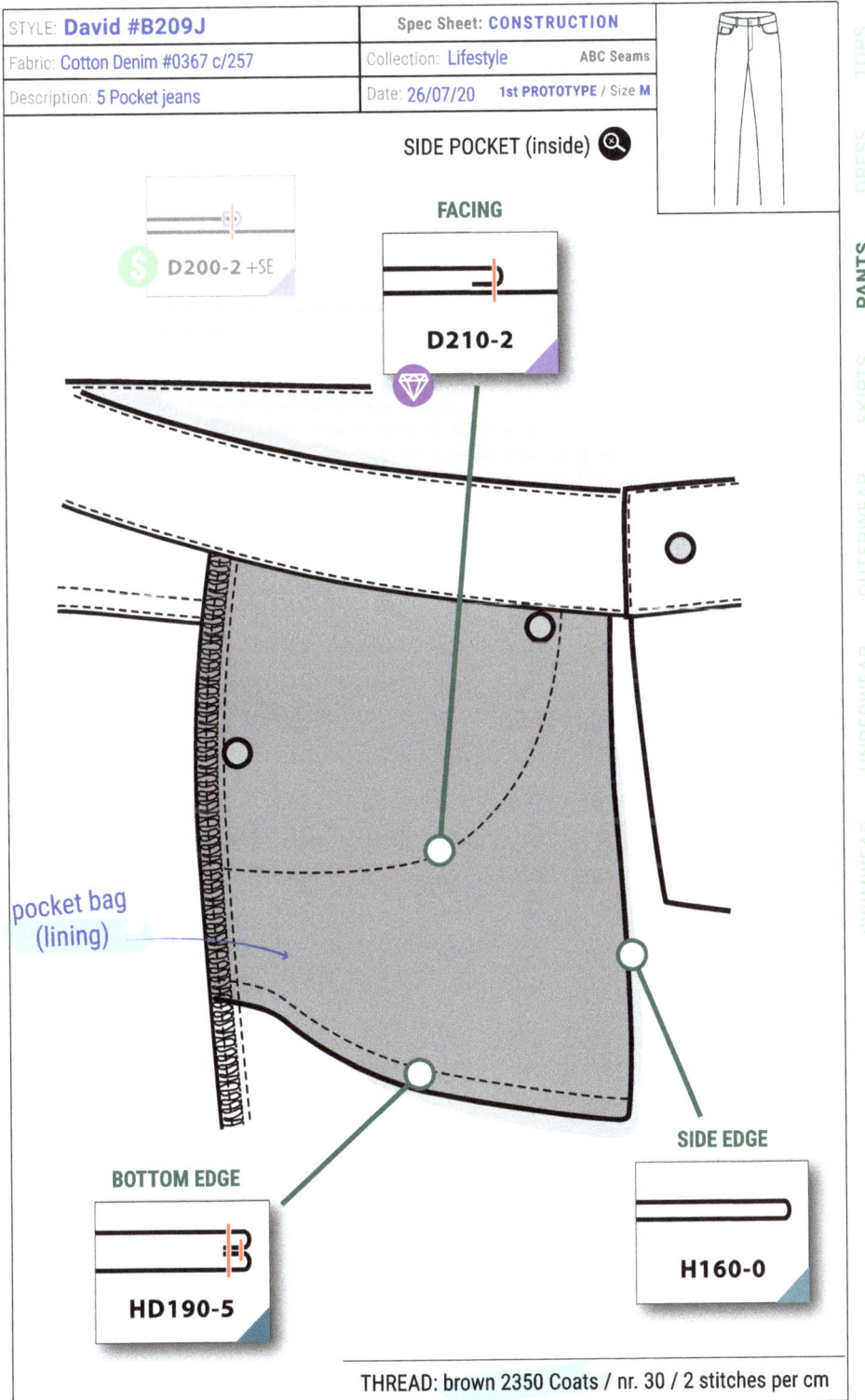

CASUAL

19-4007 TCX

16-0924 TCX

13-1008 TCX

# CHINO PANTS

Angela #B210W

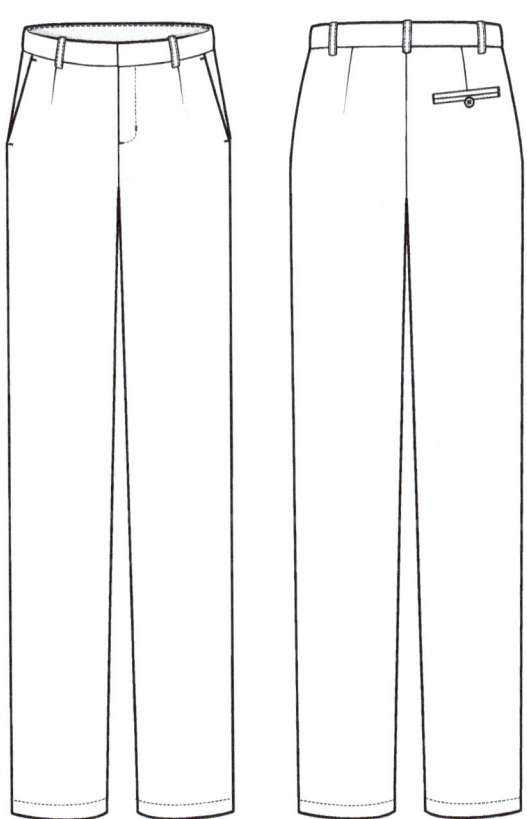

Clean look

Slant and jetted pockets

Waistband extension

Binded inner seams

Smart pleat front

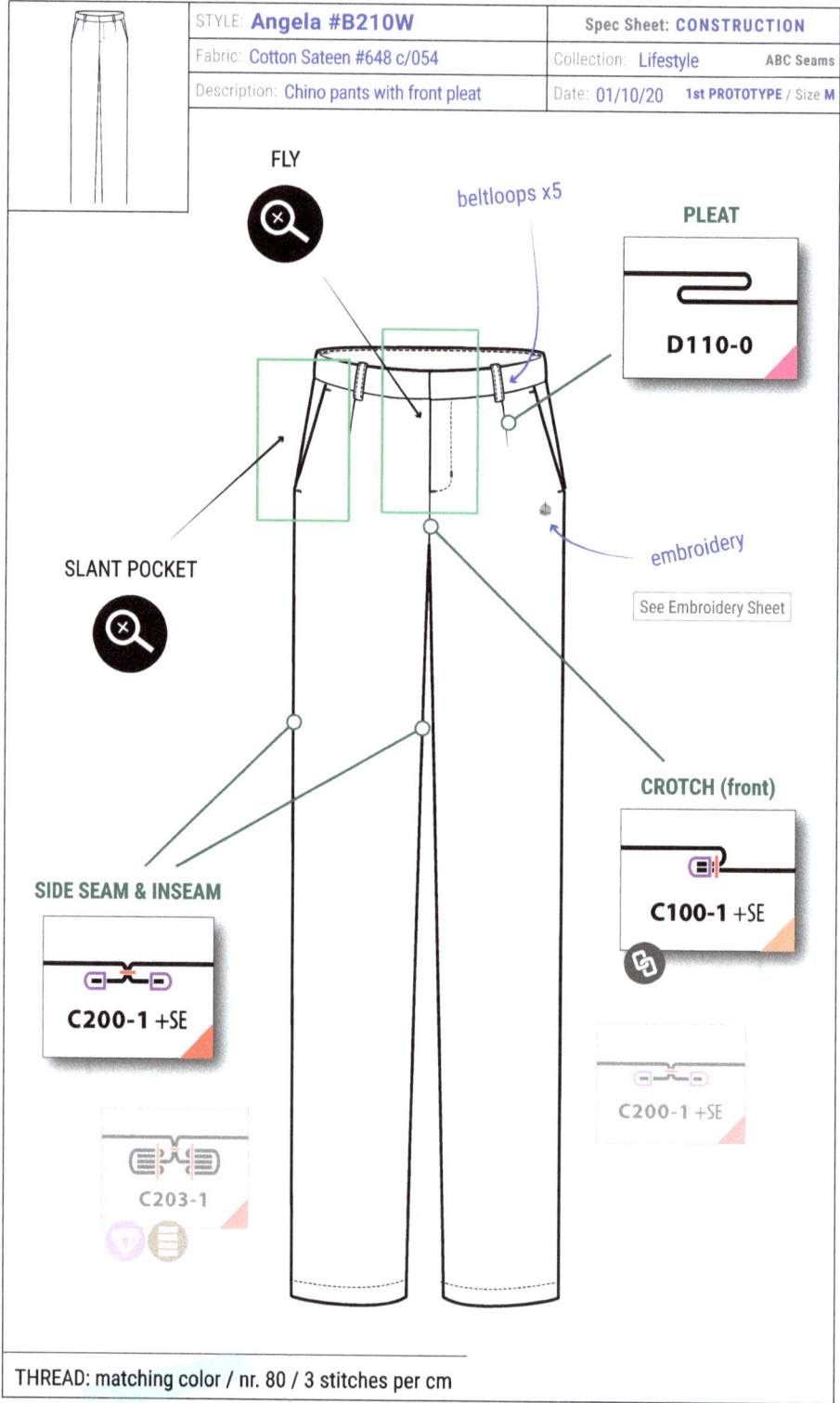

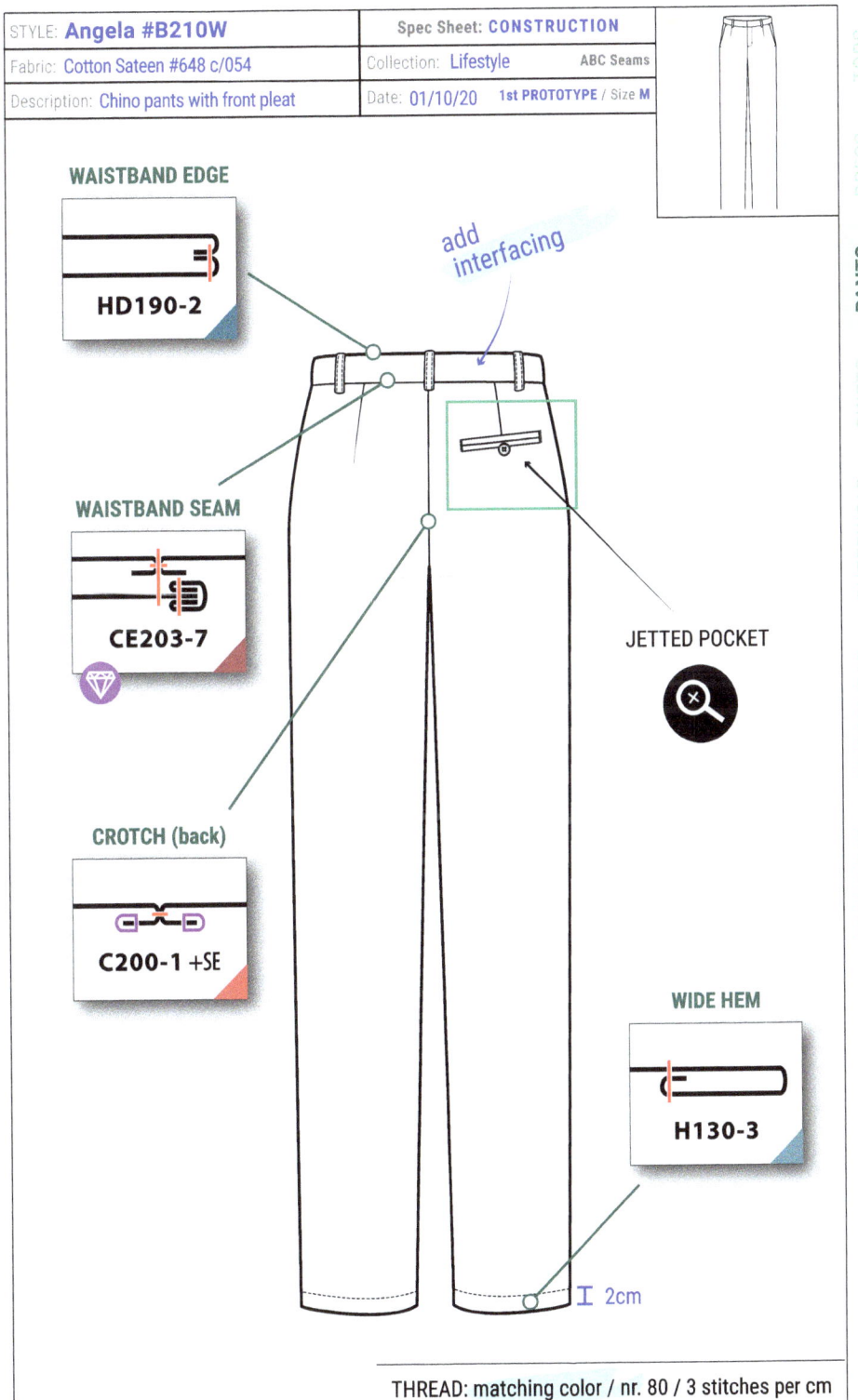

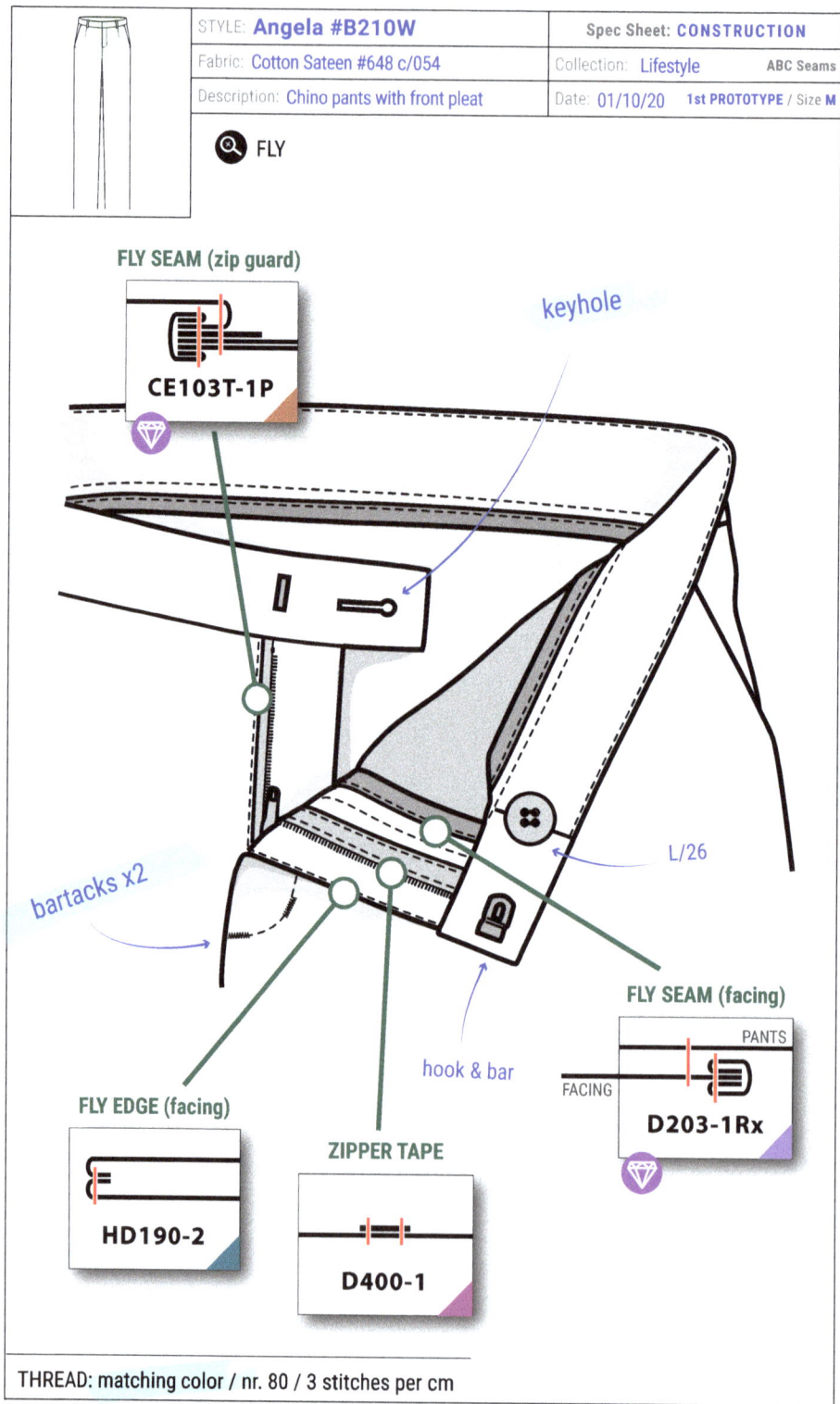

## Technical Specifications: Chinos

| STYLE: **Angela #B210W** | Spec Sheet: **CONSTRUCTION** | |
|---|---|---|
| Fabric: Cotton Sateen #648 c/054 | Collection: Lifestyle | ABC Seams |
| Description: Chino pants with front pleat | Date: **01/10/20** 1st **PROTOTYPE** / Size **M** | |

FLY (inside) 🔍

**ZIP GUARD EDGE**

H160-0

waistband extension

POCKET BAG

POCKET BAG

**ZIP GUARD BOTTOM EDGE**

HD190-1

HD000-3 +SE

THREAD: matching color / nr. 80 / 3 stitches per cm

TOPS
DRESS
PANTS
SKIRTS
OUTERWEAR
UNDERWEAR
SWIMWEAR

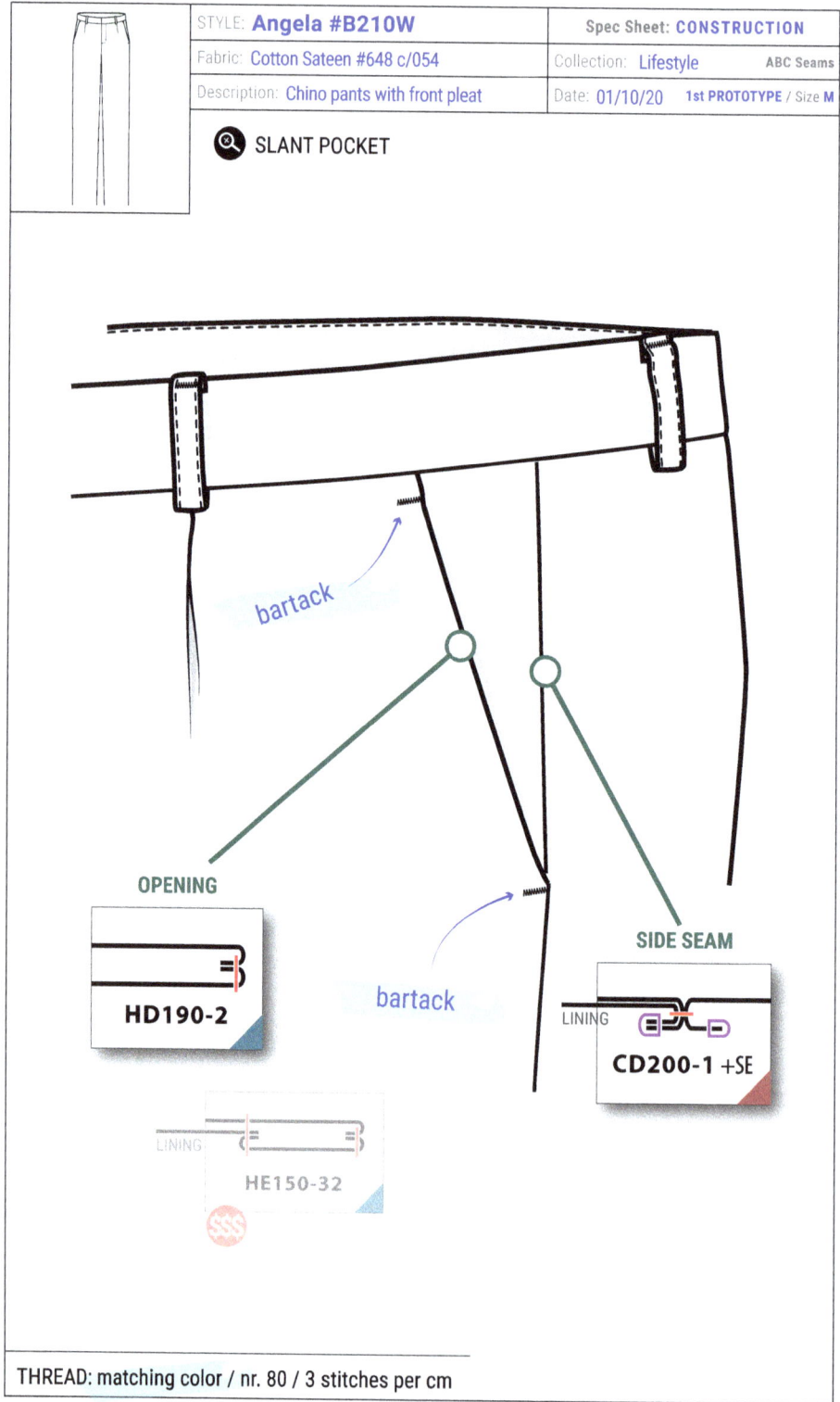

## Technical Specifications: Chinos

| STYLE: **Angela #B210W** | Spec Sheet: **CONSTRUCTION** | |
|---|---|---|
| Fabric: **Cotton Sateen #648 c/054** | Collection: **Lifestyle** | **ABC Seams** |
| Description: **Chino pants with front pleat** | Date: **01/10/20** | **1st PROTOTYPE** / Size **M** |

### SLANT POCKET (inside)

**FLY SIDE**

DD000-1

**D210-2x**

NOTE: comparing with DD000-1, this seam reduces the bulkiness of the Fly Seam

FLY SEAM

**EDGE**

pocket bag (lining)

**FACING**

**D210-2**

**HD200-1**

THREAD: matching color / nr. 80 / 3 stitches per cm

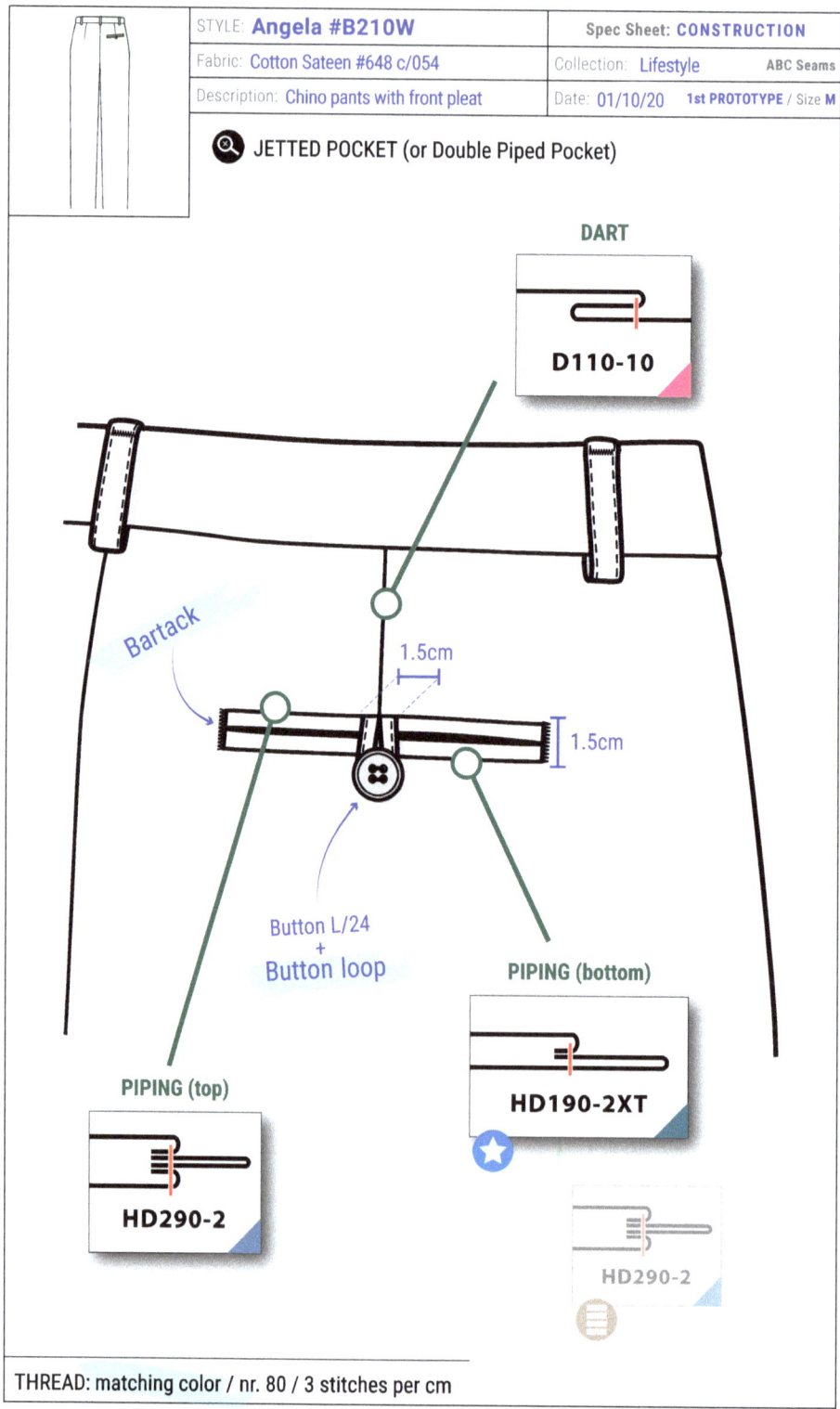

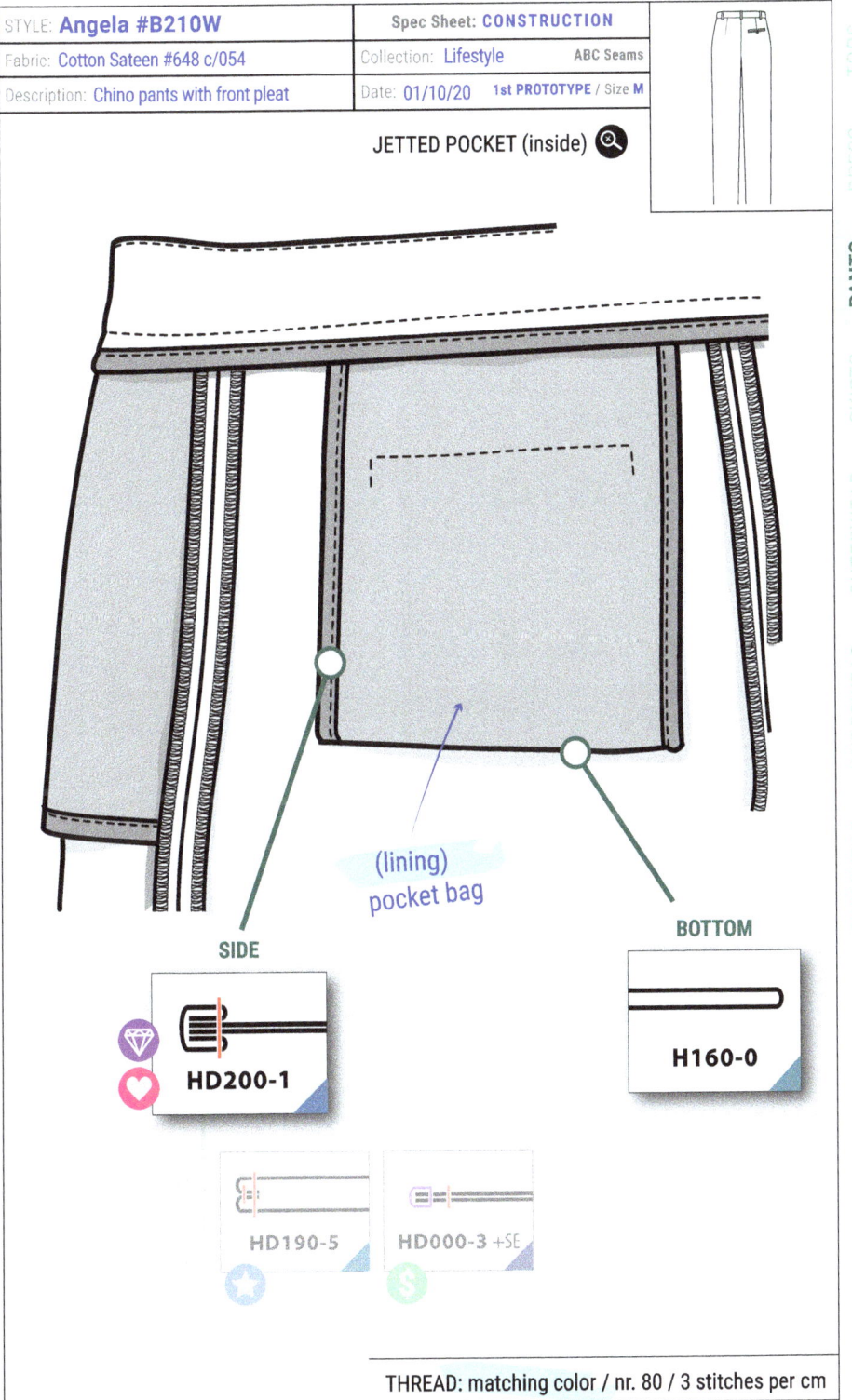

# BERMUDA SHORTS

Robert #B211W

Elastic waistband

Cargo pockets

False fly

Jetted-patch pocket (back)

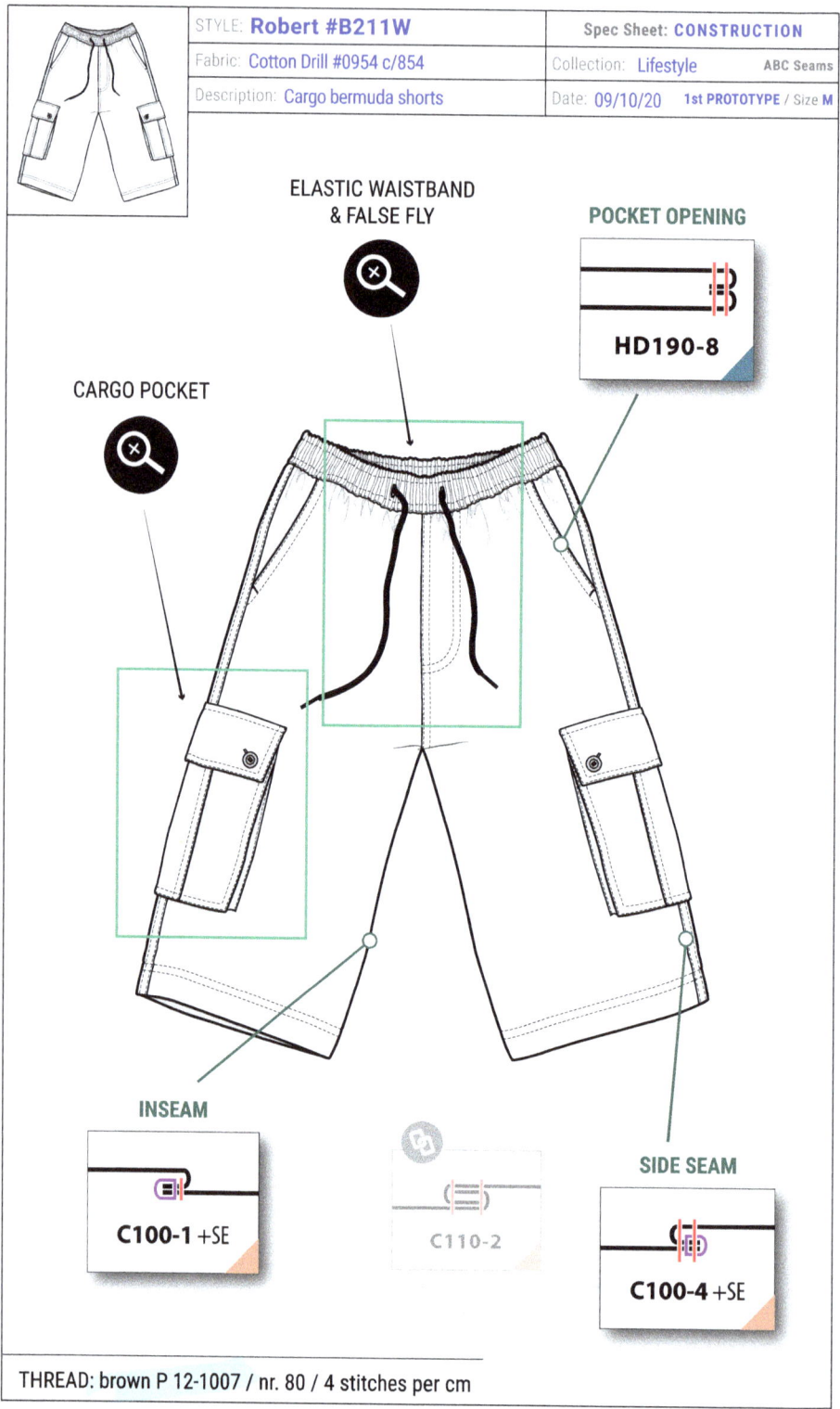

## Technical Specifications: Cargo Bermuda Shorts

| STYLE: **Robert #B211W** | Spec Sheet: **CONSTRUCTION** | |
|---|---|---|
| Fabric: Cotton Drill #0954 c/854 | Collection: Lifestyle | ABC Seams |
| Description: Cargo bermuda shorts | Date: 09/10/20 | **1st PROTOTYPE** / Size **M** |

**JETTED-PATCH POCKET**

**CROTCH**

**C100-4 +SE**

3cm

**BOTTOM**

wide hem

**H130-6**

H130-3

H130-14

THREAD: brown P 12-1007 / nr. 80 / 4 stitches per cm

TOPS · DRESS · PANTS · SKIRTS · OUTERWEAR · UNDERWEAR · SWIMWEAR

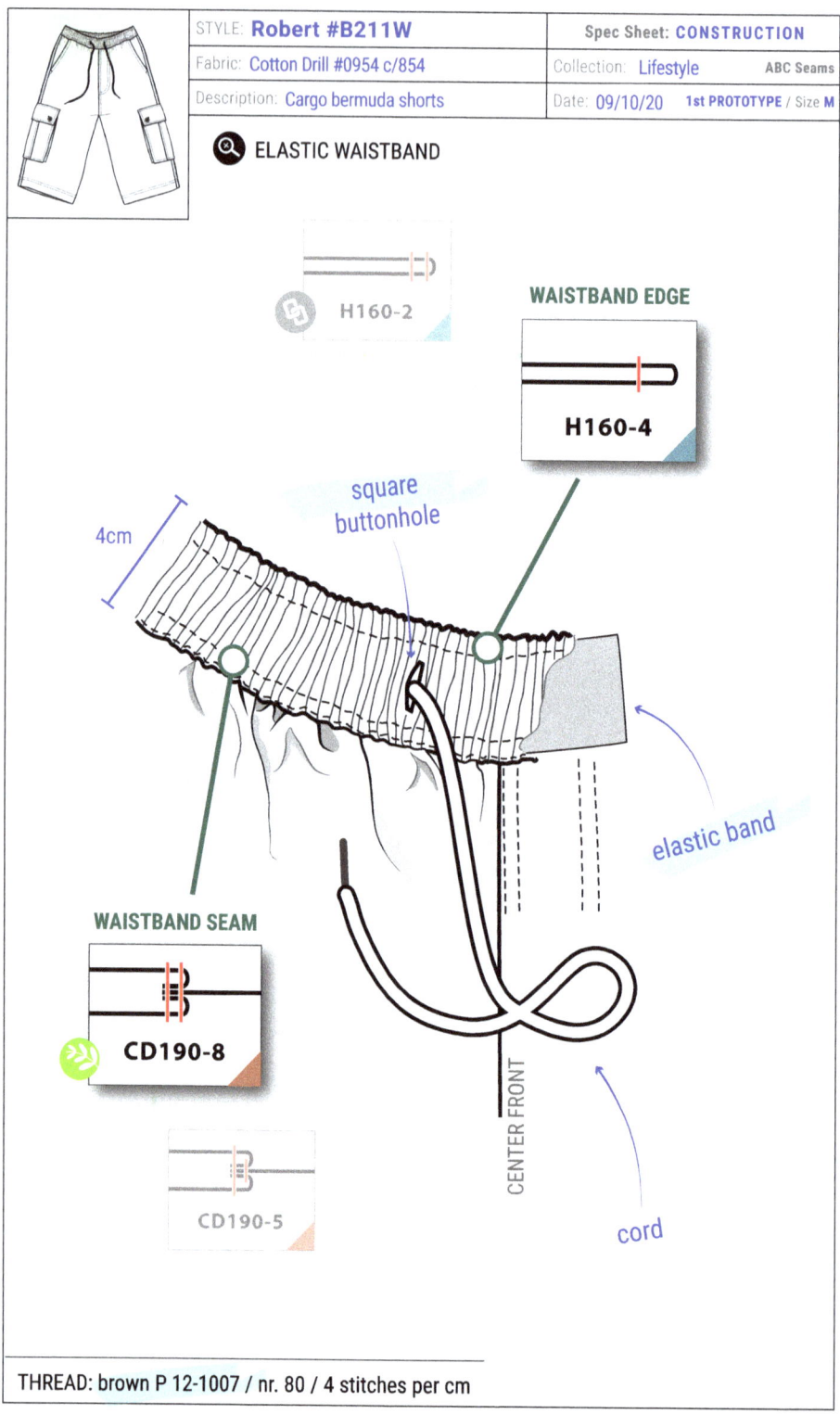

## Technical Specifications: Cargo Bermuda Shorts

| STYLE: **Robert #B211W** | Spec Sheet: **CONSTRUCTION** | |
|---|---|---|
| Fabric: Cotton Drill #0954 c/854 | Collection: Lifestyle | ABC Seams |
| Description: Cargo bermuda shorts | Date: 09/10/20 | **1st PROTOTYPE** / Size **M** |

**FALSE FLY**

**FALSE FLY (crotch)**

**HD190-8**

HD190-4

**FALSE FLY (facing)**

**D200-6x +SE**

**FRONT CROTCH (under)**

**C100-4 +SE**

C100-3 +SE

D203-1Vx

THREAD: brown P 12-1007 / nr. 80 / 4 stitches per cm

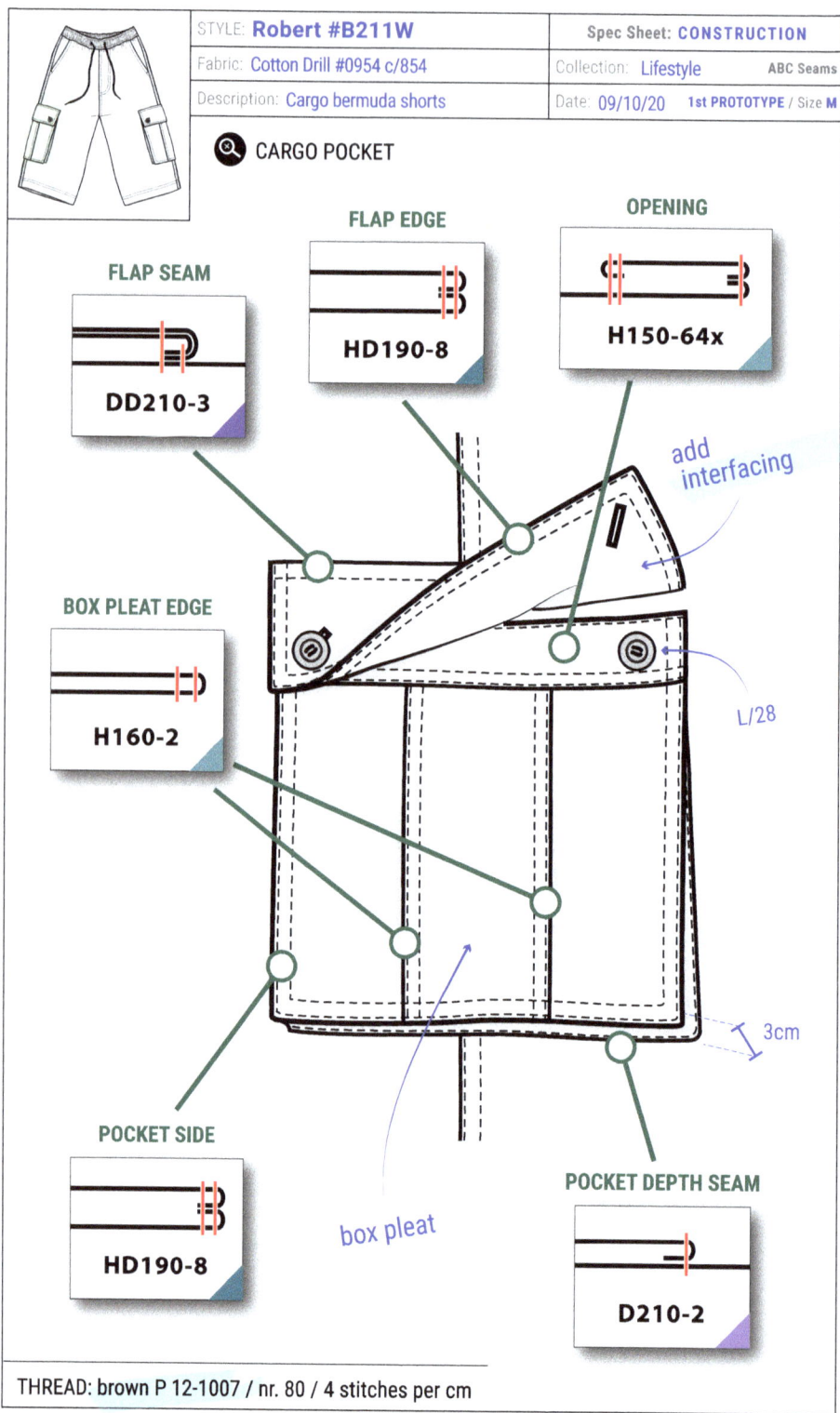

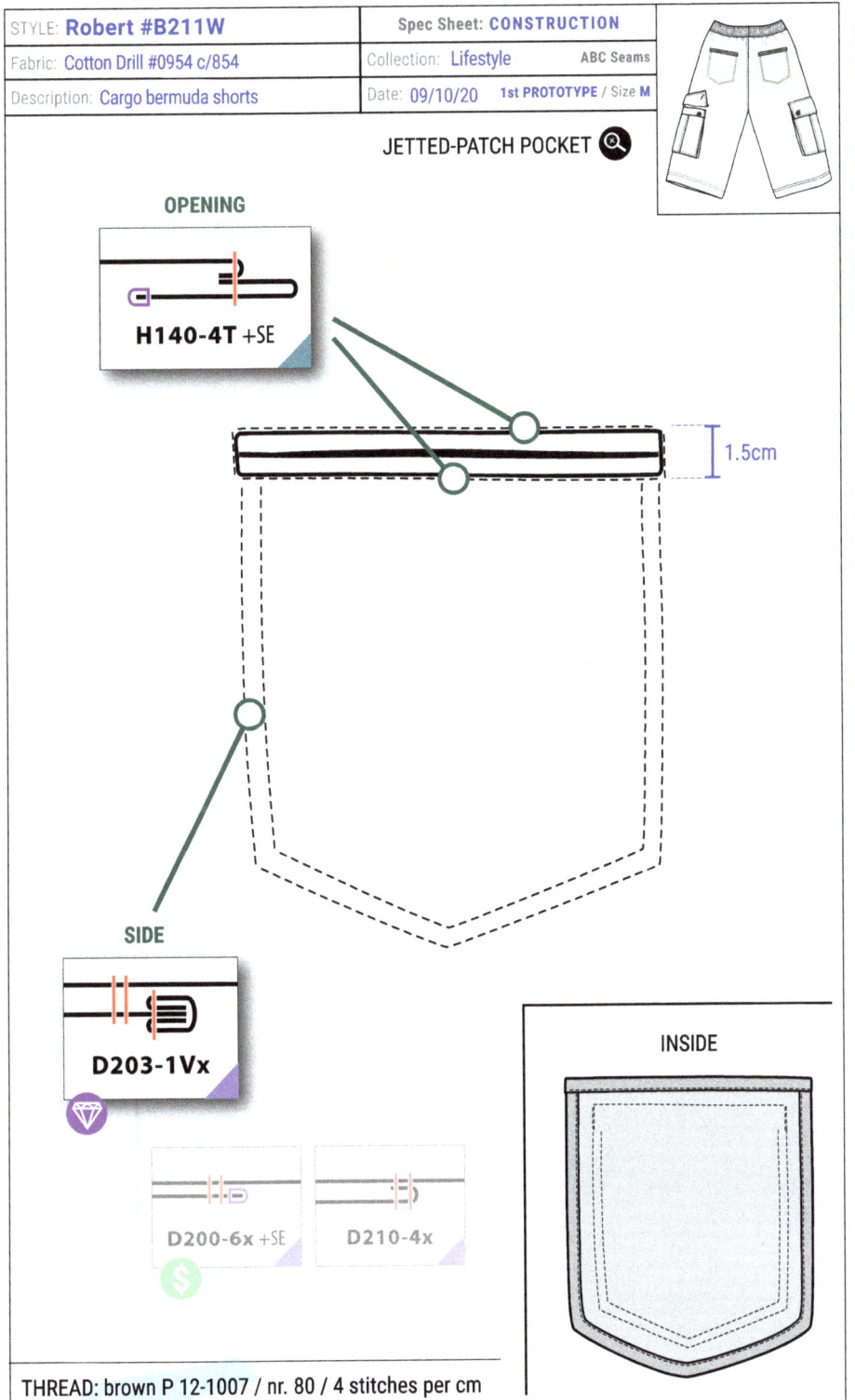

# SHORTS

Donna #B212W

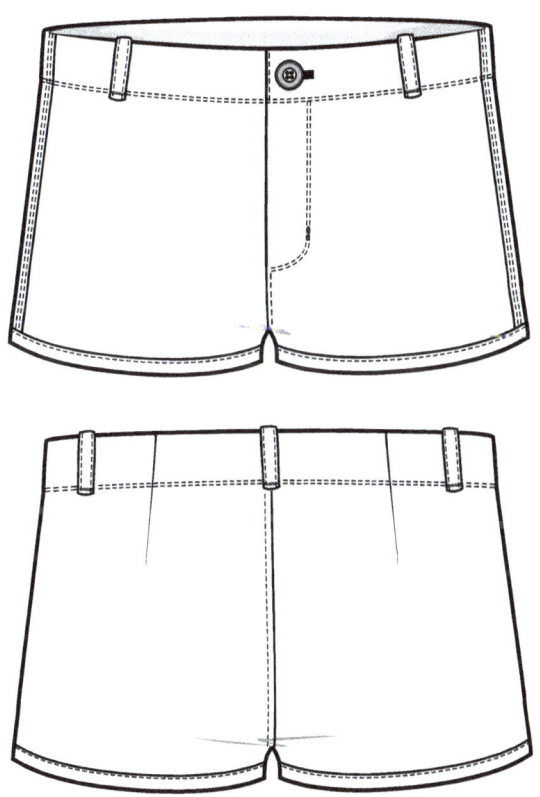

Faced waistband

Low rise

Zip fly

Binded bottom

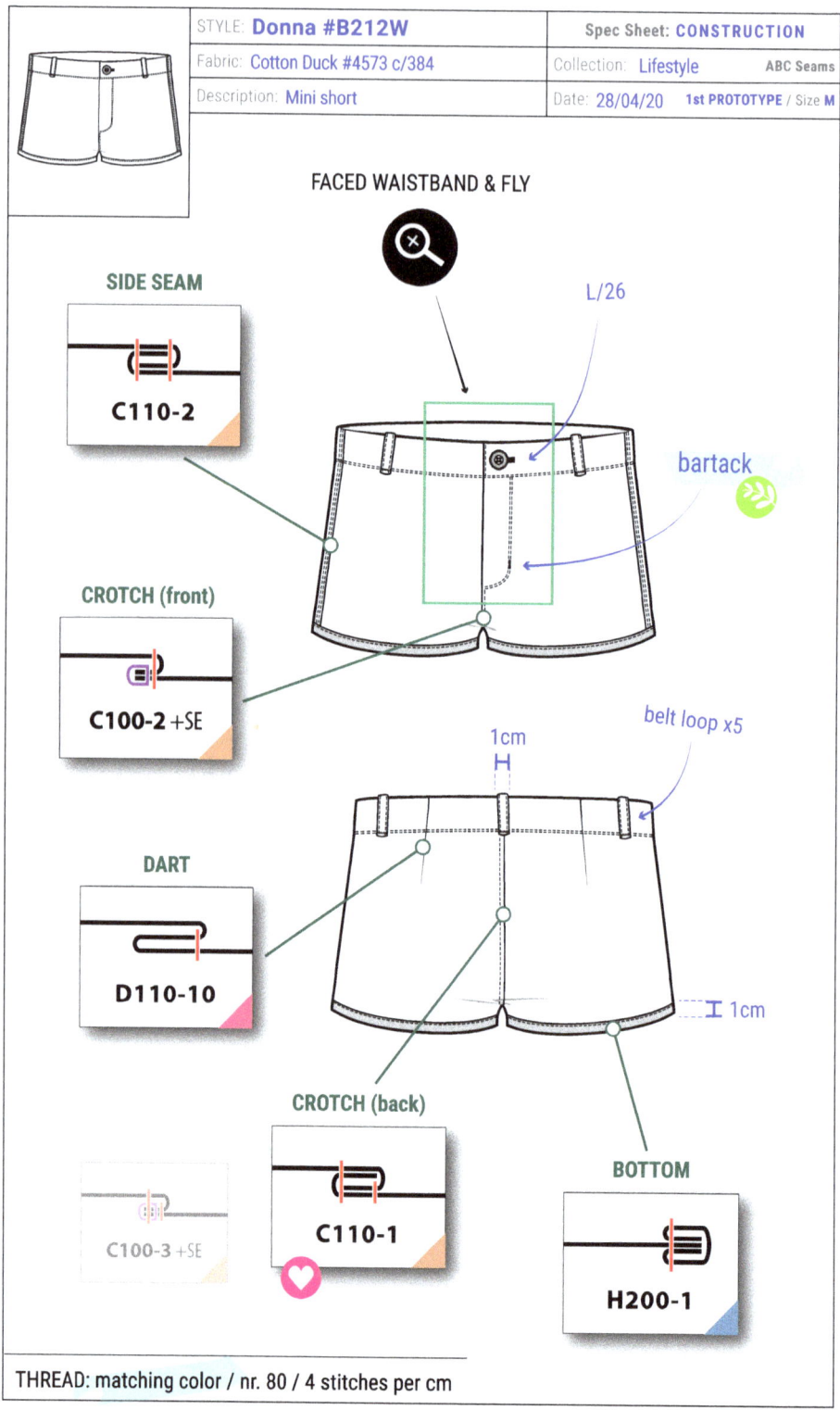

# Technical Specifications: Shorts

| STYLE: **Donna #B212W** | Spec Sheet: **CONSTRUCTION** | |
|---|---|---|
| Fabric: **Cotton Duck #4573 c/384** | Collection: **Lifestyle** | **ABC Seams** |
| Description: **Mini short** | Date: **28/04/20** **1st PROTOTYPE** / Size **M** | |

## FACED WAISTBAND and FLY

**H150-62**

### WAISTBAND
**H150-61**

### FLY SEAM (facing)
FACING
**D210-9x**

4cm

nylon zip

square buttonhole

### FLY SEAM (zip guard)
**CE100T-2 +SE**

### FLY EDGE (facing)
**HD190-2**

### ZIPPER TAPE
**D400-3x**

THREAD: matching color / nr. 80 / 4 stitches per cm

# LEGGINGS

Luisa #B213K

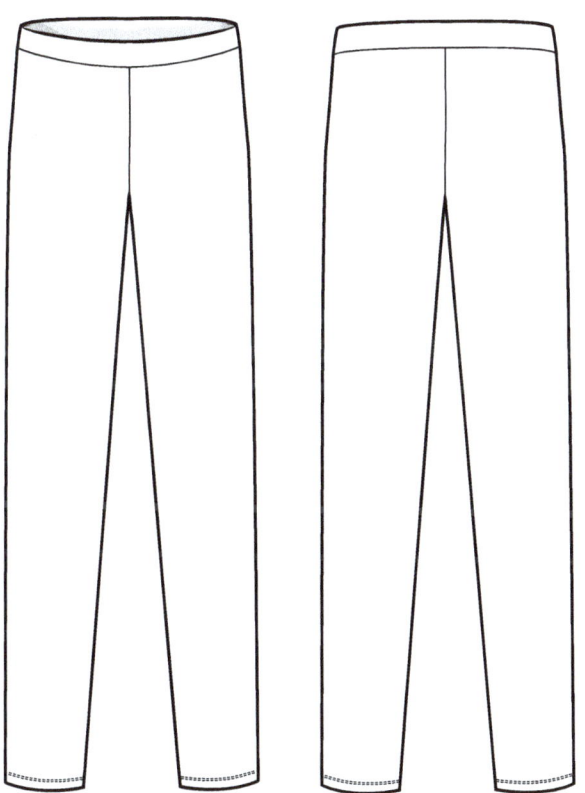

Classic style
Elastic waistband
Clean look
7/8 Length

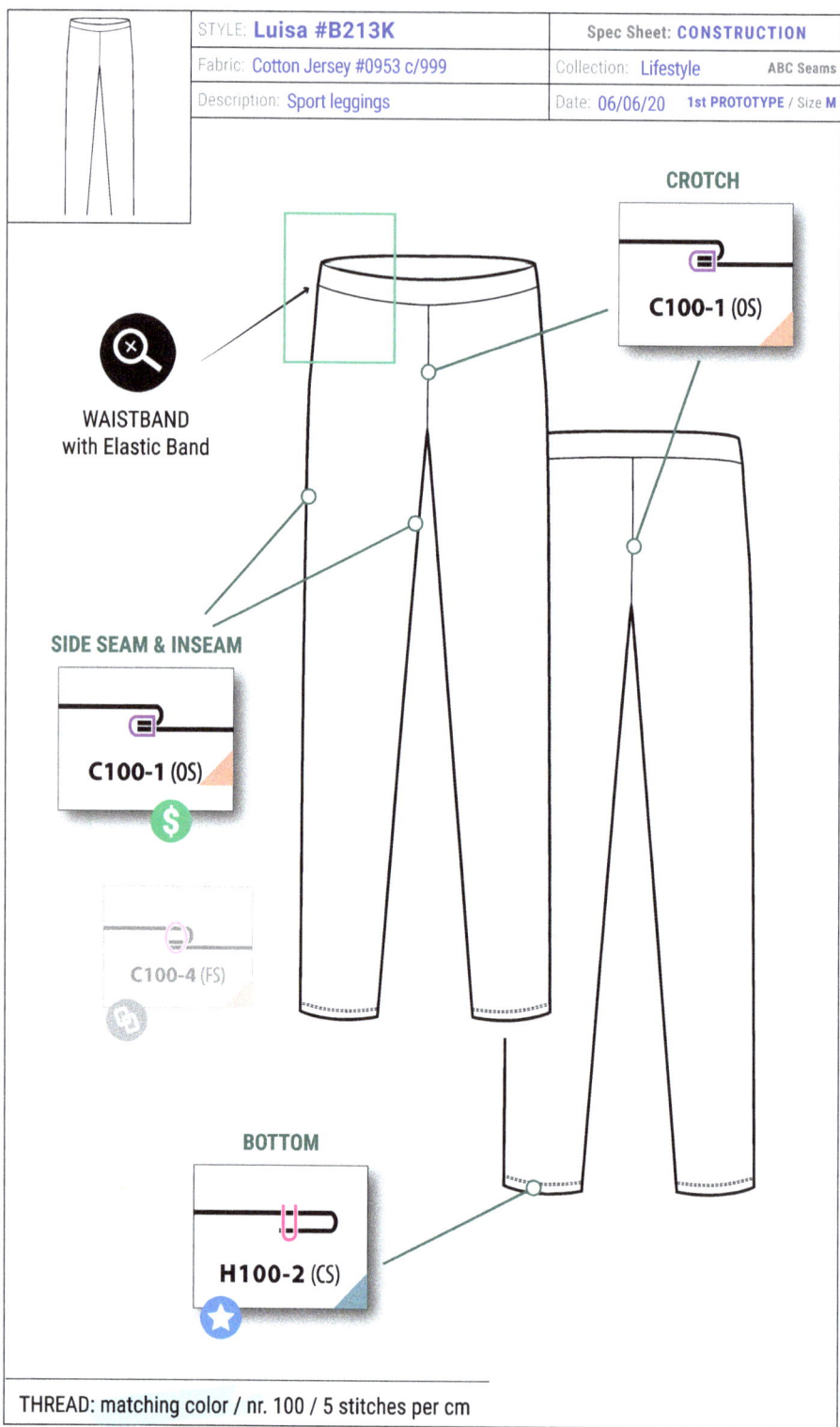

# Technical Specifications: Leggings

| STYLE: **Luisa #B213K** | Spec Sheet: **CONSTRUCTION** | |
|---|---|---|
| Fabric: **Cotton Jersey #0953 c/999** | Collection: **Lifestyle** | **ABC Seams** |
| Description: **Sport leggings** | Date: **06/06/20** | **1st PROTOTYPE** / Size **M** |

## WAISTBAND with Elastic Band

**attach the elastic band on each side seam**

H160-1

**WAISTBAND EDGE**

**H160-0**

**elastic band (3cm width)**

**WAISTBAND SEAM**

**CE100-1** (OS)

THREAD: matching color / nr. 100 / 5 stitches per cm

PANTS

# BUTTON FRONT

16-5425 TCX
17-4139 TCX
14-0852 TCX

# A-LINE SKIRT

### Patricia #B214W

Buttoned front opening
Straight waistband (one- piece)
False pocket
Wide bottom

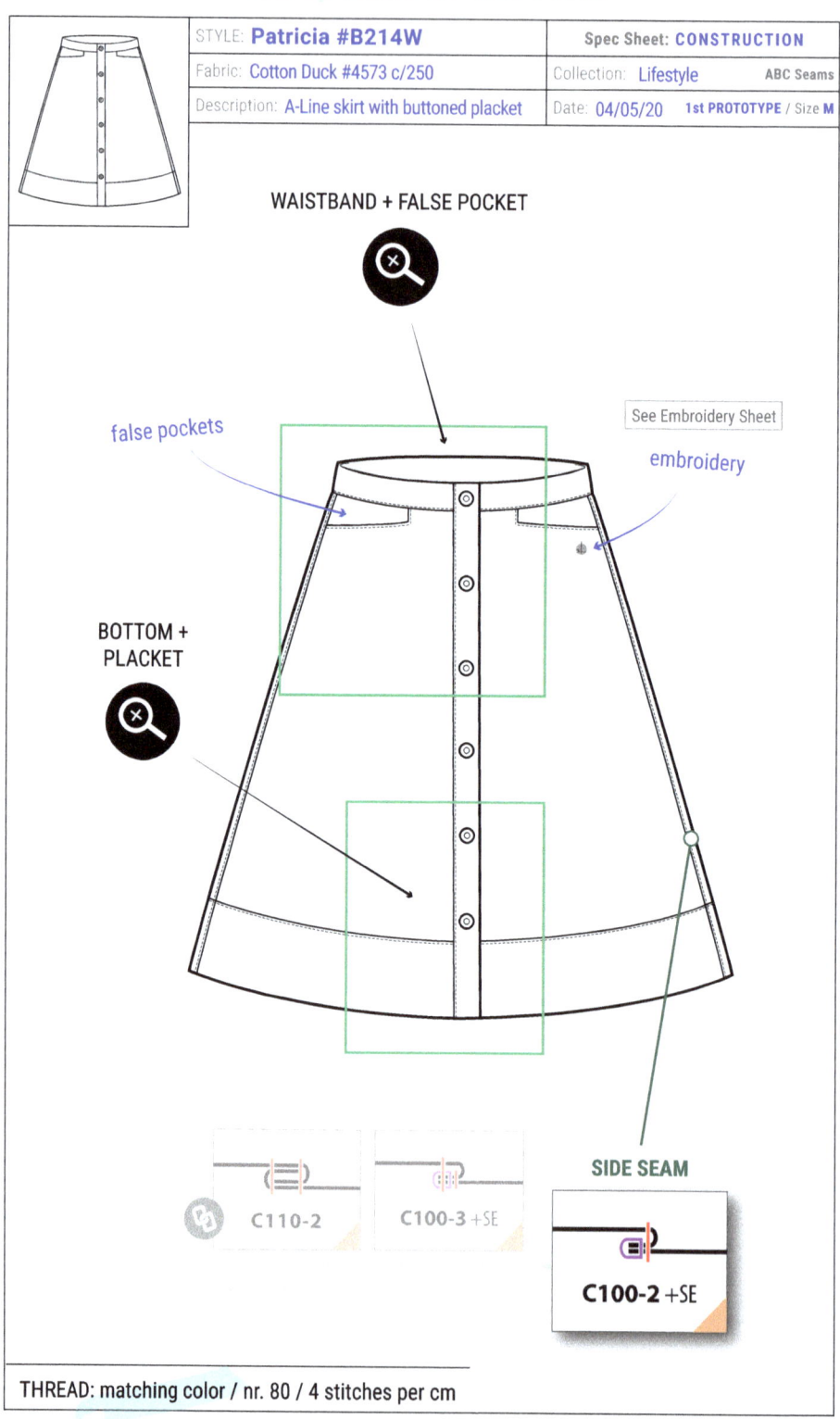

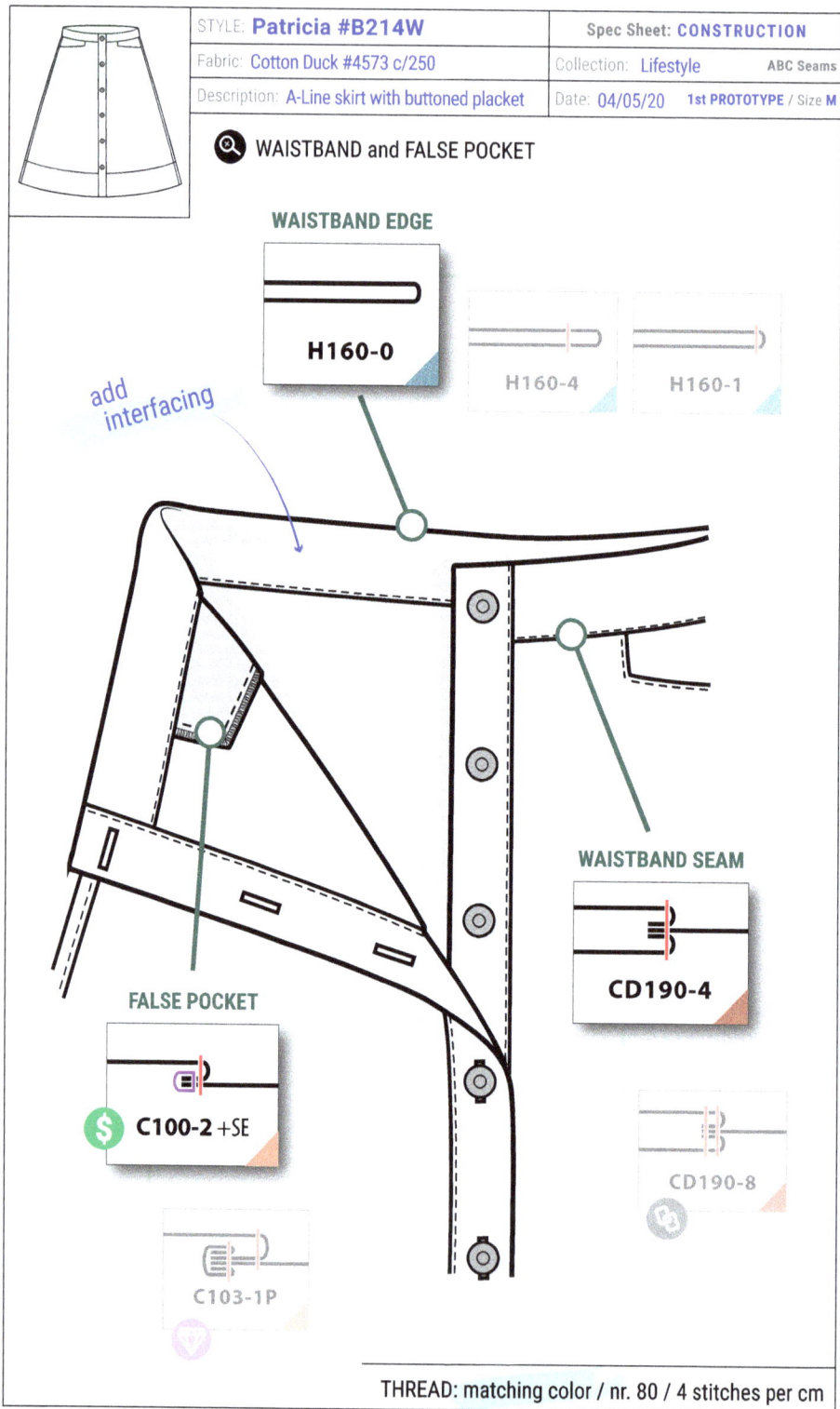

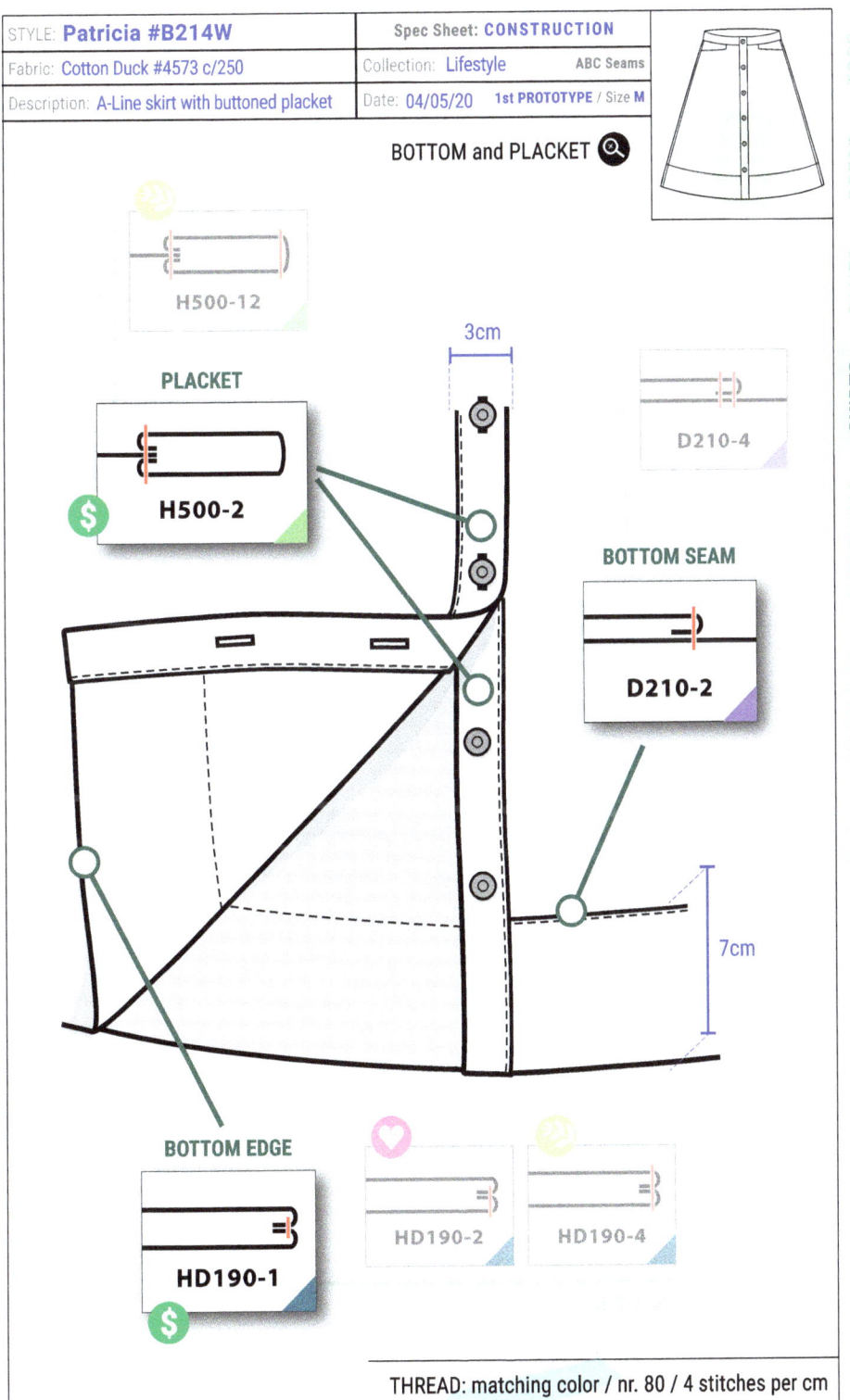

# MINI

| | |
|---|---|
| | 18-4436 TCX |
| | 19-4007 TCX |
| | 16-1305 TCX |

# DENIM SKIRT

Linda #B215J

Button fly
Straight waistband (two pieces)
Patch pocket with flap (front)
Welt pocket (back)

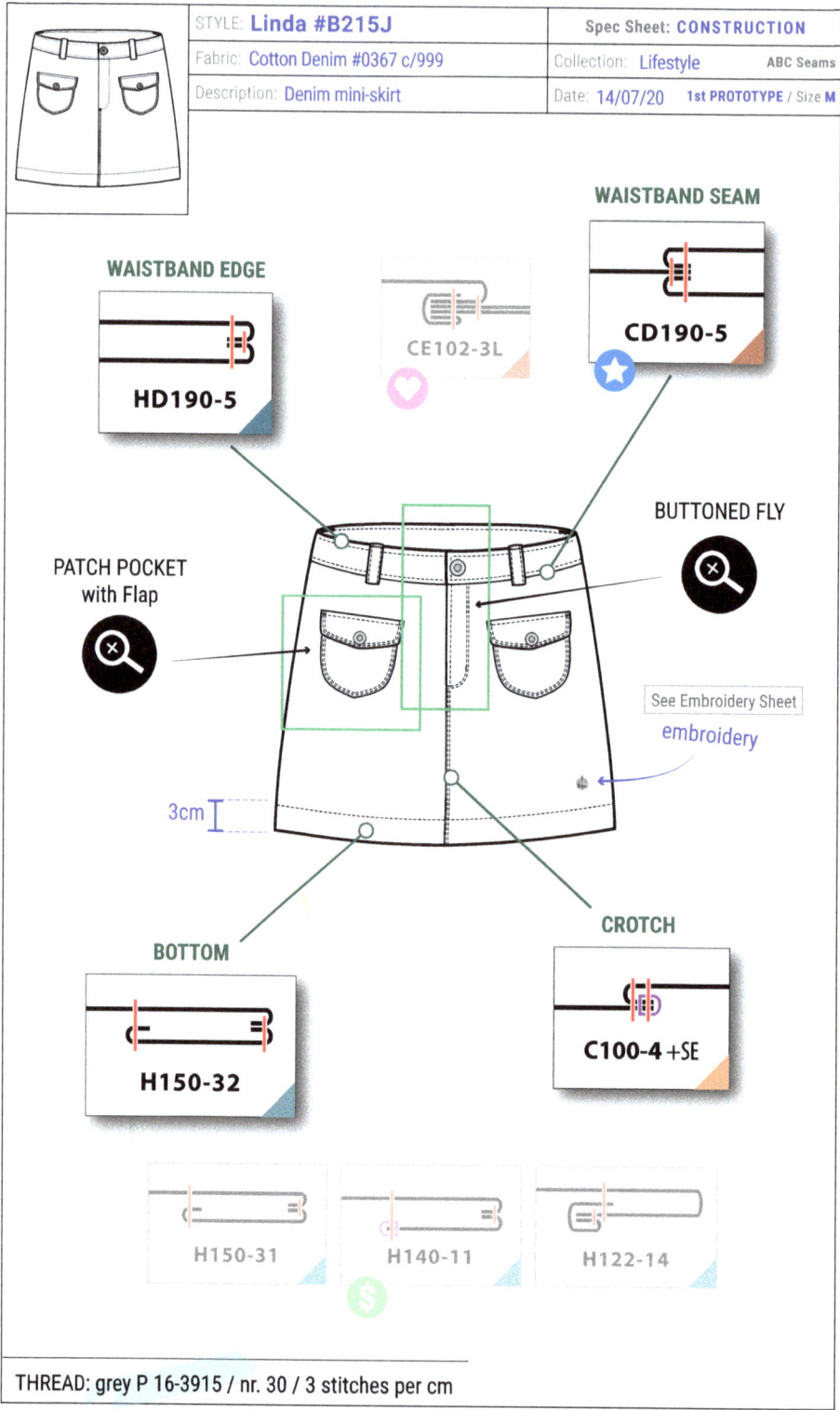

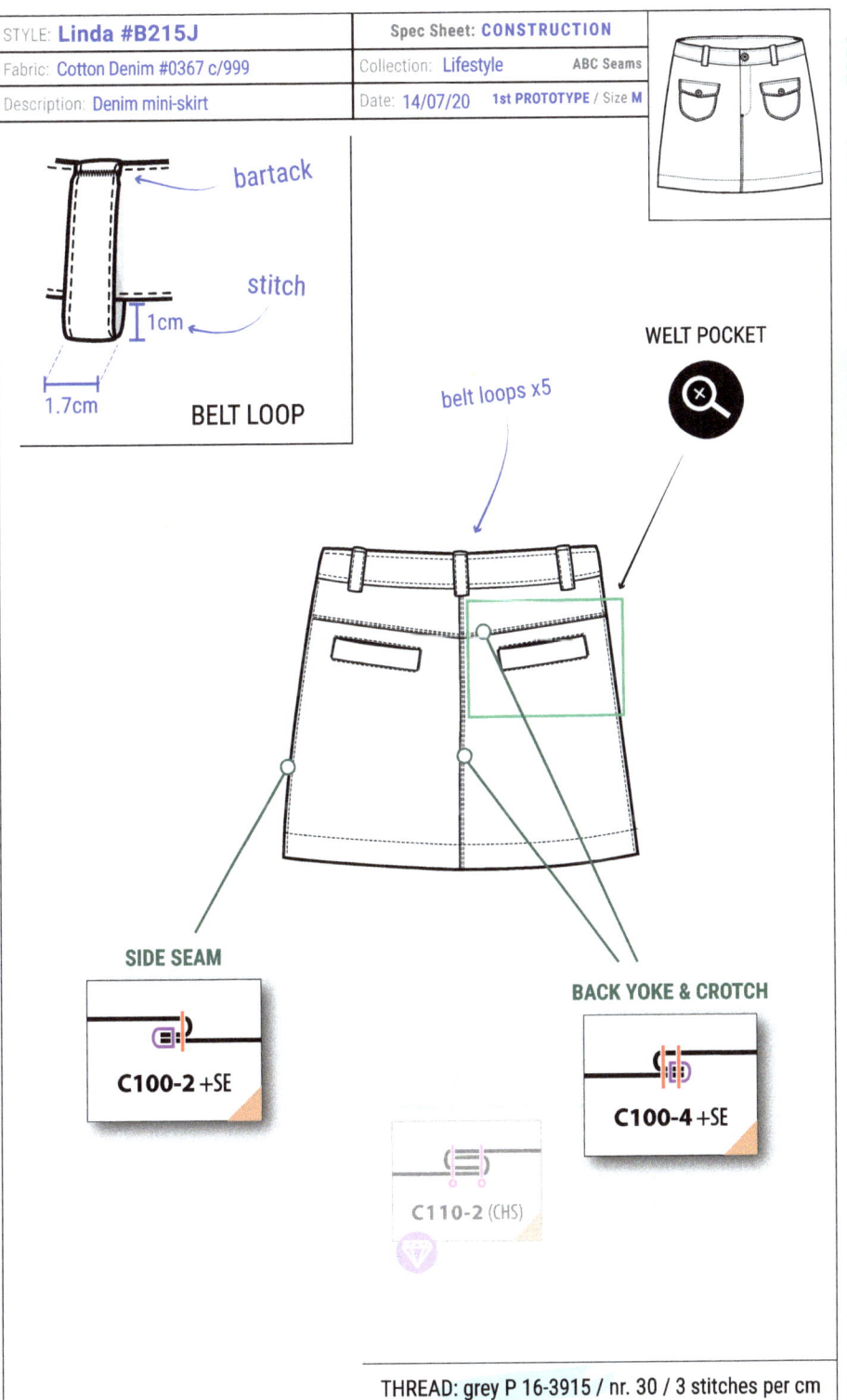

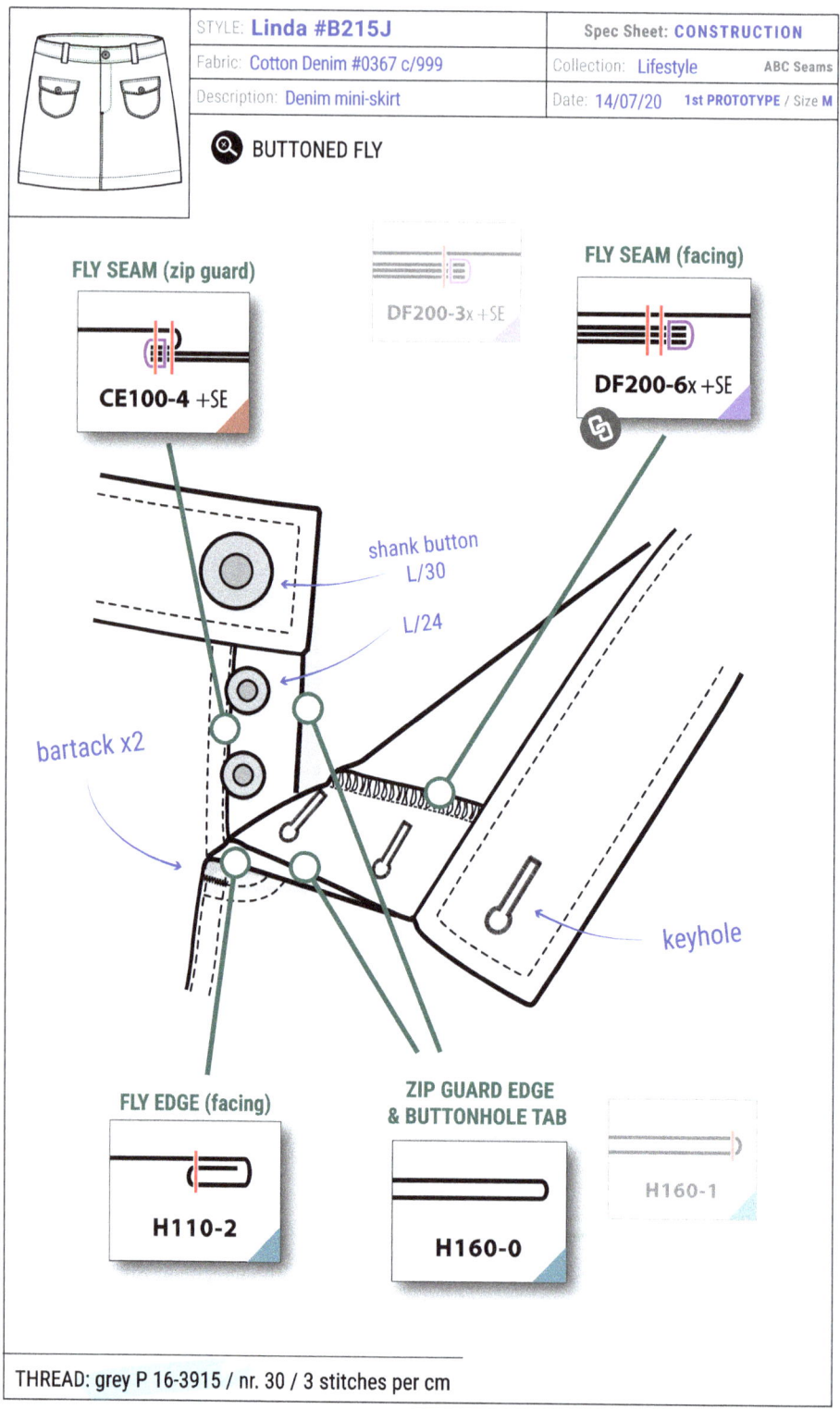

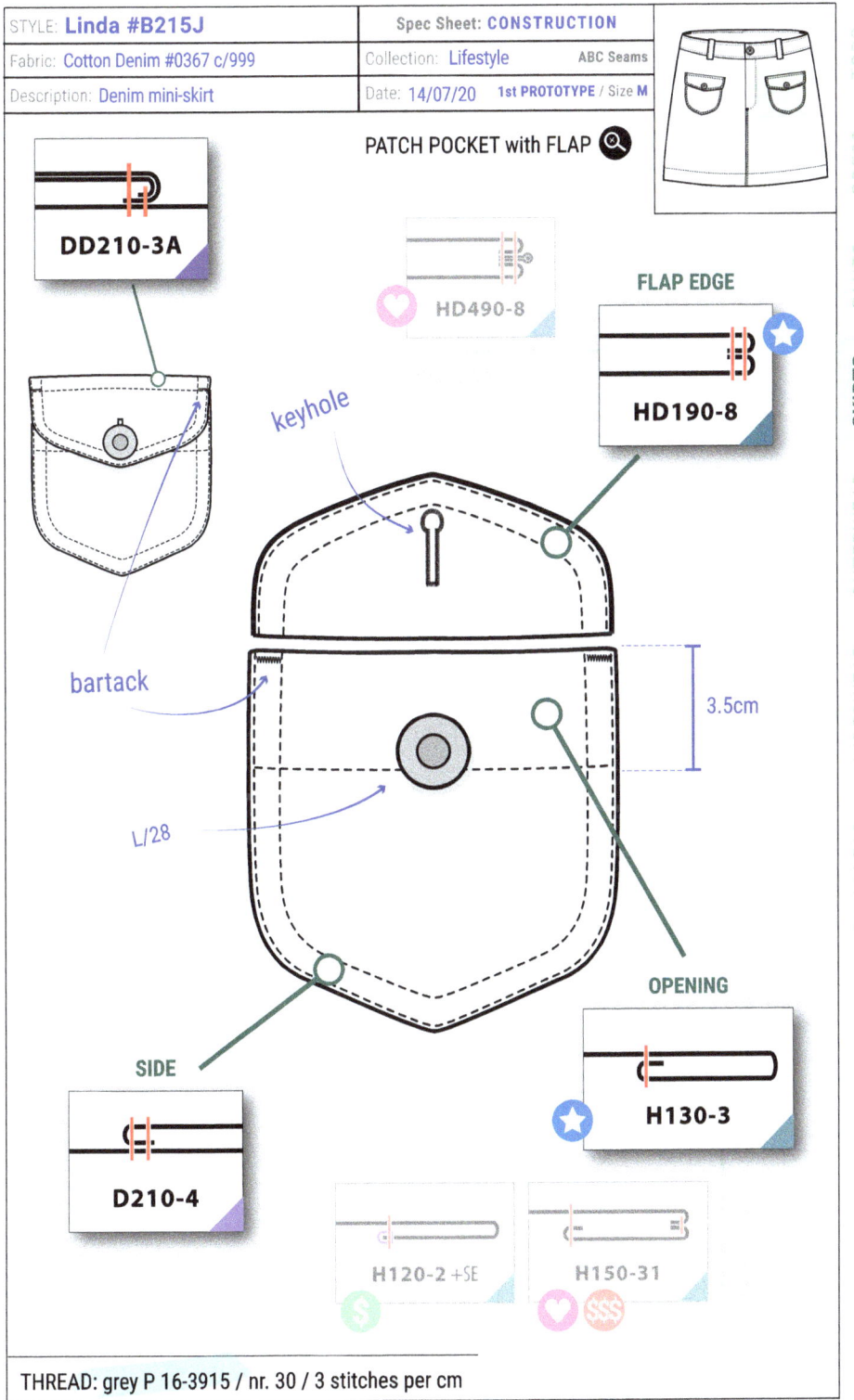

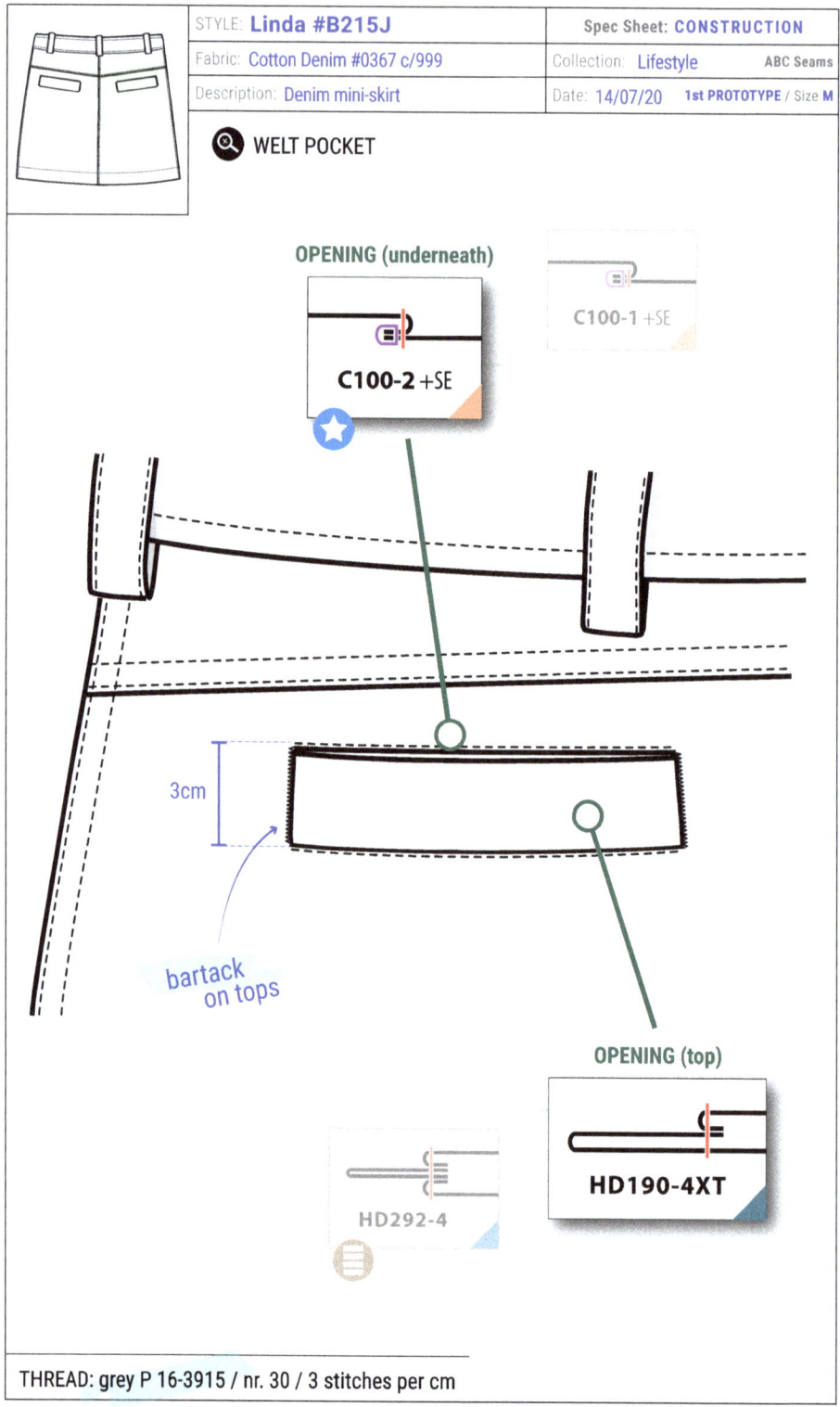

Technical Specifications: Denim Skirt

| STYLE: **Linda #B215J** | Spec Sheet: **CONSTRUCTION** | |
|---|---|---|
| Fabric: Cotton Denim #0367 c/999 | Collection: Lifestyle | ABC Seams |
| Description: Denim mini-skirt | Date: 14/07/20 | **1st PROTOTYPE** / Size **M** |

**WELT POCKET** (inside)

BACK YOKE

CB

**BOTTOM**

H160-0

(lining) pocket bag

**SIDE**

HD190-5

HD200-1

HD000-3 +SE

THREAD: grey P 16-3915 / nr. 30 / 3 stitches per cm

TOPS · DRESS · PANTS · SKIRTS · OUTERWEAR · UNDERWEAR · SWIMWEAR

# SWEATSHIRT

### Simon #B216J

CF Zipper with facing

Knitted cuff and bottom

Kangaroo pocket

Lined hood

## Technical Specifications: Sweatshirt

| | | |
|---|---|---|
| STYLE: **Simon #B216J** | Spec Sheet: **CONSTRUCTION** | |
| Fabric: **Jersey Sweatshirt #01454 c/026** | Collection: **Lifestyle** | **ABC Seams** |
| Description: **Hooded sweatshirt** | Date: **16/05/20** **1st PROTOTYPE** / Size **M** | |

**ARMHOLE**
- C100-3 (OS)
- C100-4 (FS)
- **C100-1 (OS)**

**LINED HOOD**

**INNER HALF-MOON YOKE** — fabric 2
- **D200-2x +SE**
- D200-4x (FS)

**BOTTOM SEAM**
- CE100-4 (FS)
- **CE100-1 (OS)**

**BOTTOM EDGE**
- **H160-0**

THREAD: matching color / nr. 80 / 4 stitches per cm

TOPS · DRESS · PANTS · SKIRTS · OUTERWEAR · UNDERWEAR · SWIMWEAR

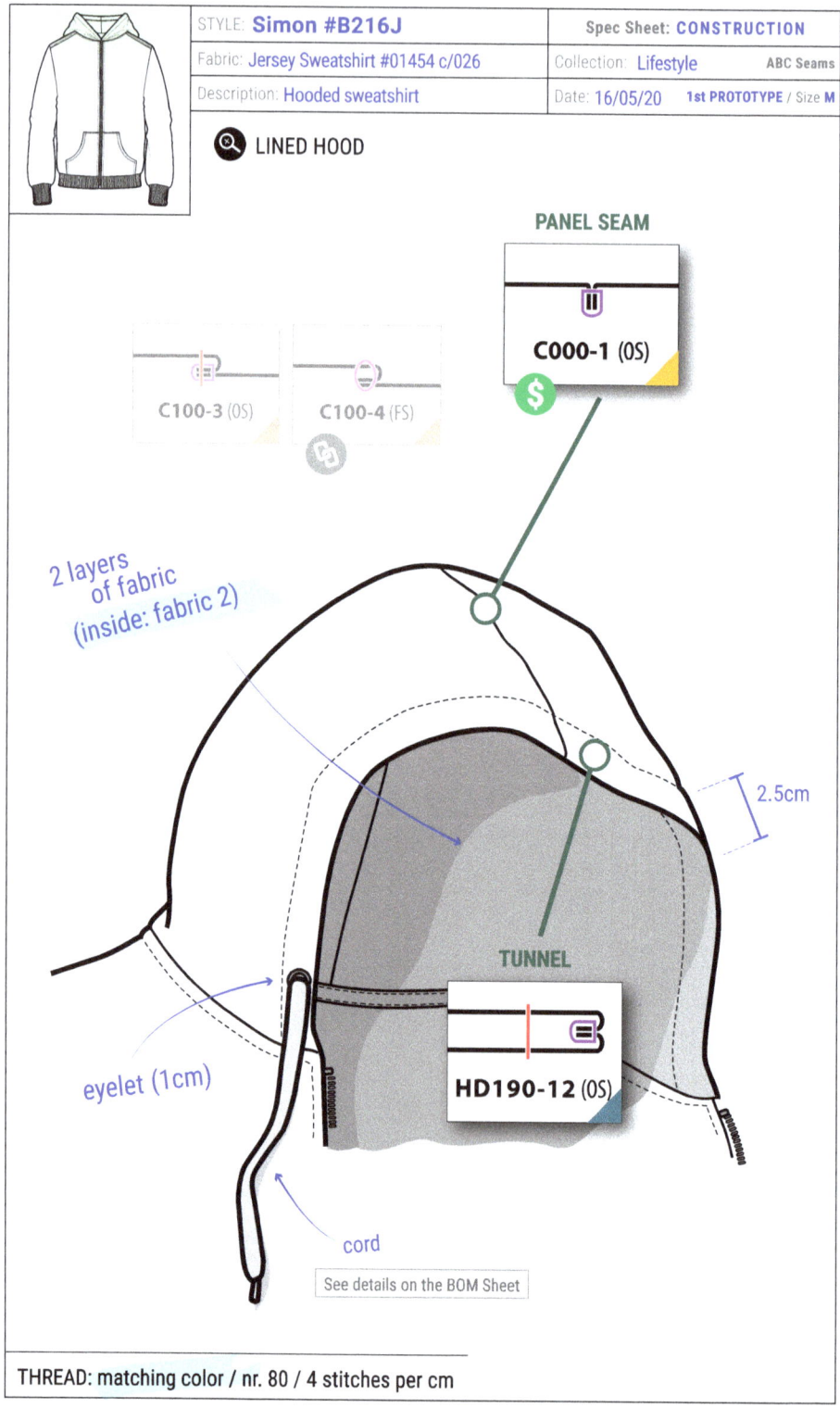

## Technical Specifications: Sweatshirt

| | | |
|---|---|---|
| STYLE: **Simon #B216J** | Spec Sheet: **CONSTRUCTION** | |
| Fabric: **Jersey Sweatshirt #01454 c/026** | Collection: **Lifestyle** — **ABC Seams** | |
| Description: **Hooded sweatshirt** | Date: **16/05/20** — **1st PROTOTYPE** / Size **M** | |

### NECKLINE & CF ZIP with Facing

**NECKLINE (back)**
CF104-3

**NECKLINE (front)**
CD190-5 +SE

hood lining and yoke: fabric 2

grosgrain tape (1cm)

facing (main fabric)

HD390-4

**CF ZIPPER**
HD390-5

**INNER YOKE**
See back sketch

**FACING EDGE**
H000-0 +SE

H100-2 (CS)

H200-1

THREAD: matching color / nr. 80 / 4 stitches per cm

TOPS · DRESS · PANTS · SKIRTS · OUTERWEAR · UNDERWEAR · SWIMWEAR

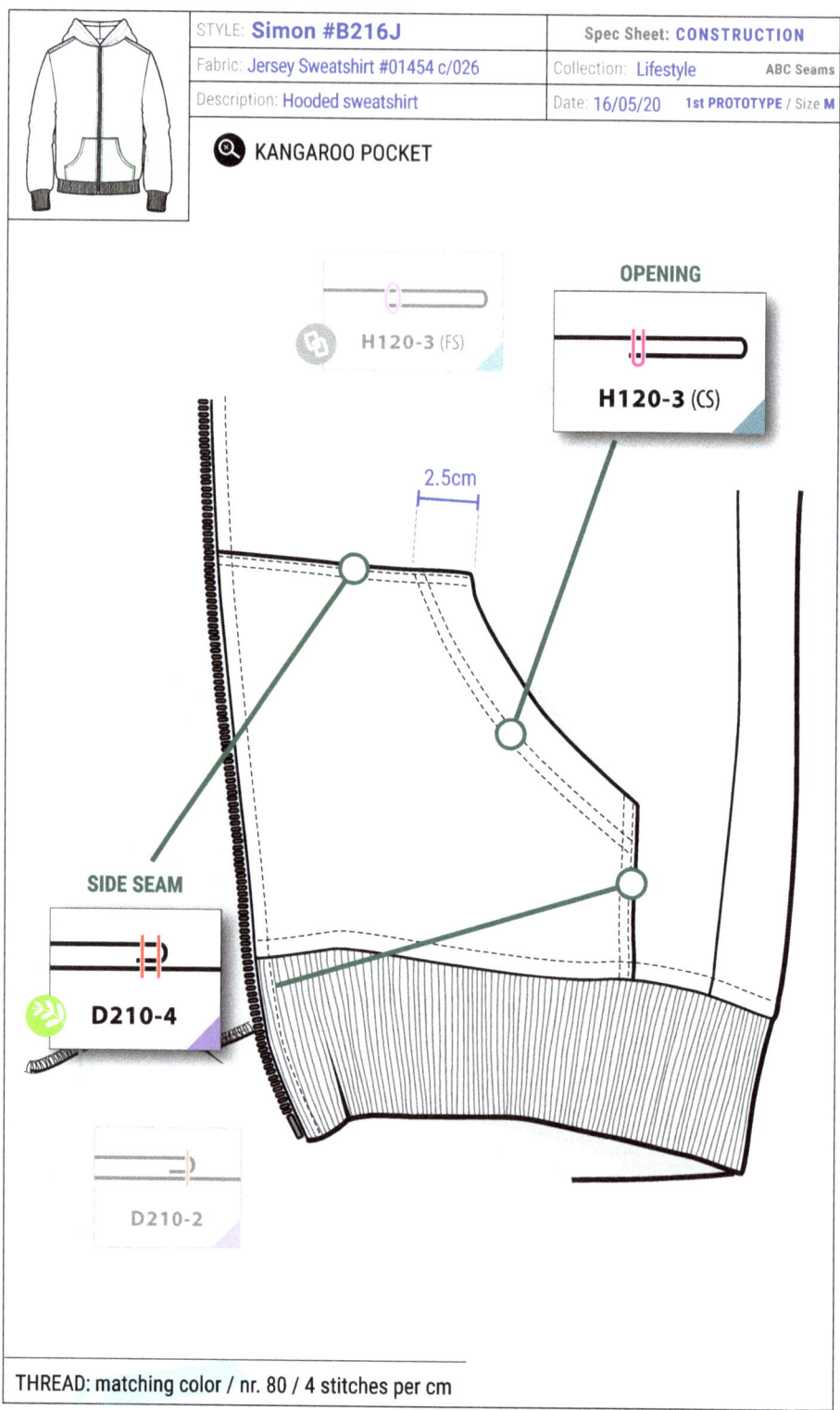

## Technical Specifications: Sweatshirt

| STYLE: **Simon #B216J** | Spec Sheet: **CONSTRUCTION** | |
|---|---|---|
| Fabric: **Jersey Sweatshirt #01454 c/026** | Collection: **Lifestyle** | **ABC Seams** |
| Description: **Hooded sweatshirt** | Date: **16/05/20** | **1st PROTOTYPE** / Size **M** |

**RIBBED CUFF**

**CUFF EDGE**
**H160-0**

**SIDE SEAM**
**C000-1** (OS)

rib 2x2
( fabric 3 )

WRONG SIDE

**CE100-4** (FS)

**CUFF SEAM**
**CE100-1** (OS)

THREAD: matching color / nr. 80 / 4 stitches per cm

# SMART

18-4436 TCX

15-1316 TCX

16-1305 TCX

# BLAZER
Tom #B217W

Classic lapel
Lined
Sleeve button vent
Double back vent
Clean look

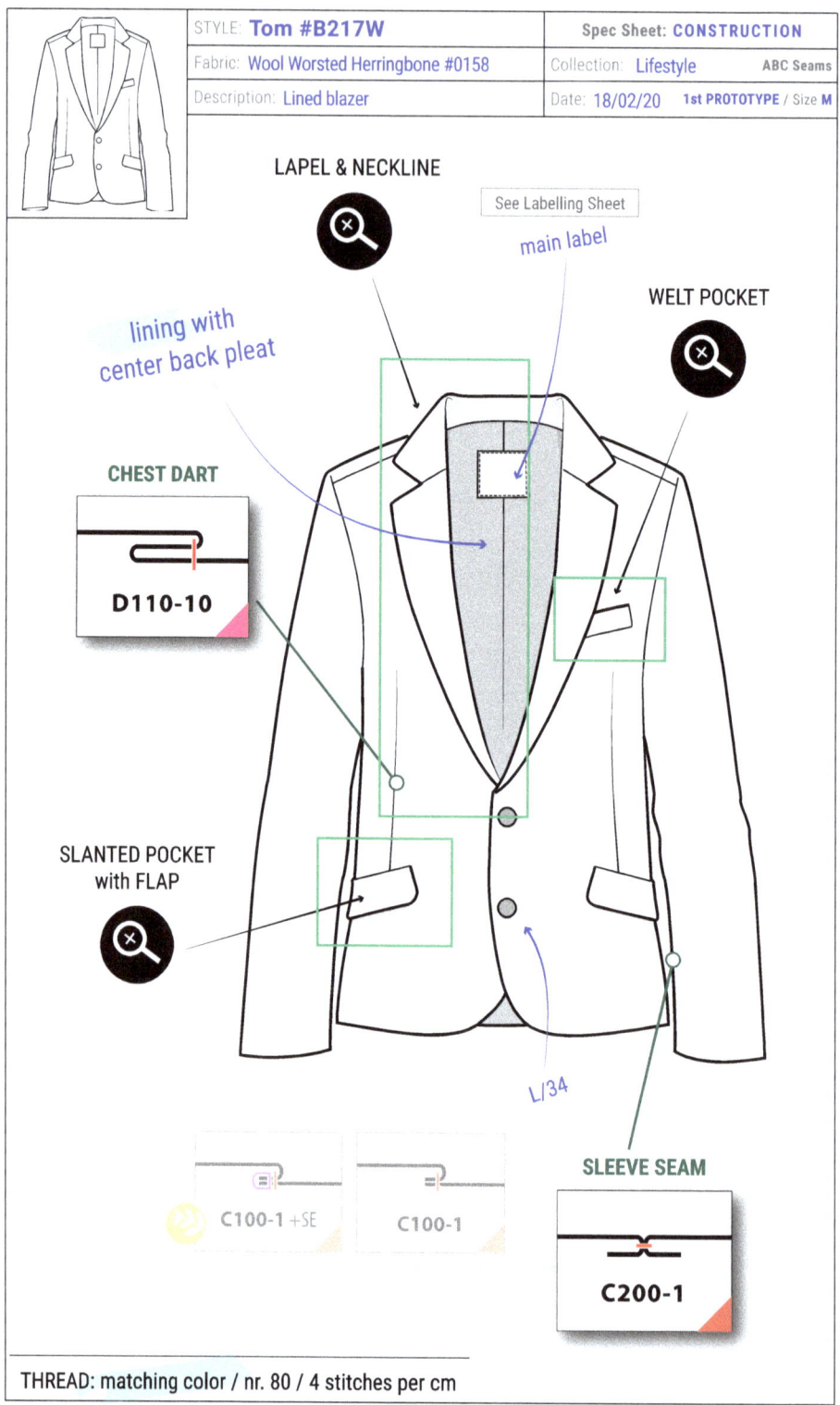

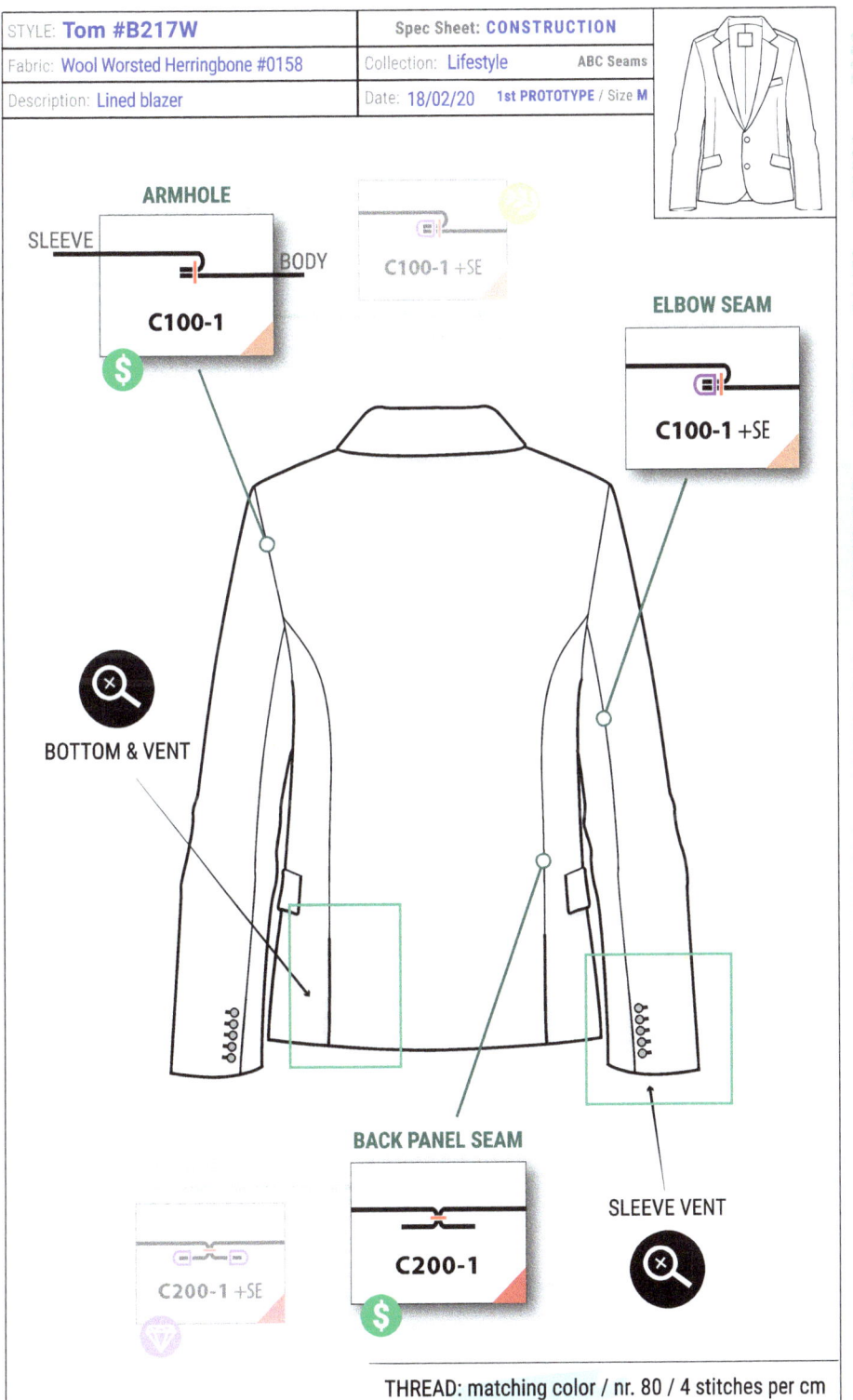

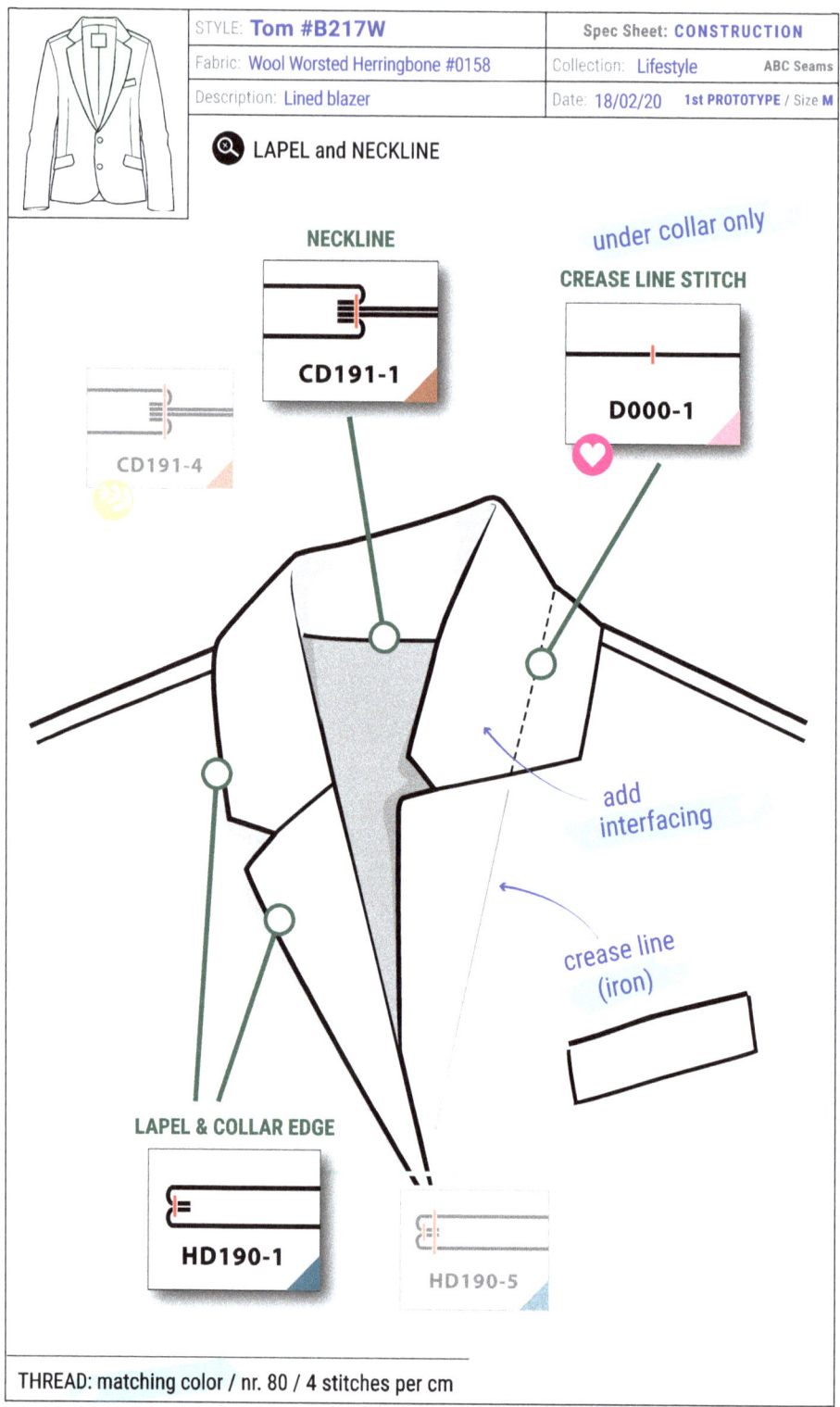

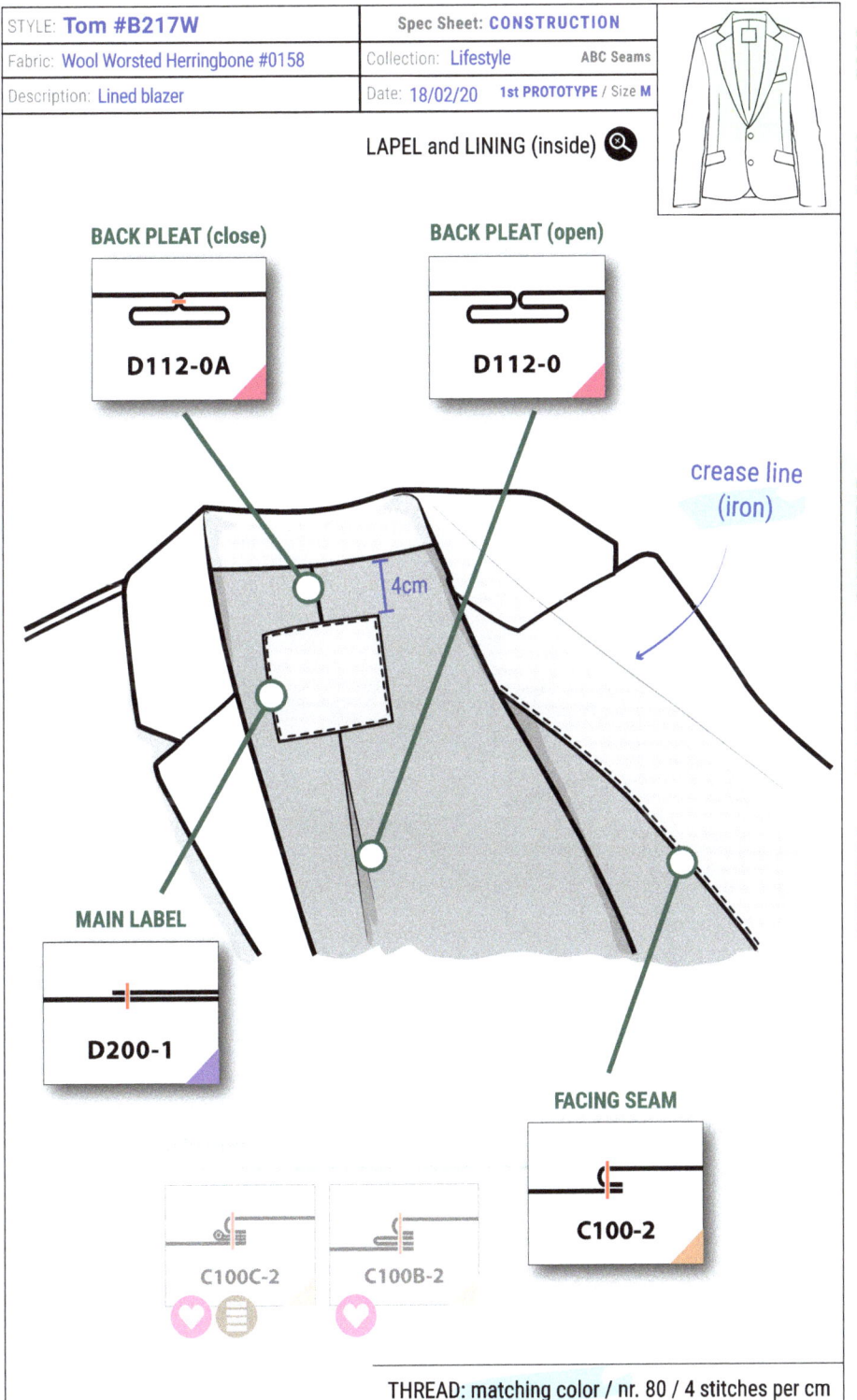

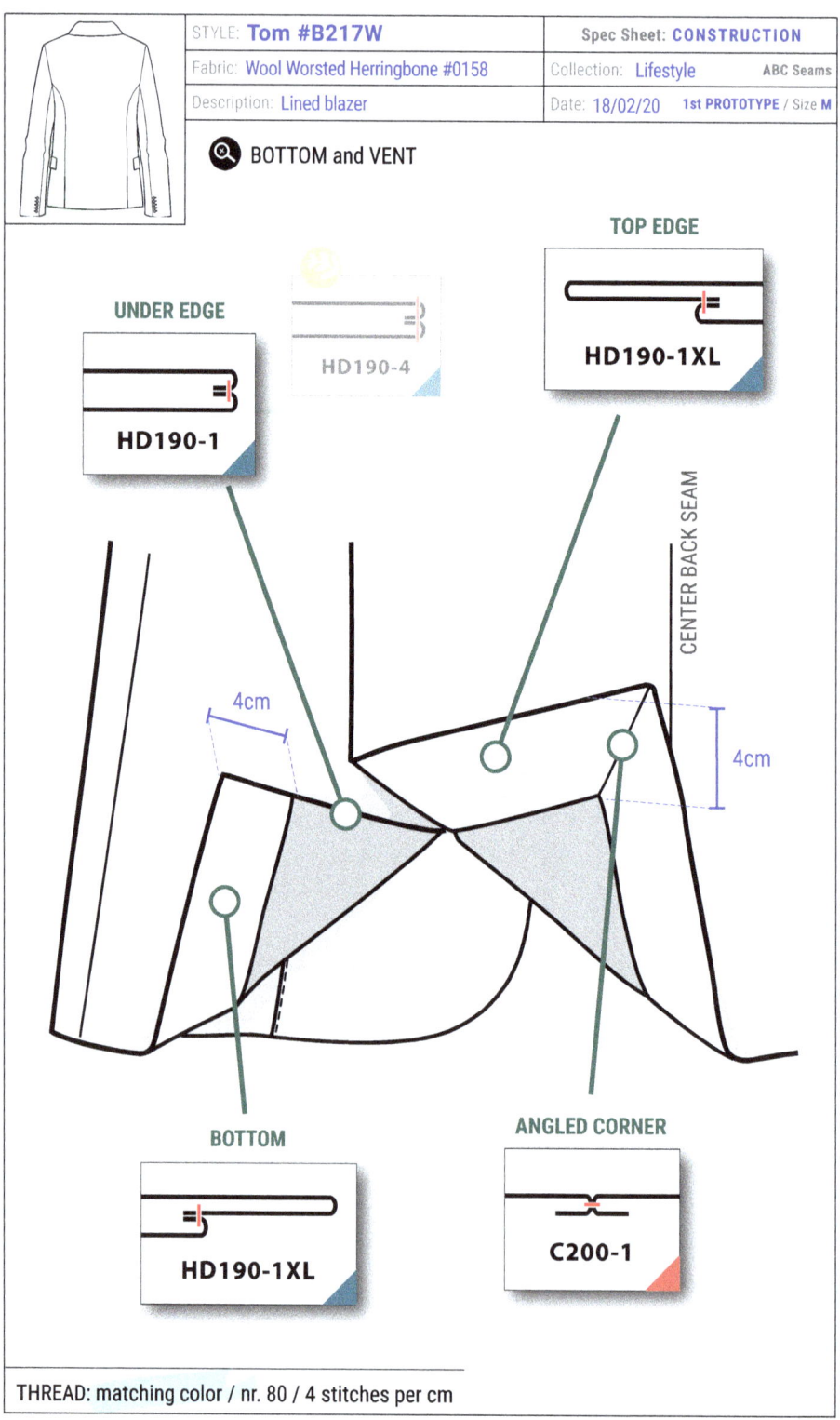

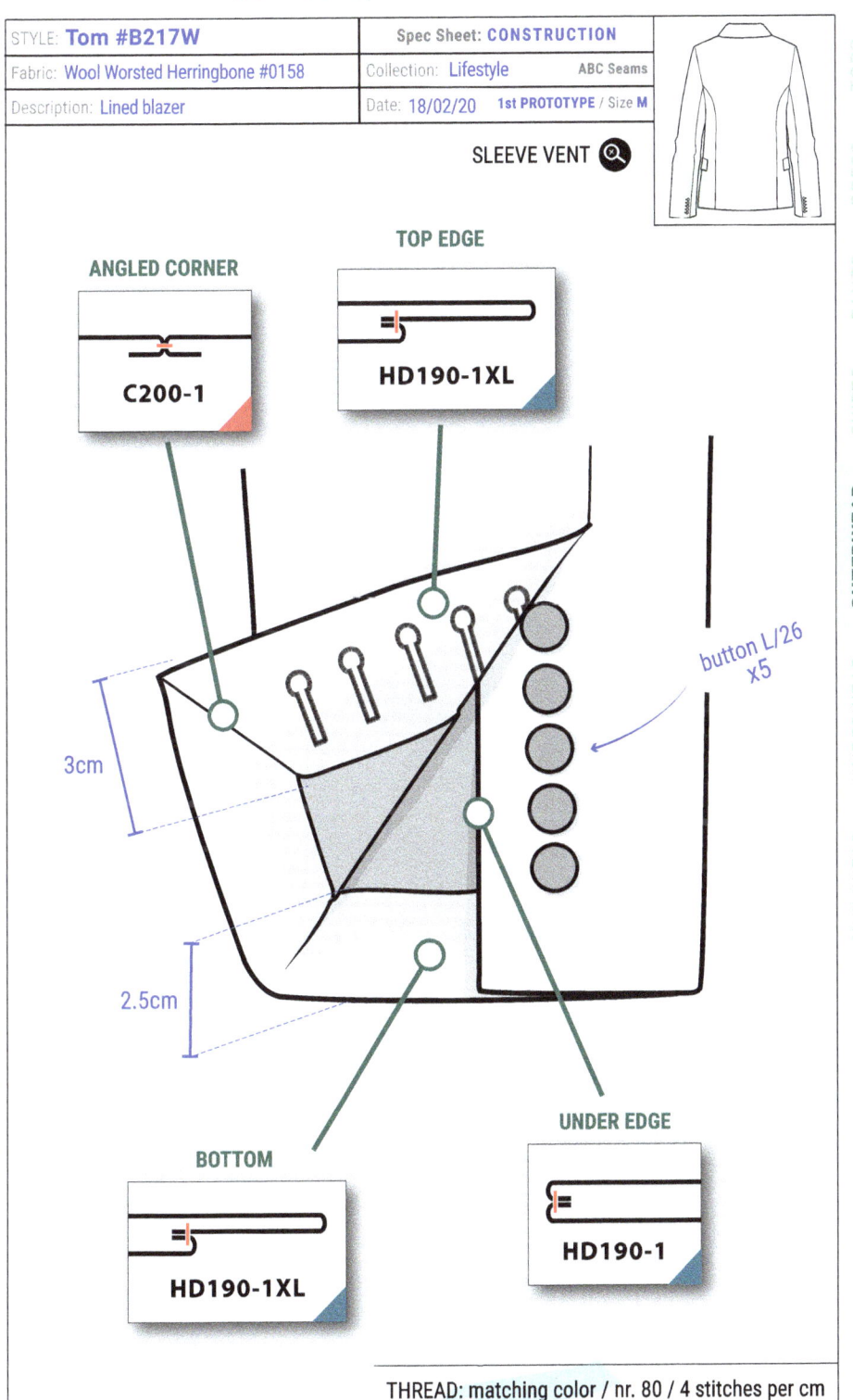

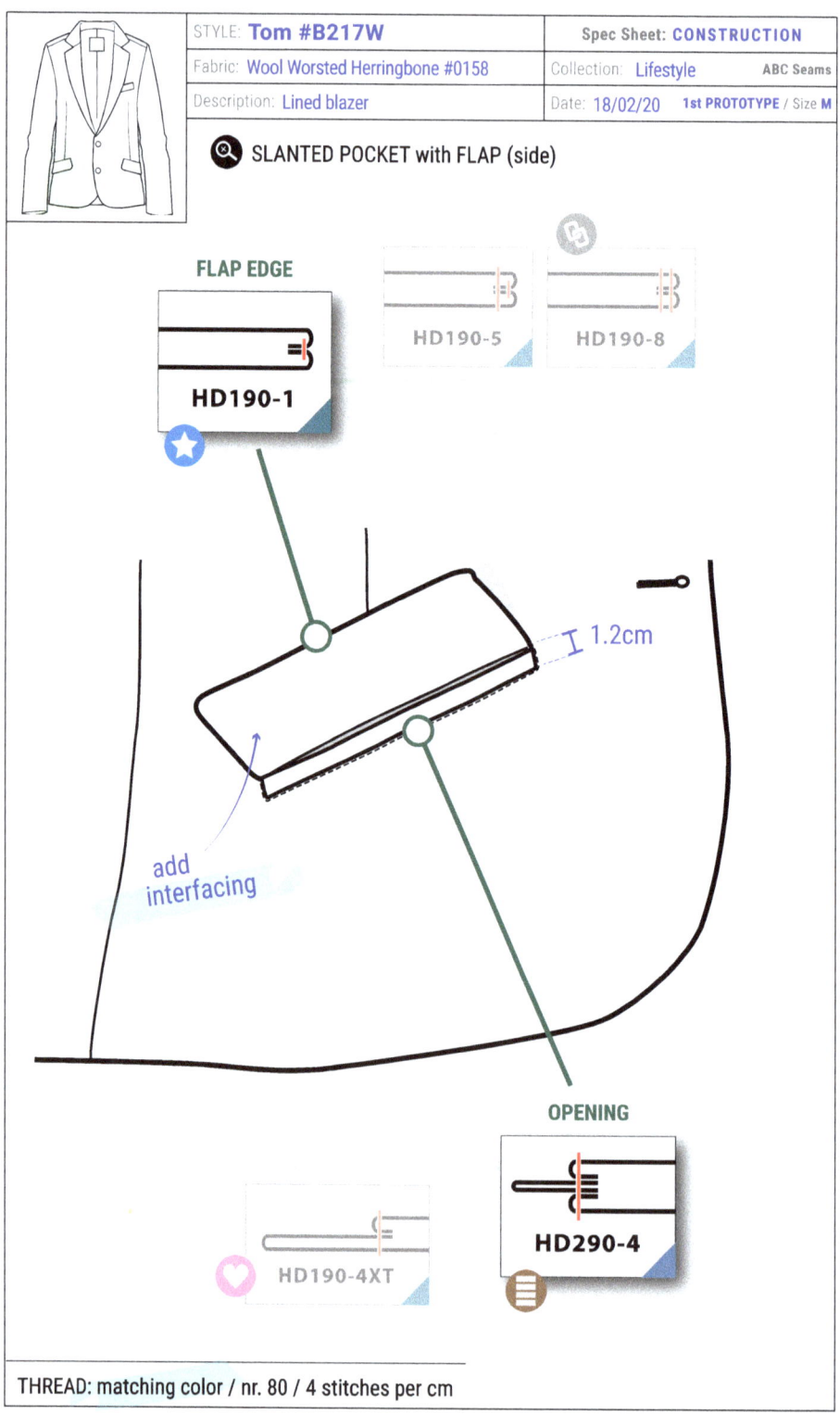

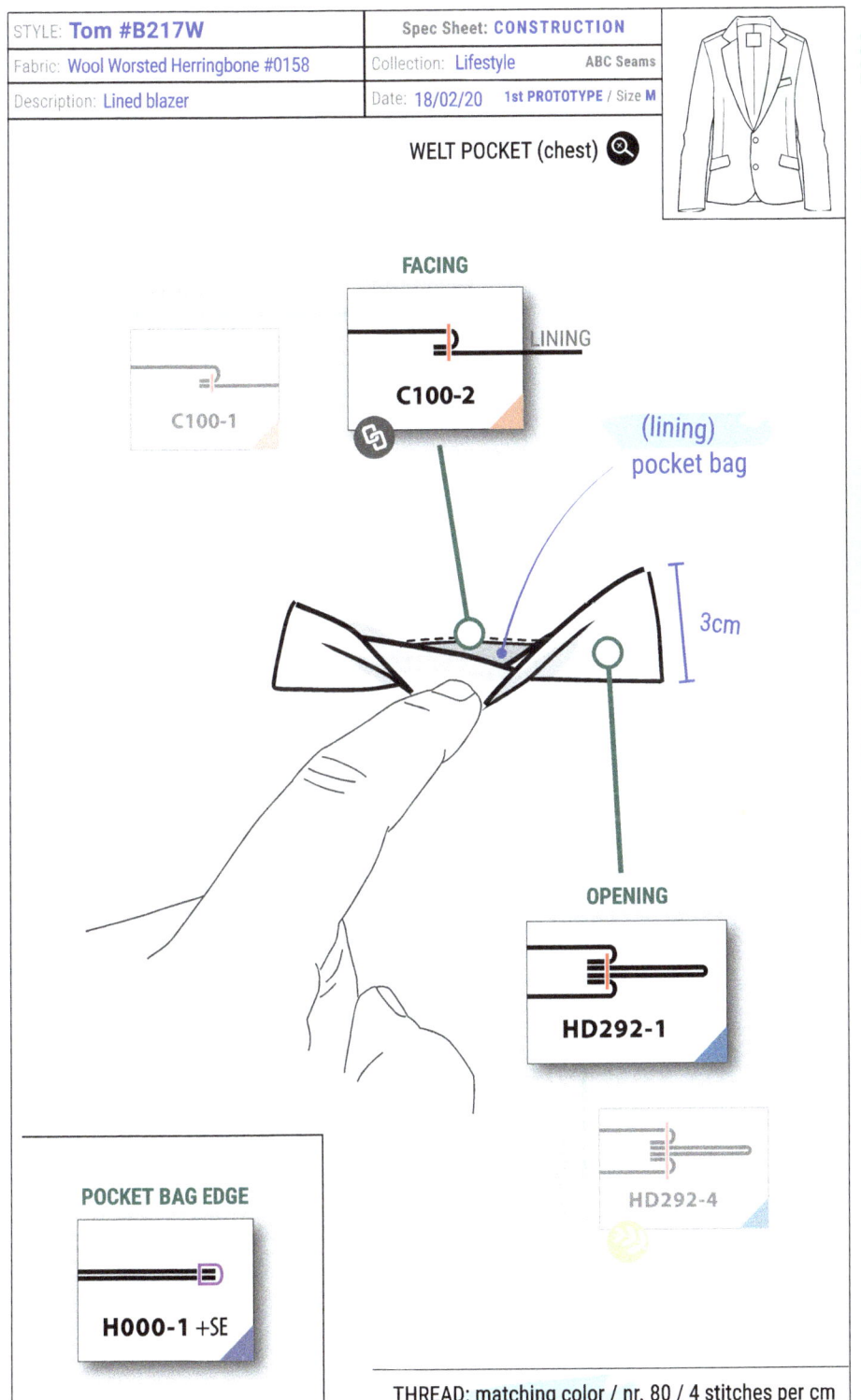

18-4436 TCX
16-3929 TCX
14-4310 TCX

DENIM CODE

# DENIM JACKET

Karen #B218J

Shirt collar (one-piece)

Cuff vent

Bottom with adjustable tabs

Double topstitch

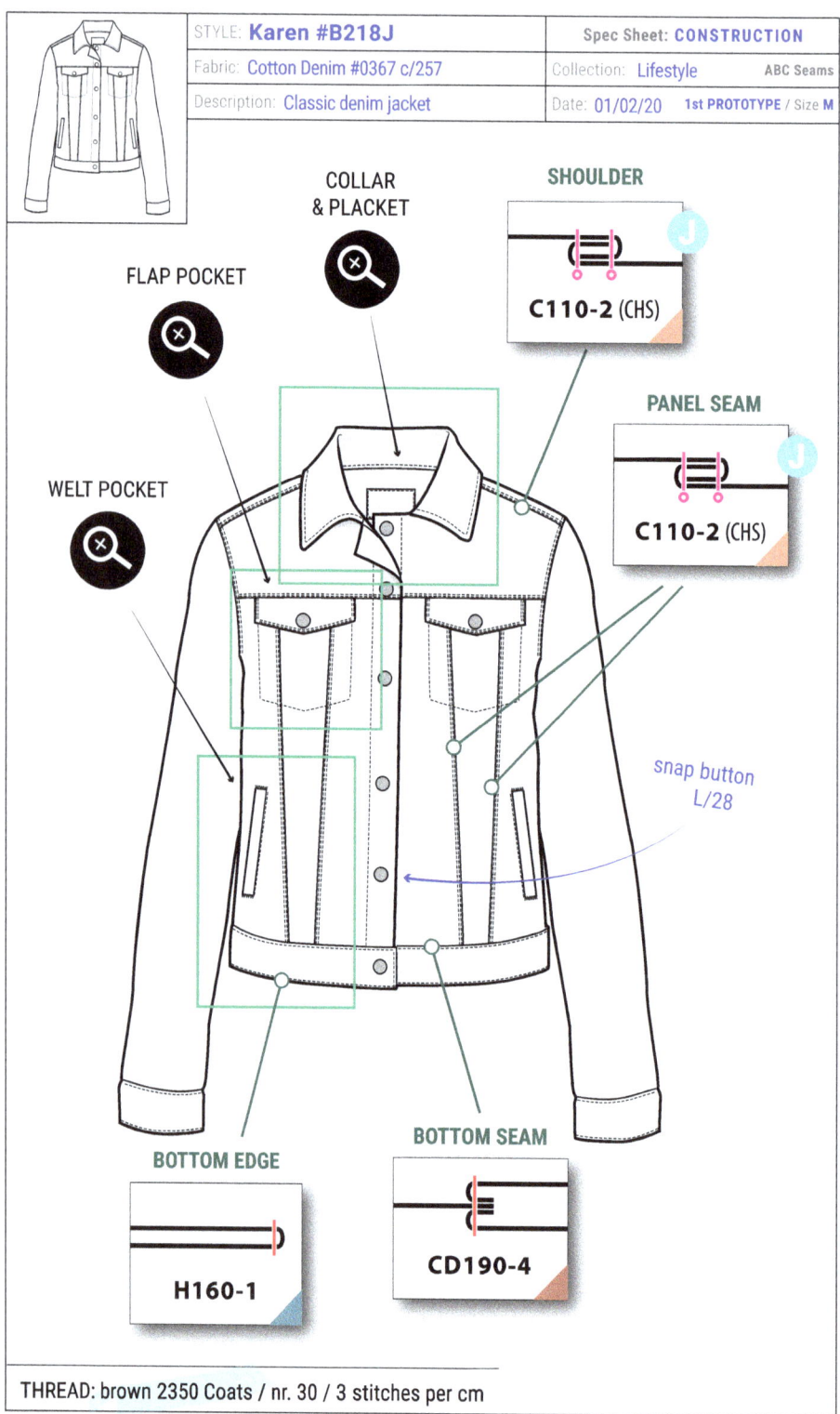

# Technical Specifications: Denim Jacket

| STYLE: **Karen #B218J** | Spec Sheet: **CONSTRUCTION** | |
|---|---|---|
| Fabric: Cotton Denim #0367 c/257 | Collection: Lifestyle | ABC Seams |
| Description: Classic denim jacket | Date: 01/02/20 | **1st PROTOTYPE** / Size **M** |

## SIDE, BACK YOKE & PANEL SEAMS
**C110-2** (CHS)

## ARMHOLE
**C100-4** +SE

## ELBOW & SLEEVE SIDE SEAMS
**C110-2** (CHS)

adjustable waist tab

CUFF with VENT

## TAB SEAM
**DF210-3**

## TAB EDGE
**HD190-4**

TOPS · DRESS · PANTS · SKIRTS · **OUTERWEAR** · UNDERWEAR · SWIMWEAR

THREAD: brown 2350 Coats / nr. 30 / 3 stitches per cm

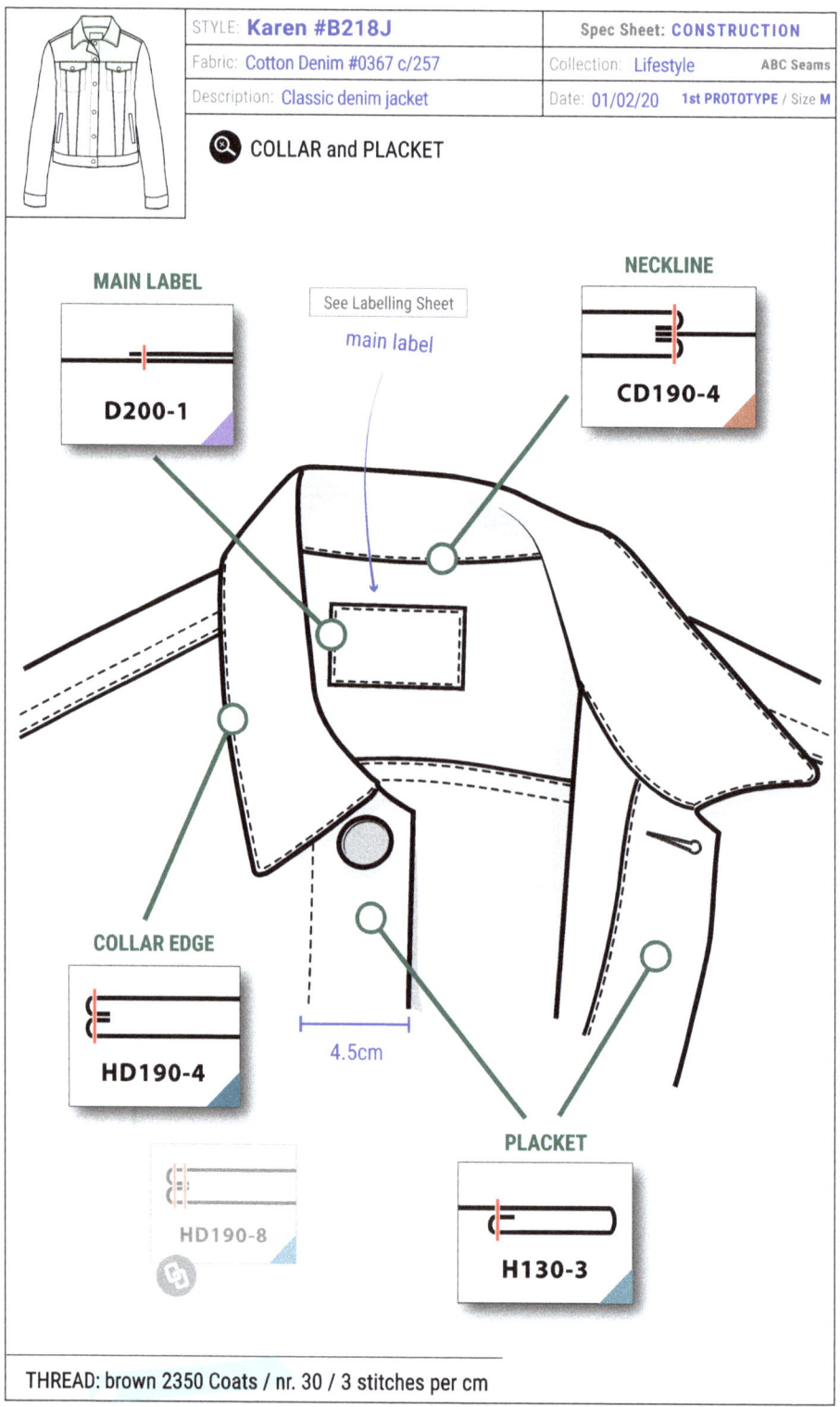

| STYLE: **Karen #B218J** | Spec Sheet: **CONSTRUCTION** | |
|---|---|---|
| Fabric: **Cotton Denim #0367 c/257** | Collection: **Lifestyle** | **ABC Seams** |
| Description: **Classic denim jacket** | Date: **01/02/20** | **1st PROTOTYPE** / Size **M** |

## CUFF with VENT

### VENT EDGE (top)
**H110-7**

### ELBOW SEAM
**C110-2** (CHS)

### VENT EDGE (underneath)
**H110-2**

bartack

L/28

5cm

### CUFF EDGE
**H160-1**

### CUFF SEAM
**CD190-4**

THREAD: brown 2350 Coats / nr. 30 / 3 stitches per cm

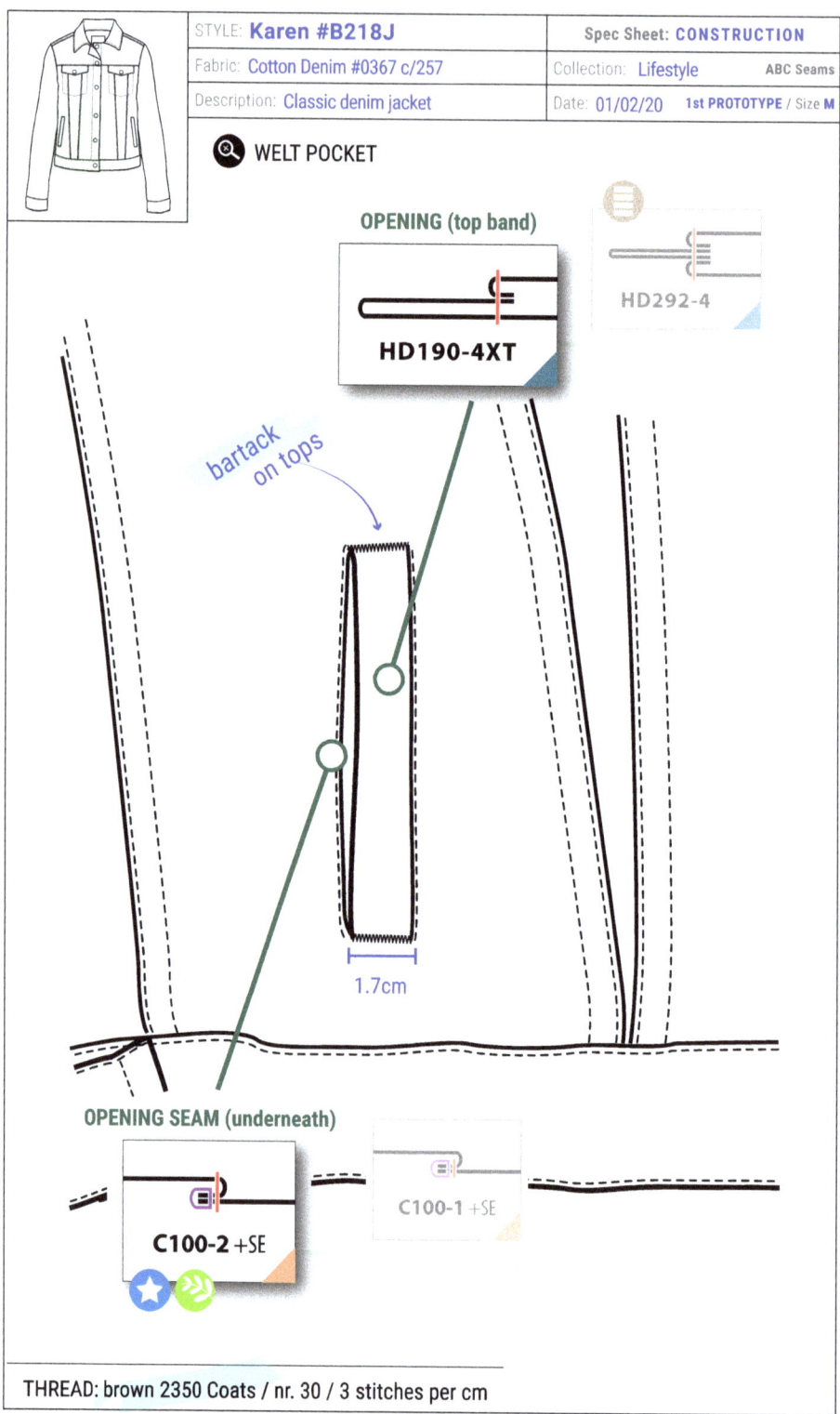

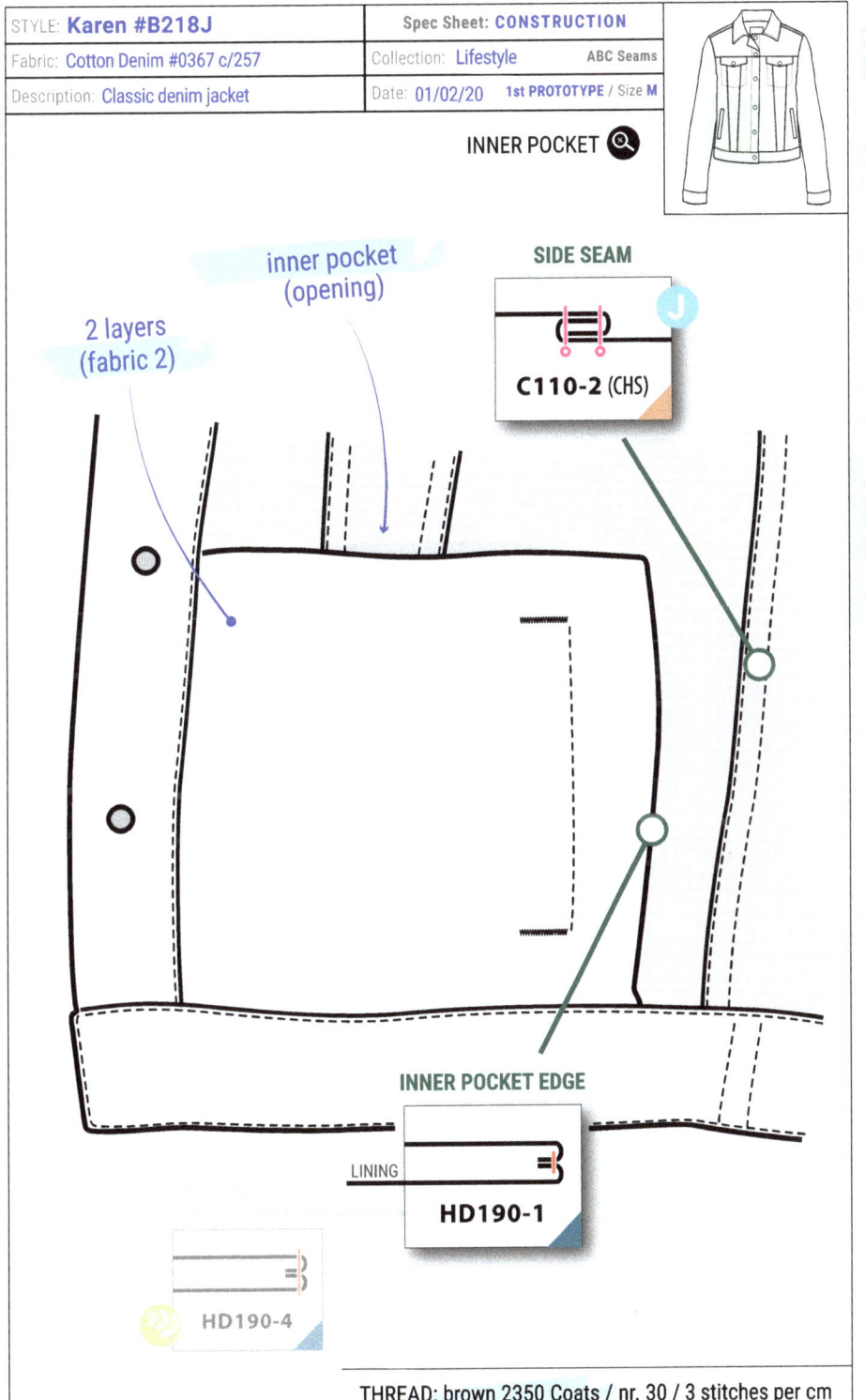

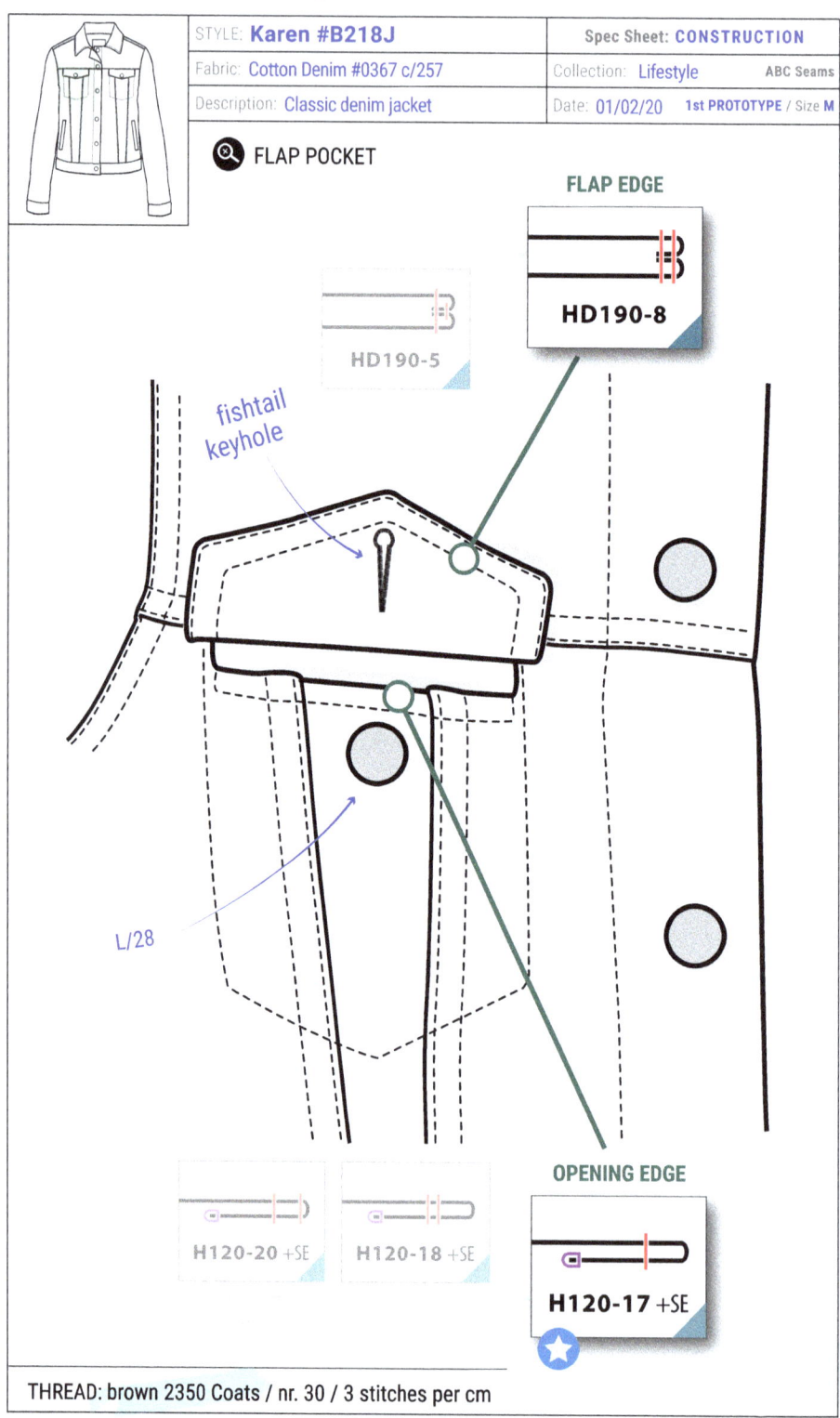

# Technical Specifications: Denim Jacket

| STYLE: **Karen #B218J** | Spec Sheet: **CONSTRUCTION** | |
|---|---|---|
| Fabric: Cotton Denim #0367 c/257 | Collection: Lifestyle | ABC Seams |
| Description: Classic denim jacket | Date: 01/02/20 | **1st PROTOTYPE** / Size **M** |

**FLAP PLACKET** (inside)

C100-3 +SE

**FLAP SEAM** (front yoke)

C100-4 +SE

**POCKET BAG EDGE**

D210-2x

D210-4x

THREAD: brown 2350 Coats / nr. 30 / 3 stitches per cm

OUTERWEAR

Technical Specifications_Bomber Jacket

# BOMBER JACKET

Mark #B219W

Turtle neck

Lined

Ribbed cuff and bottom

Zip pocket

Center front zip

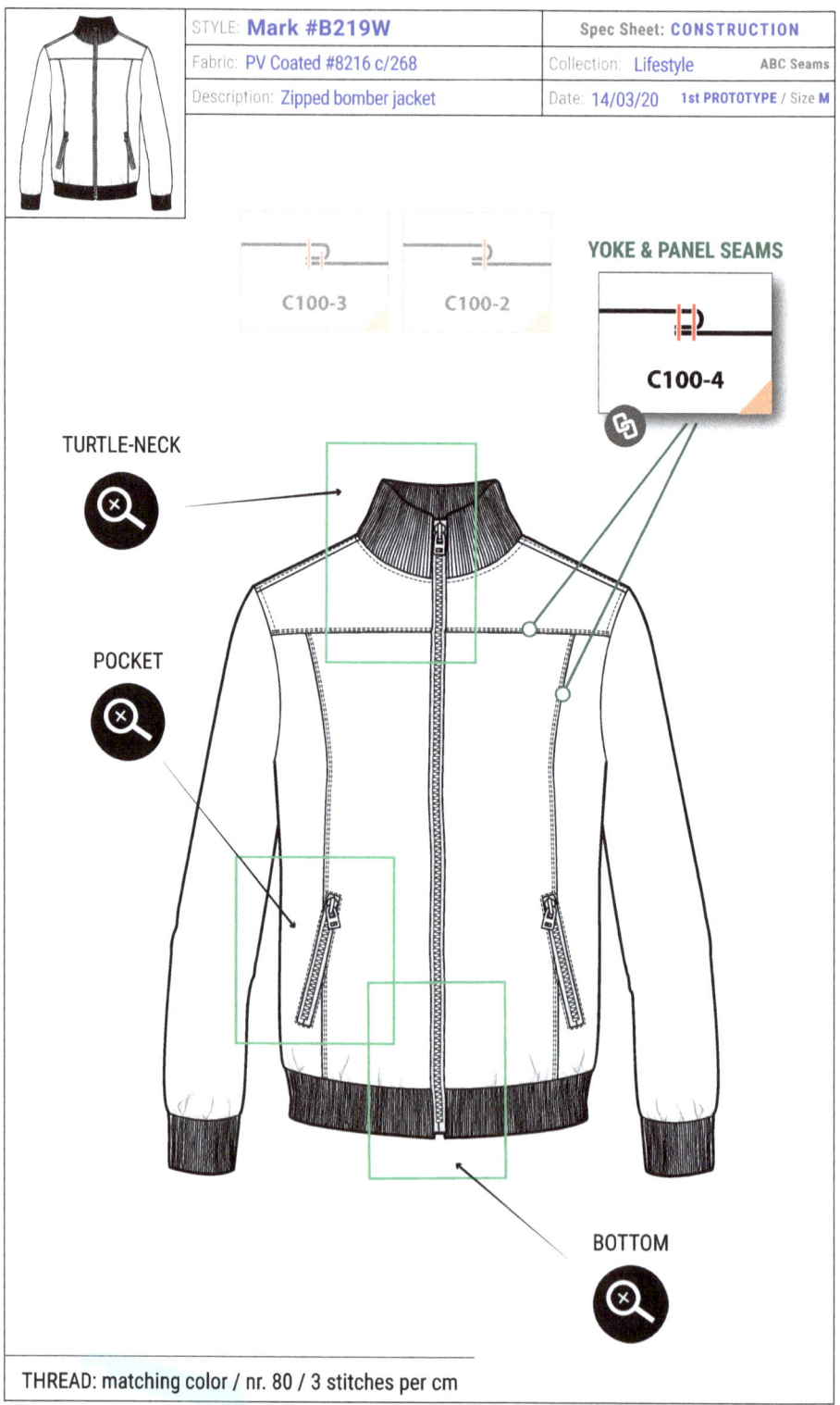

# Technical Specifications: Bomber Jacket

| STYLE: **Mark #B219W** | Spec Sheet: **CONSTRUCTION** | |
|---|---|---|
| Fabric: **PV Coated #8216 c/268** | Collection: **Lifestyle** | **ABC Seams** |
| Description: **Zipped bomber jacket** | Date: **14/03/20** | **1st PROTOTYPE** / Size **M** |

**TOPS · DRESS · PANTS · SKIRTS · OUTERWEAR · UNDERWEAR · SWIMWEAR**

### ARMHOLE (top)
**C100-3**

### ARMHOLE (bottom)
**C100-1**

### YOKE & PANEL SEAMS
**C100-4**

### CUFF

*puckers*

### SIDE SEAMS
**C100-1**

**C100-1 +SE**

---

THREAD: matching color / nr. 80 / 3 stitches per cm

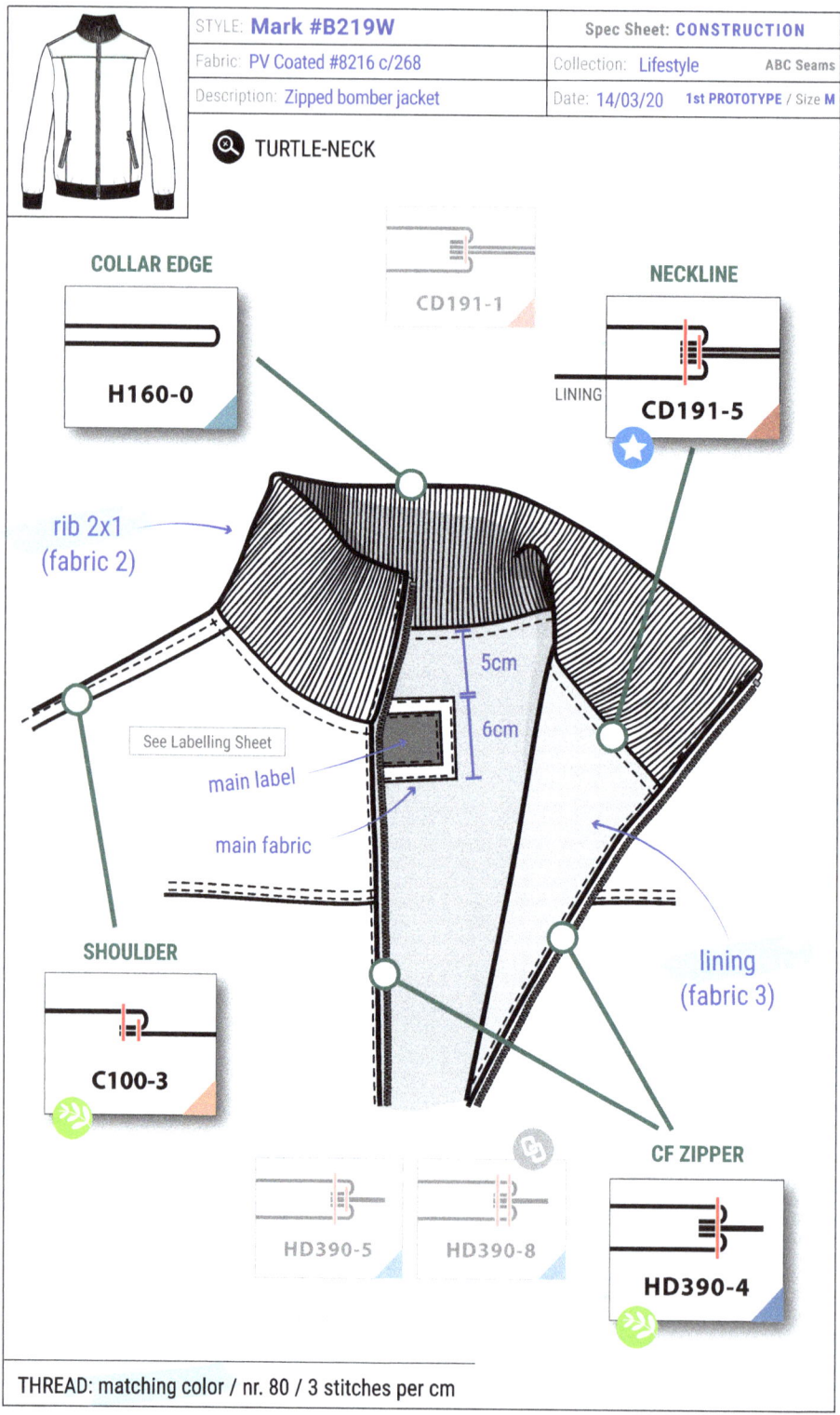

# Technical Specifications: Bomber Jacket

| STYLE: **Mark #B219W** | Spec Sheet: **CONSTRUCTION** | |
|---|---|---|
| Fabric: **PV Coated #8216 c/268** | Collection: **Lifestyle** | ABC Seams |
| Description: **Zipped bomber jacket** | Date: **14/03/20** **1st PROTOTYPE** / Size **M** | |

**BOTTOM** 🔍

**BOTTOM SEAM**

LINING

**CD191-1**

CD191-4

CD191-5

lining (fabric 3)

**BOTTOM EDGE**

**H160-0**

rib 2x1 (fabric 2)

THREAD: matching color / nr. 80 / 3 stitches per cm

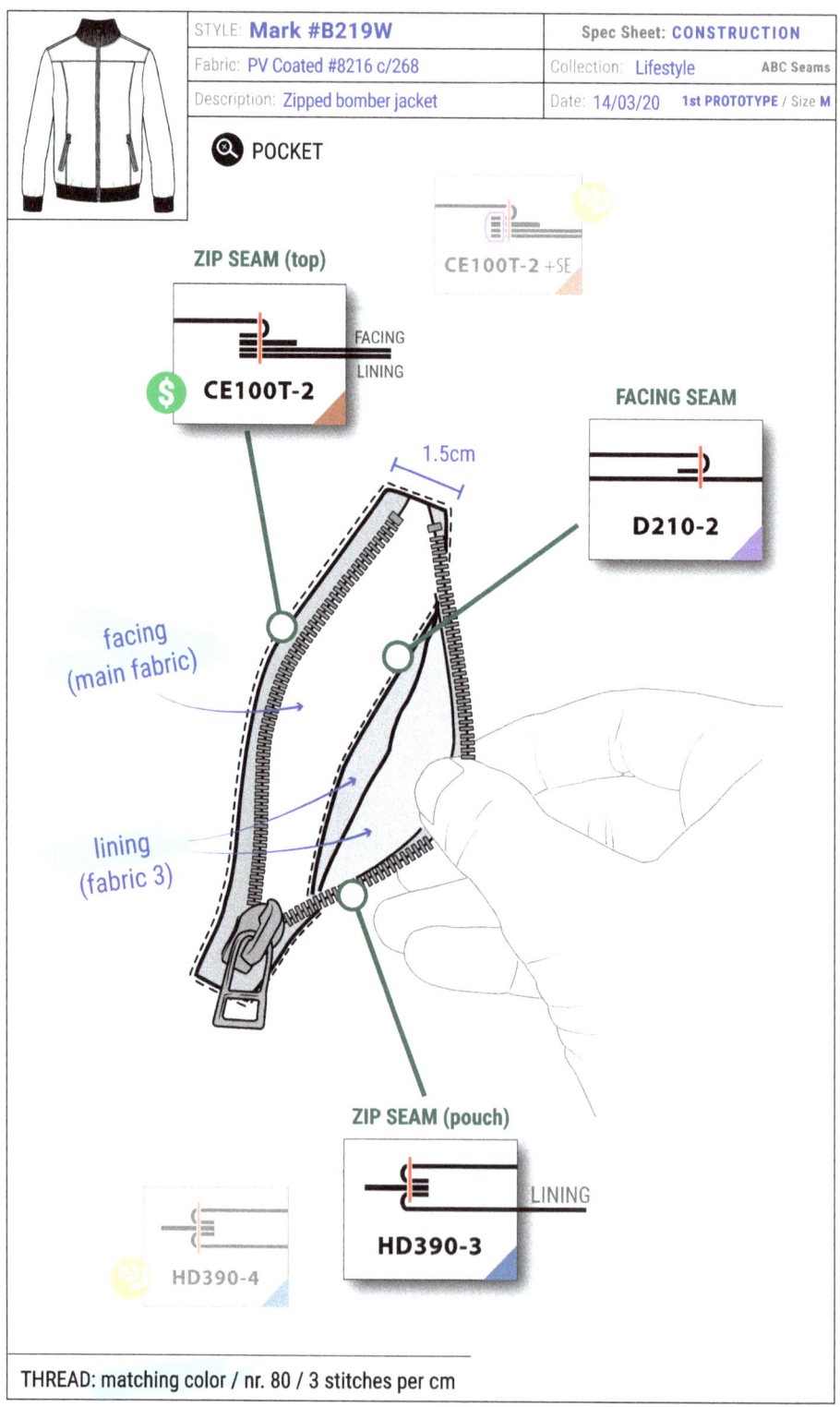

Technical Specifications_Bomber Jacket

| STYLE: **Mark #B219W** | Spec Sheet: **CONSTRUCTION** | |
|---|---|---|
| Fabric: PV Coated #8216 c/268 | Collection: Lifestyle | ABC Seams |
| Description: Zipped bomber jacket | Date: 14/03/20 | **1st PROTOTYPE** / Size **M** |

CUFF 🔍

**CUFF EDGE**

H160-0

rib 2x1 (fabric 2)

lining (fabric 3)

**CUFF SEAM**

LINING

CD191-1

CD191-4    CD191-5

THREAD: matching color / nr. 80 / 3 stitches per cm

TOPS | DRESS | PANTS | SKIRTS | OUTERWEAR | UNDERWEAR | SWIMWEAR

# PARKA

Lisa #B220W

Unlined (smart finishes)
Oversized hood
In-seam pockets
Belt and belt loop
CB pleat

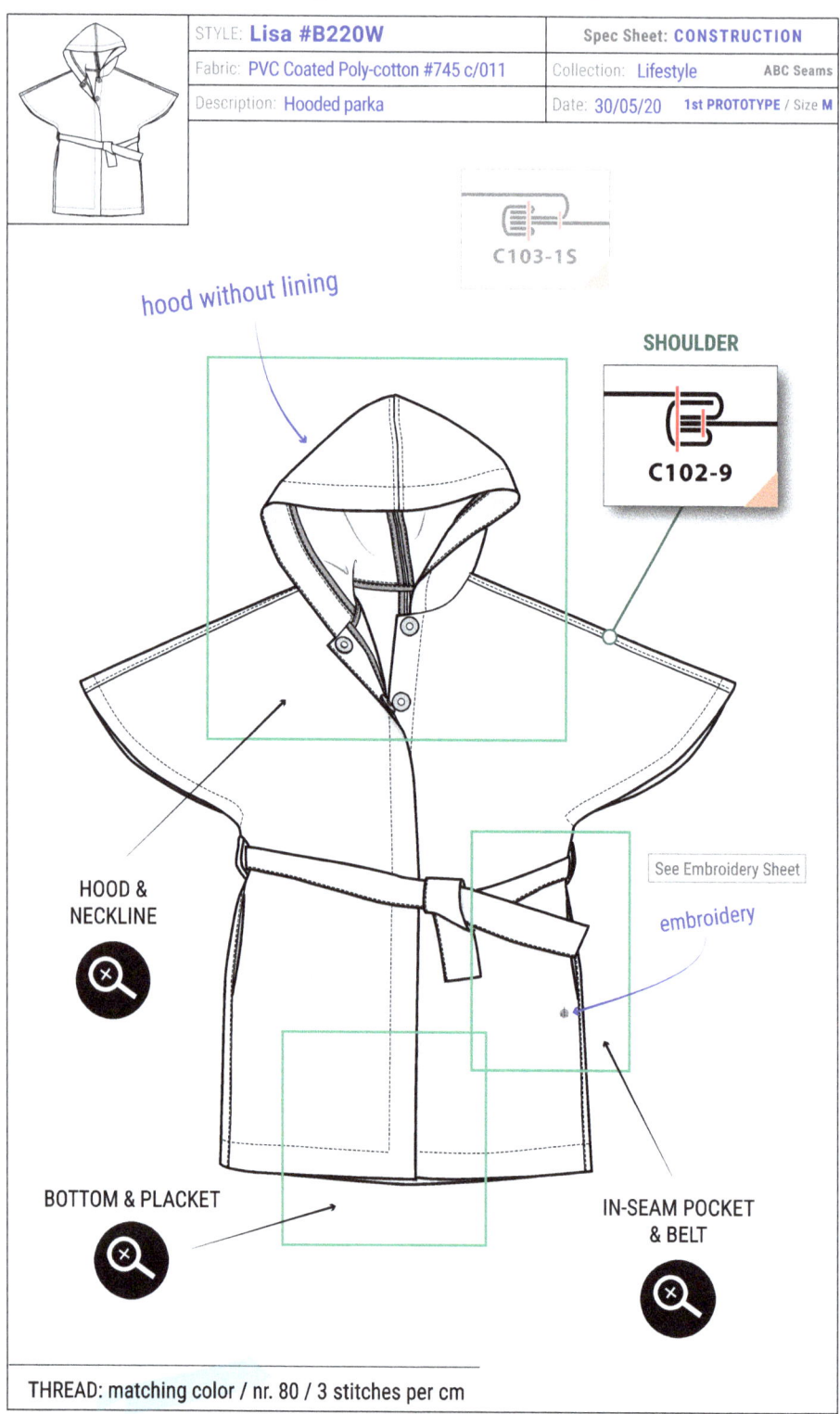

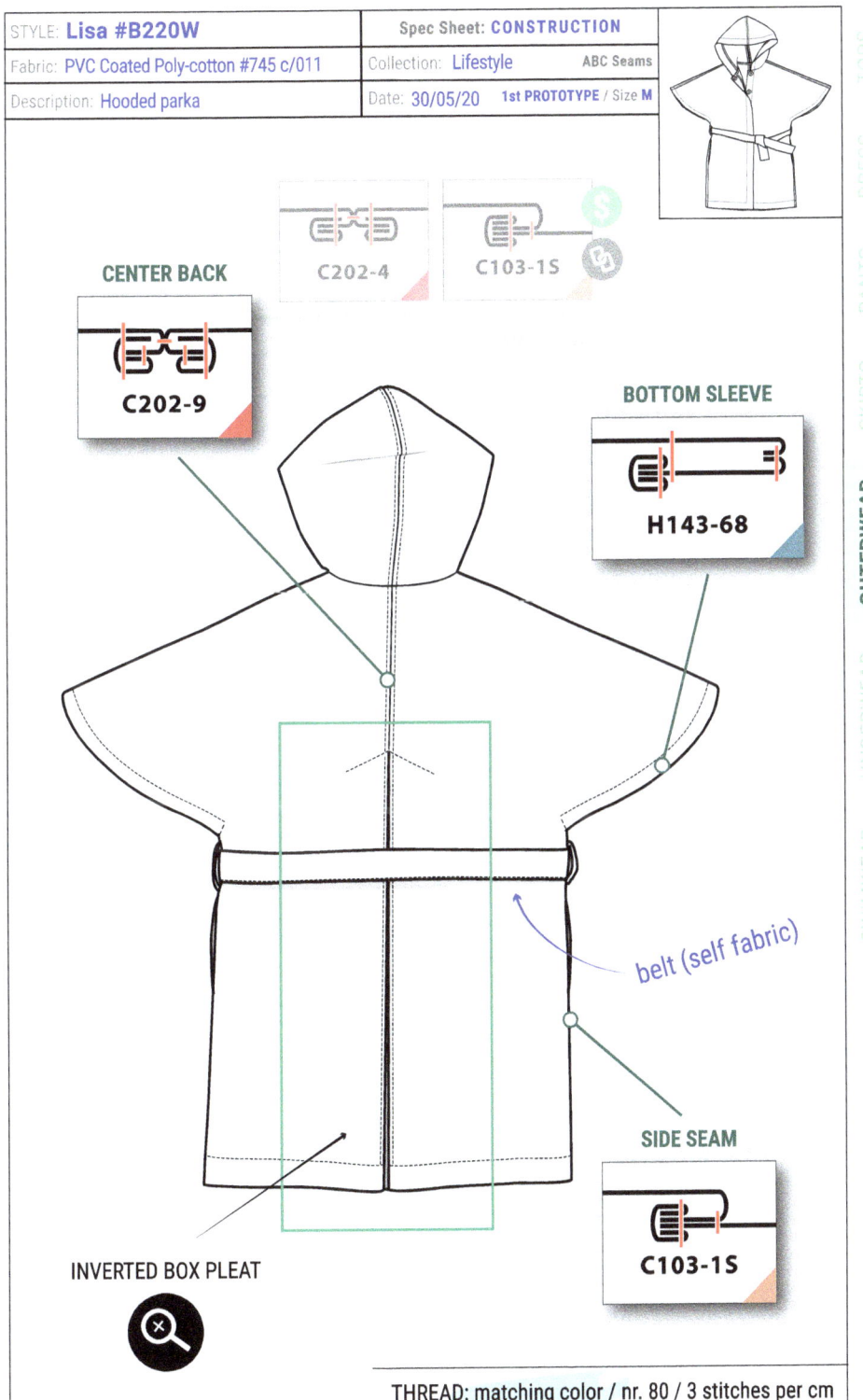

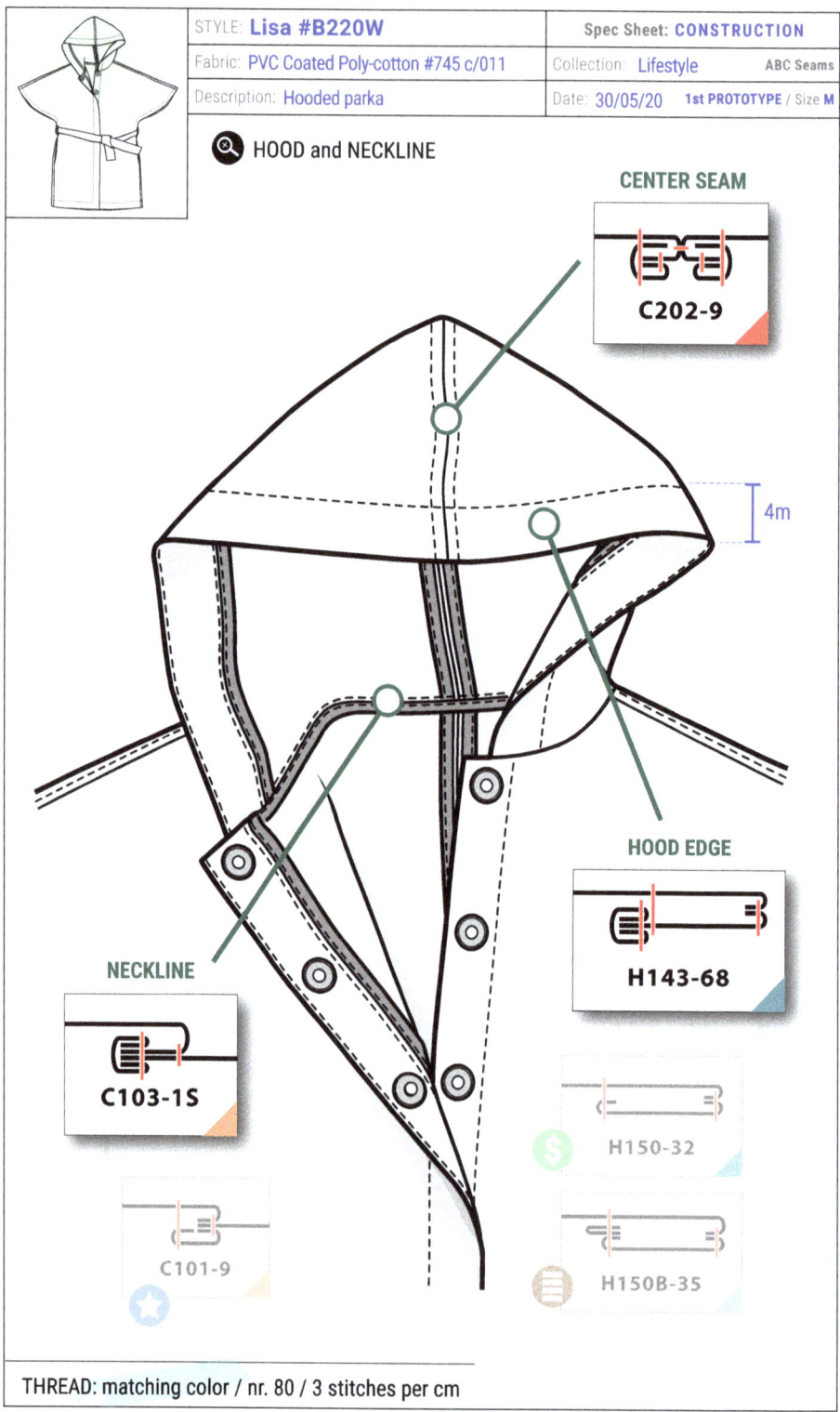

Technical Specifications: Parka

| STYLE: **Lisa #B220W** | Spec Sheet: **CONSTRUCTION** | |
|---|---|---|
| Fabric: PVC Coated Poly-cotton #745 c/011 | Collection: Lifestyle | ABC Seams |
| Description: Hooded parka | Date: 30/05/20 | **1st PROTOTYPE** / Size **M** |

BOTTOM and PLACKET

**TOP PLACKET**

H143-68

4m

**UNDER PLACKET**

H130-3

snap button L/30

4cm

**BOTTOM**

H150B-35

H130B-3

H130-3

THREAD: matching color / nr. 80 / 3 stitches per cm

OUTERWEAR

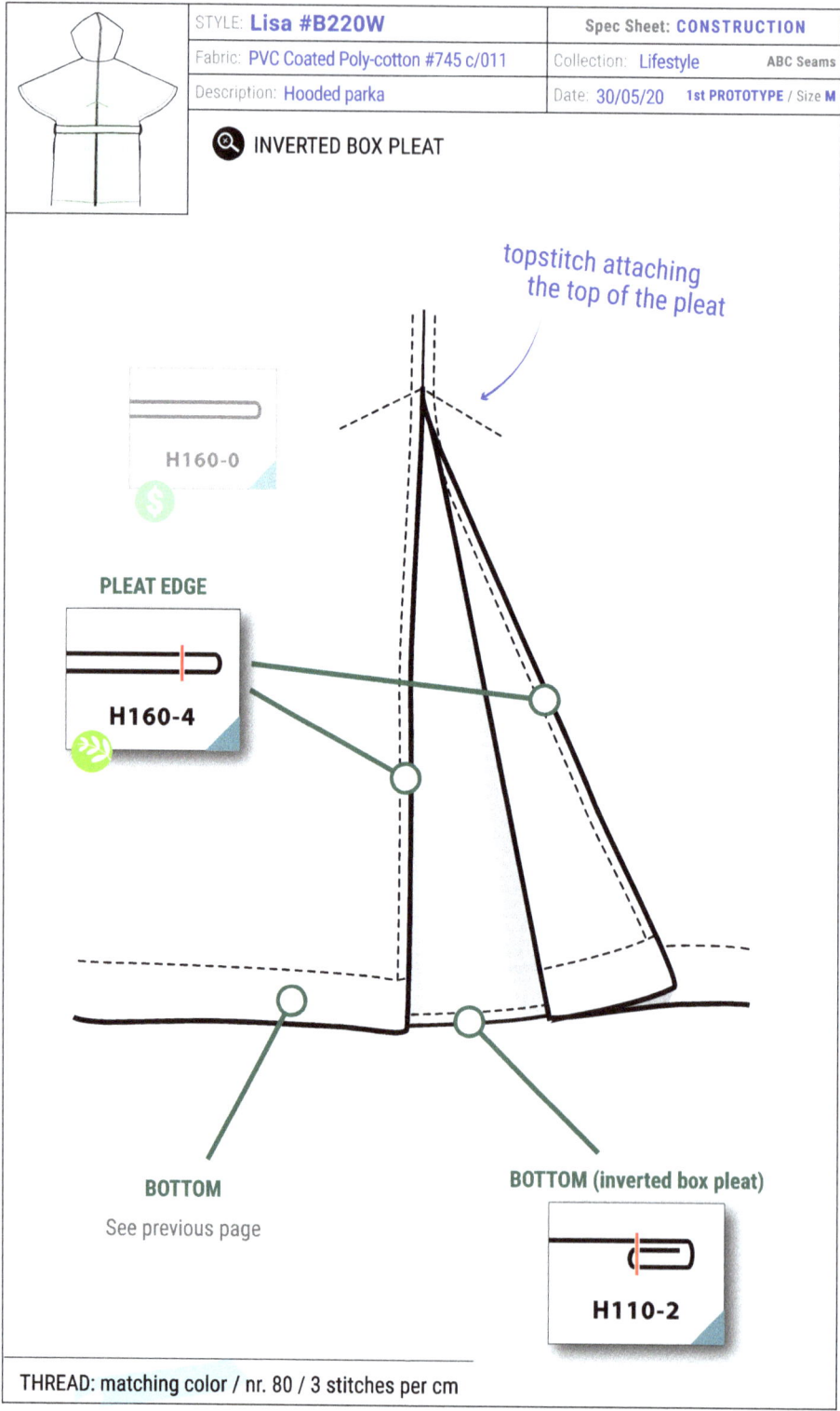

Technical Specifications: Parka

| STYLE: **Lisa #B220W** | Spec Sheet: **CONSTRUCTION** | |
|---|---|---|
| Fabric: **PVC Coated Poly-cotton #745 c/011** | Collection: **Lifestyle** | **ABC Seams** |
| Description: **Hooded parka** | Date: **30/05/20** | **1st PROTOTYPE** / Size **M** |

**INVERTED BOX PLEAT** (inside)

**CENTER BACK**
See back sketch

HD200-2R

HD000-3 +SE

**PLEAT INNER EDGE**

HD200-1R

THREAD: matching color / nr. 80 / 3 stitches per cm

TOPS · DRESS · PANTS · SKIRTS · **OUTERWEAR** · UNDERWEAR · SWIMWEAR

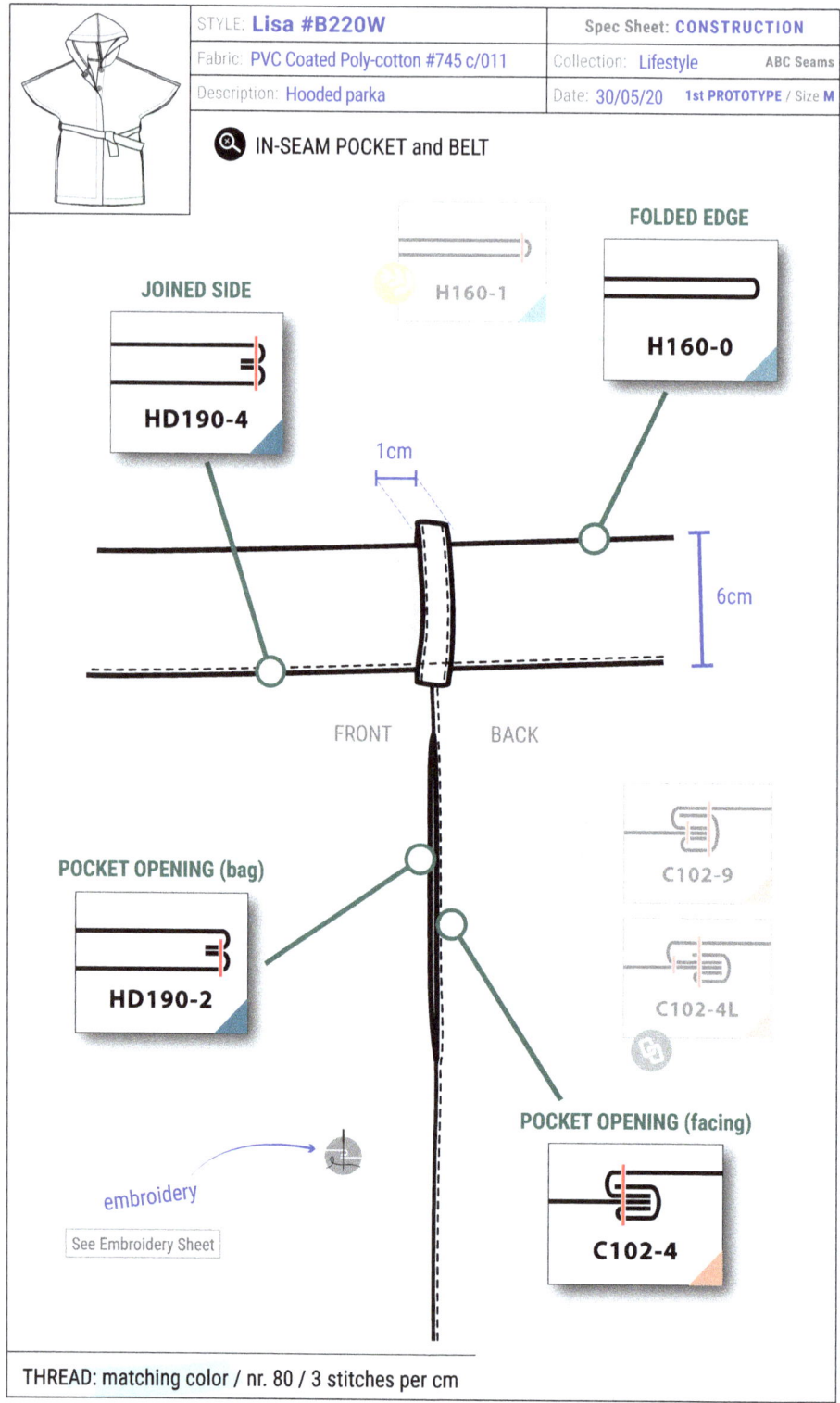

## Technical Specifications: Parka

| STYLE: Lisa #B220W | Spec Sheet: CONSTRUCTION | |
|---|---|---|
| Fabric: PVC Coated Poly-cotton #745 c/011 | Collection: Lifestyle | ABC Seams |
| Description: Hooded parka | Date: 30/05/20 | 1st PROTOTYPE / Size M |

IN-SEAM POCKET (inside)

**POUCH EDGE**

HD200-1

HD200-1R

pouch holder

**SIDE SEAM**
See back sketch

THREAD: matching color / nr. 80 / 3 stitches per cm

# PANTIES

Stella #B221K and Sally #B222K

Decorative lace

Wide waistband

CB gathering

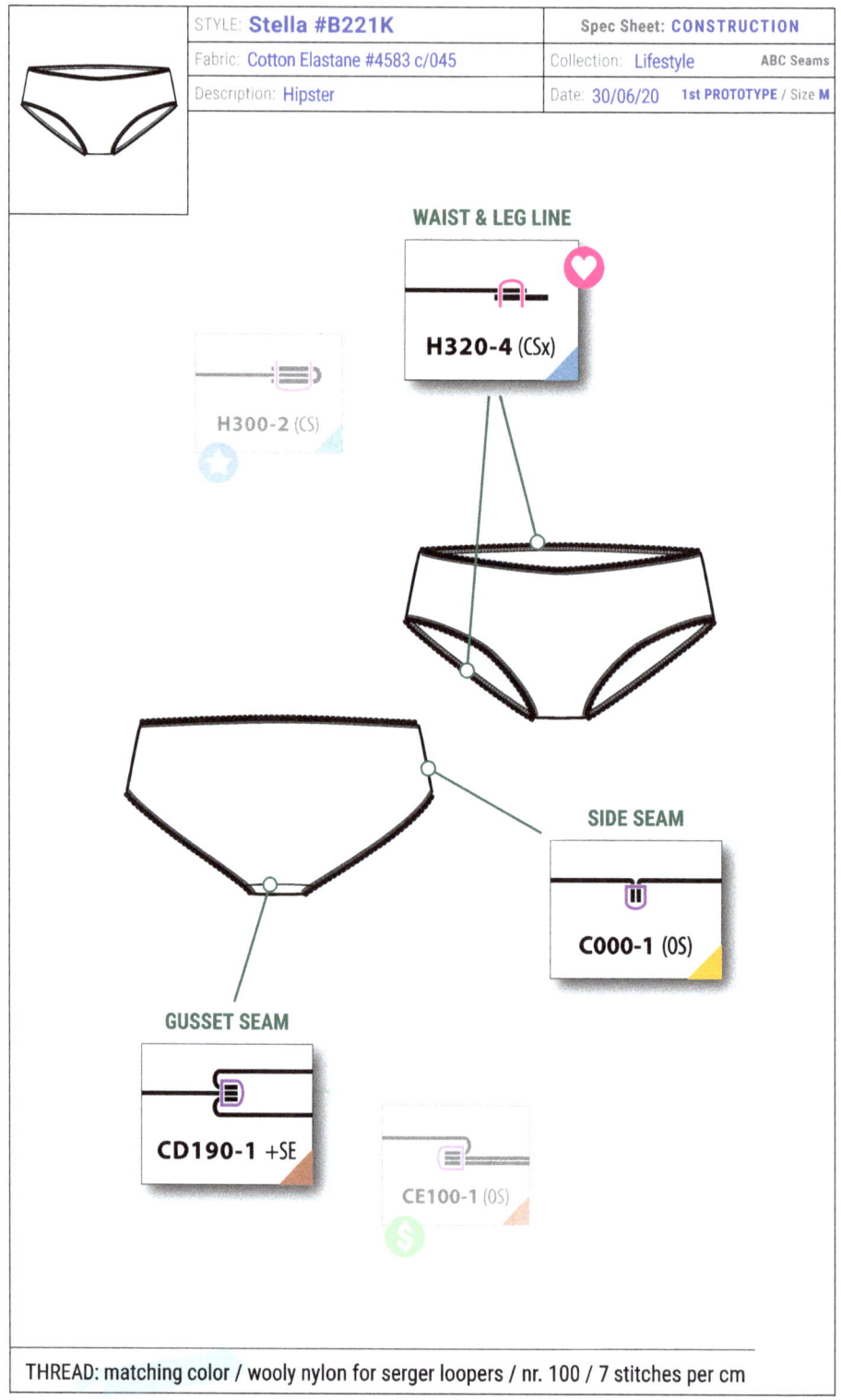

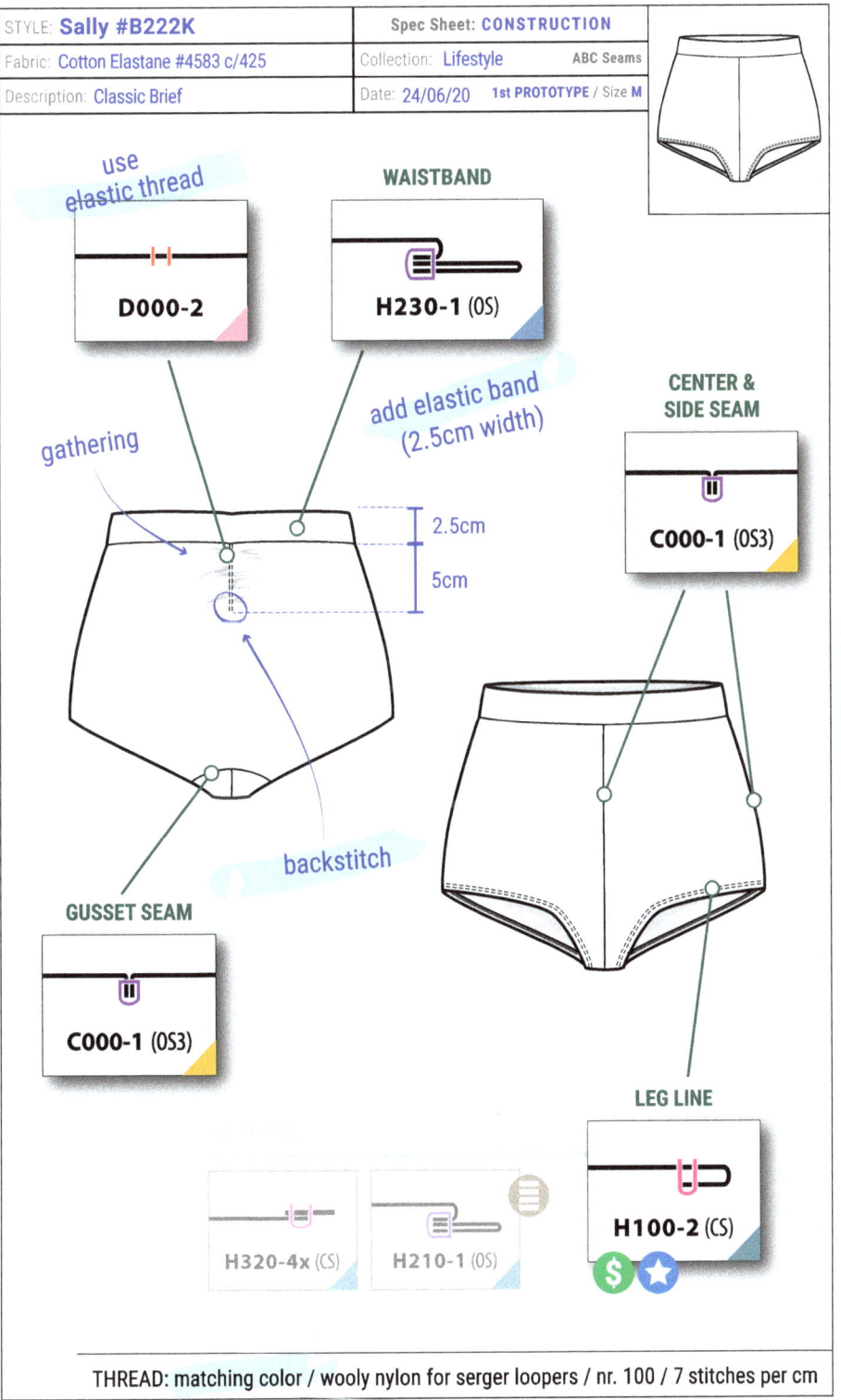

# BRAS

Barbara #B223K and Michelle #B224K

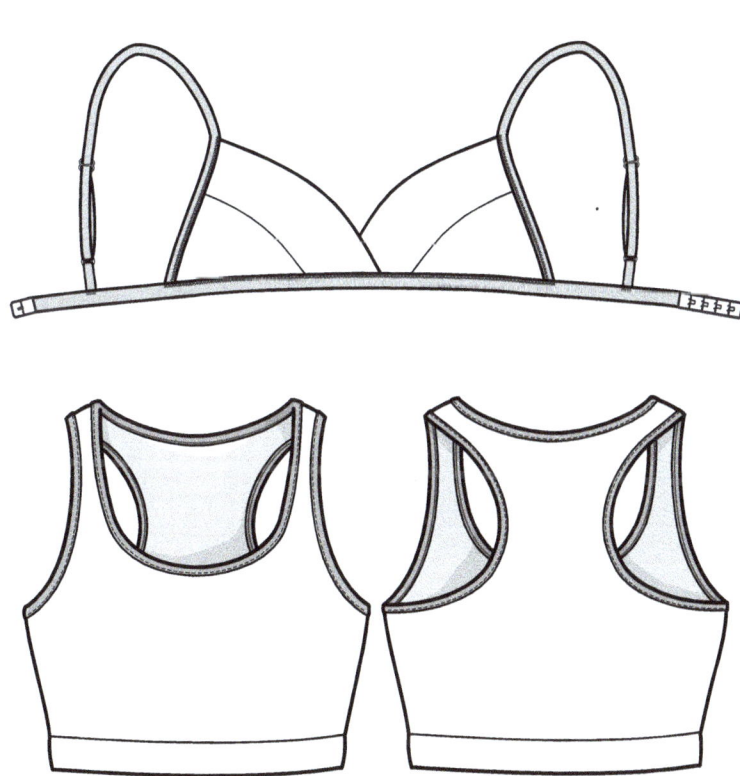

Adjustable straps

Lingerie elastic

Binded edges

Edge with elastic band

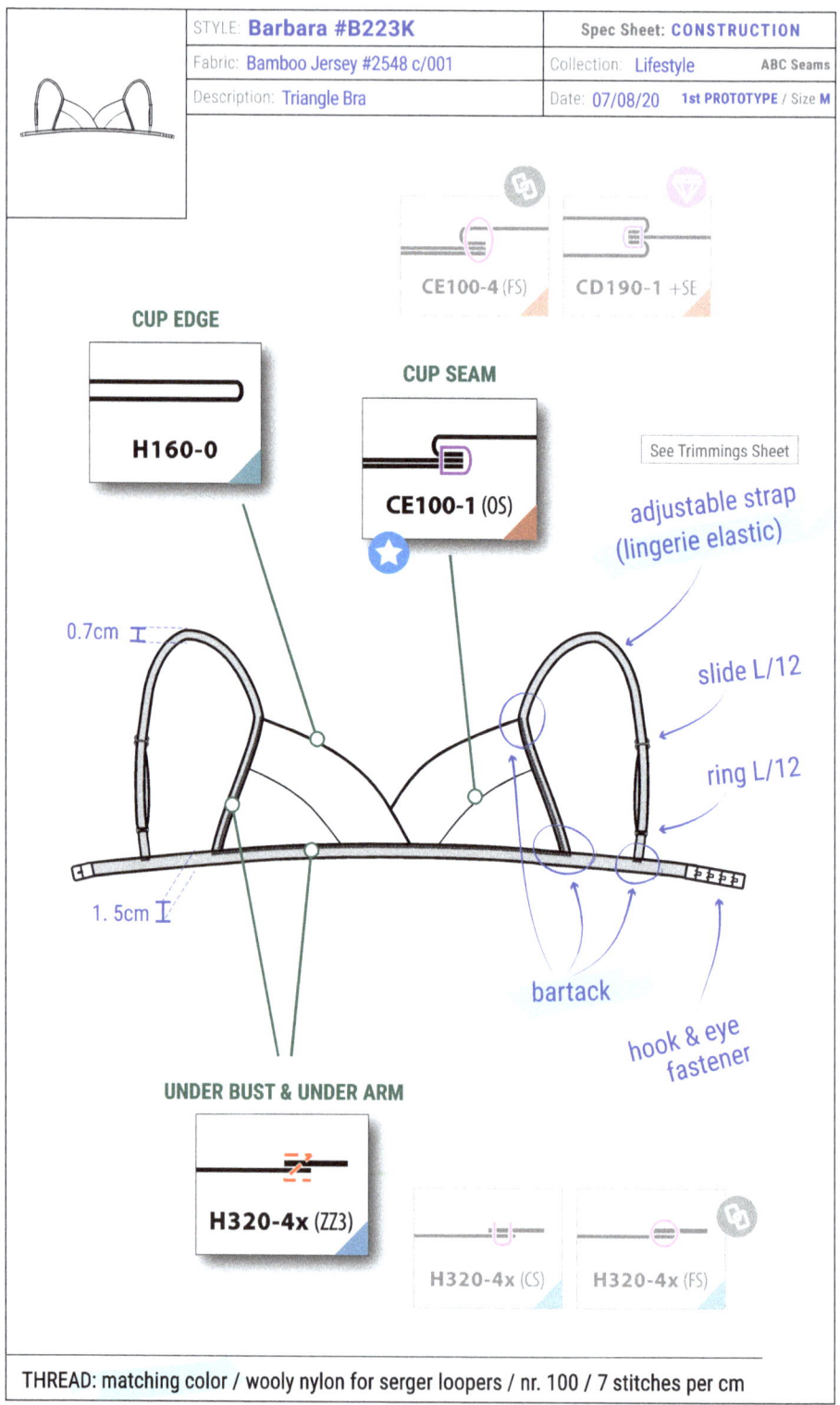

# Technical Specifications: Bras

| STYLE: **Michelle #B224K** | Spec Sheet: **CONSTRUCTION** | |
|---|---|---|
| Fabric: **Cotton Elastane #4583 c/425** | Collection: **Lifestyle** | ABC Seams |
| Description: **Sport Bra** | Date: **26/08/20** | **1st PROTOTYPE** / Size **M** |

**NECKLINE & ARMHOLE**

**H200-1** (CHS)

**H200-2** (CS)  **H200-2** (FS)

**SIDE SEAM**

**C000-1** (OS)

add elastic band (3cm width)

**BOTTOM**

3cm

**H120-3** (CS)   **H230-4** (CS)   **H230-1** (OS)

THREAD: matching color / wooly nylon for serger loopers / nr. 100 / 7 stitches per cm

# BIKINI

Sarah #B225K and Anna #B226K

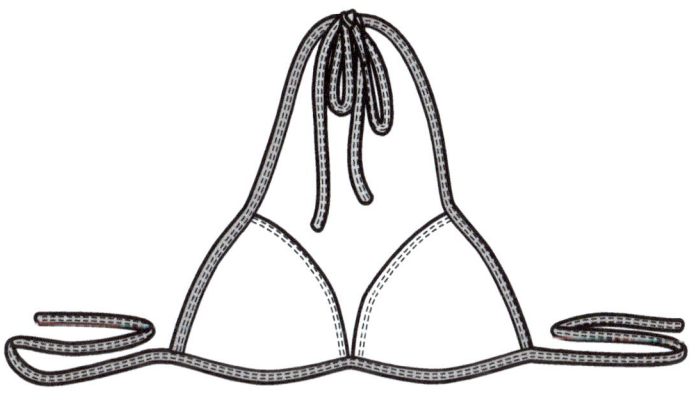

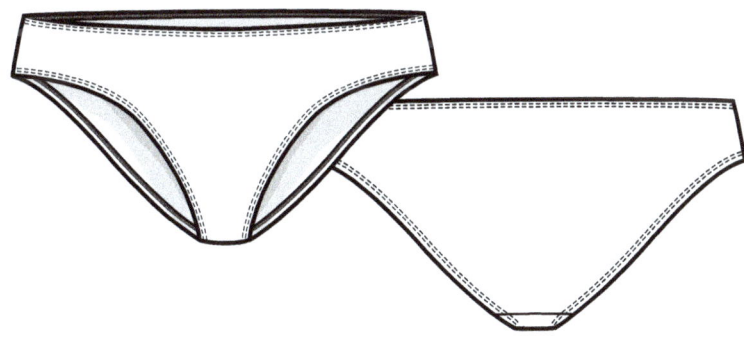

Hem with elastic band

Lined front

Binded edge

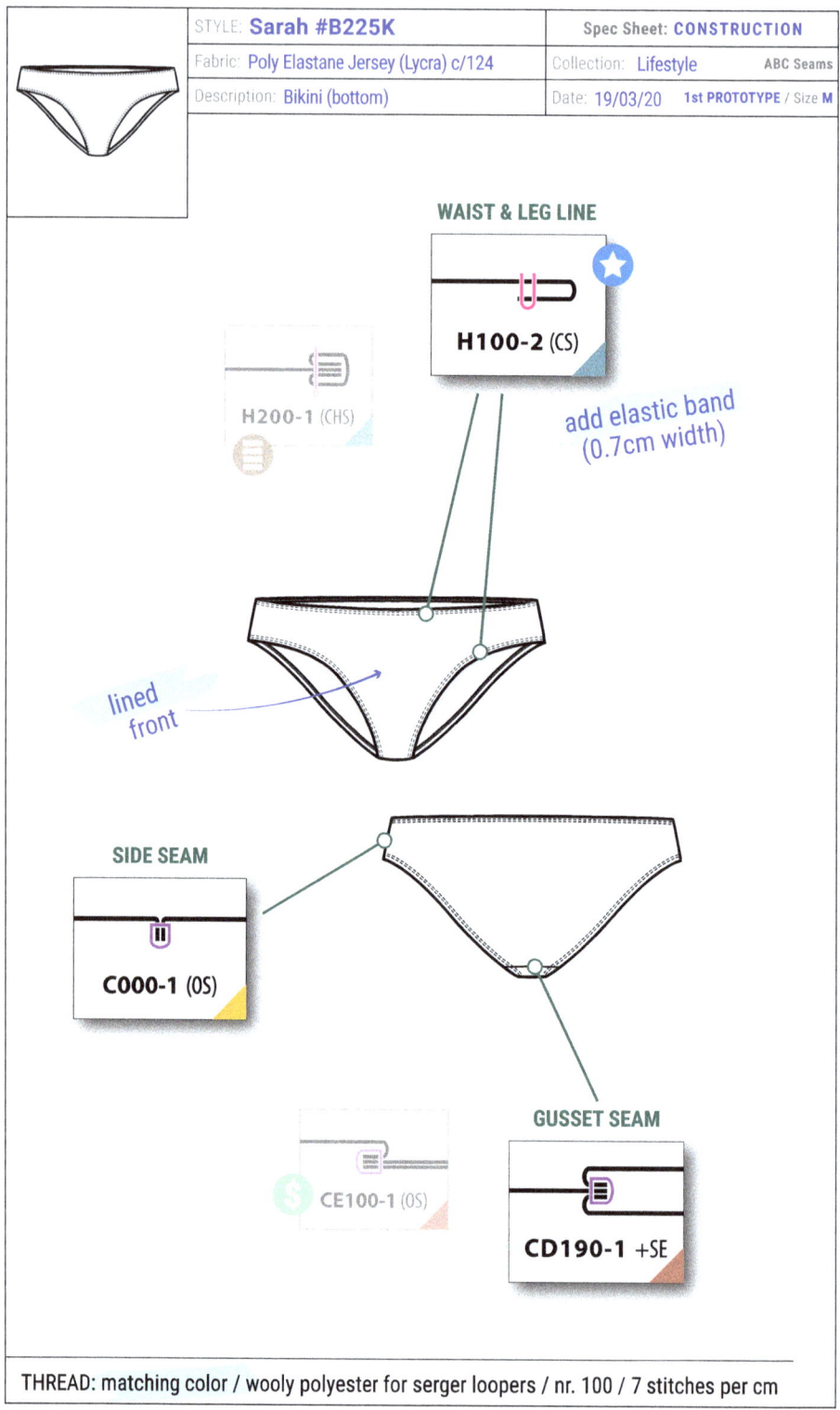

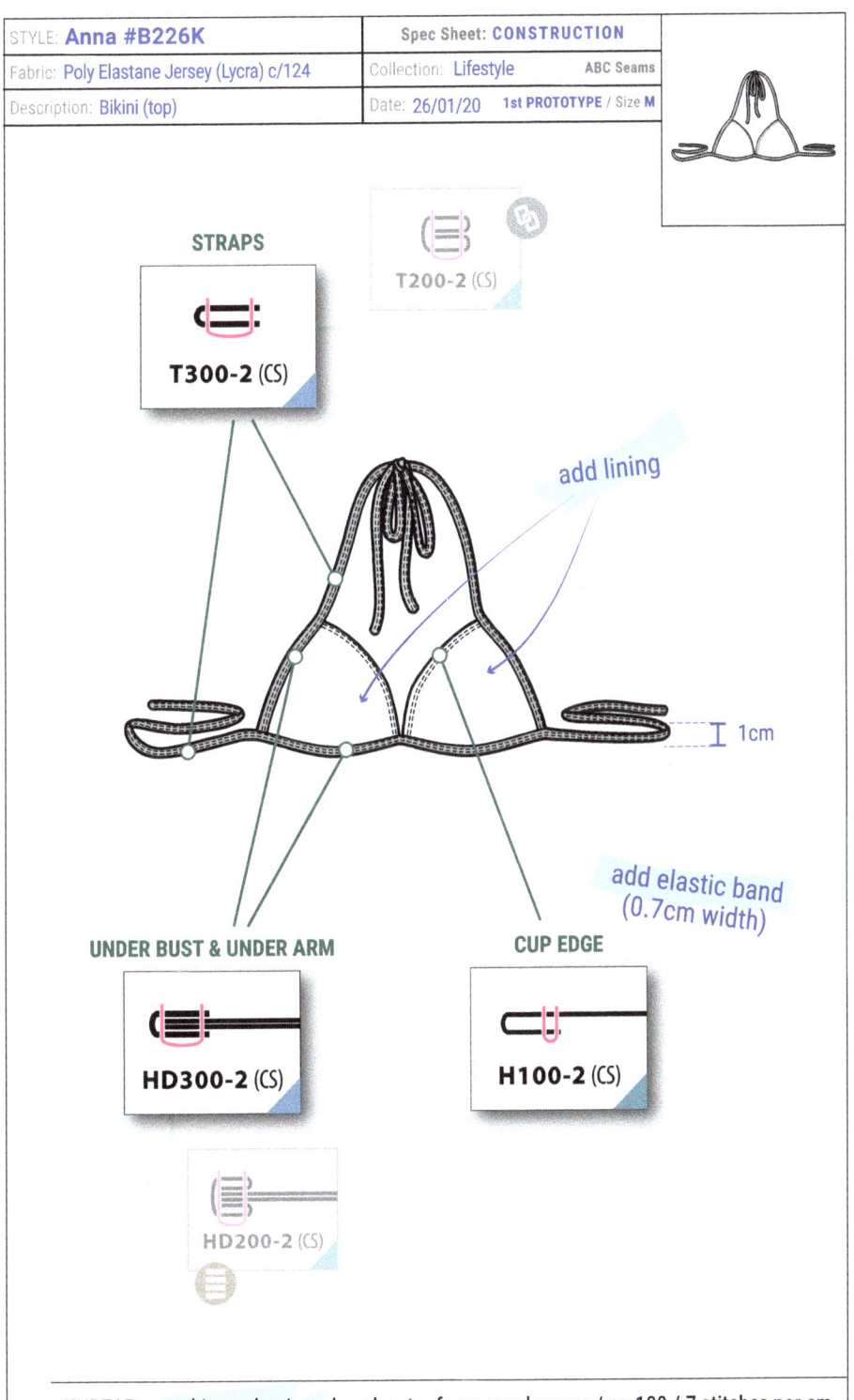

# ONE PIECE SWIMSUIT

Rita #B227K

Binded edge

Lined front

Hem with elastic band

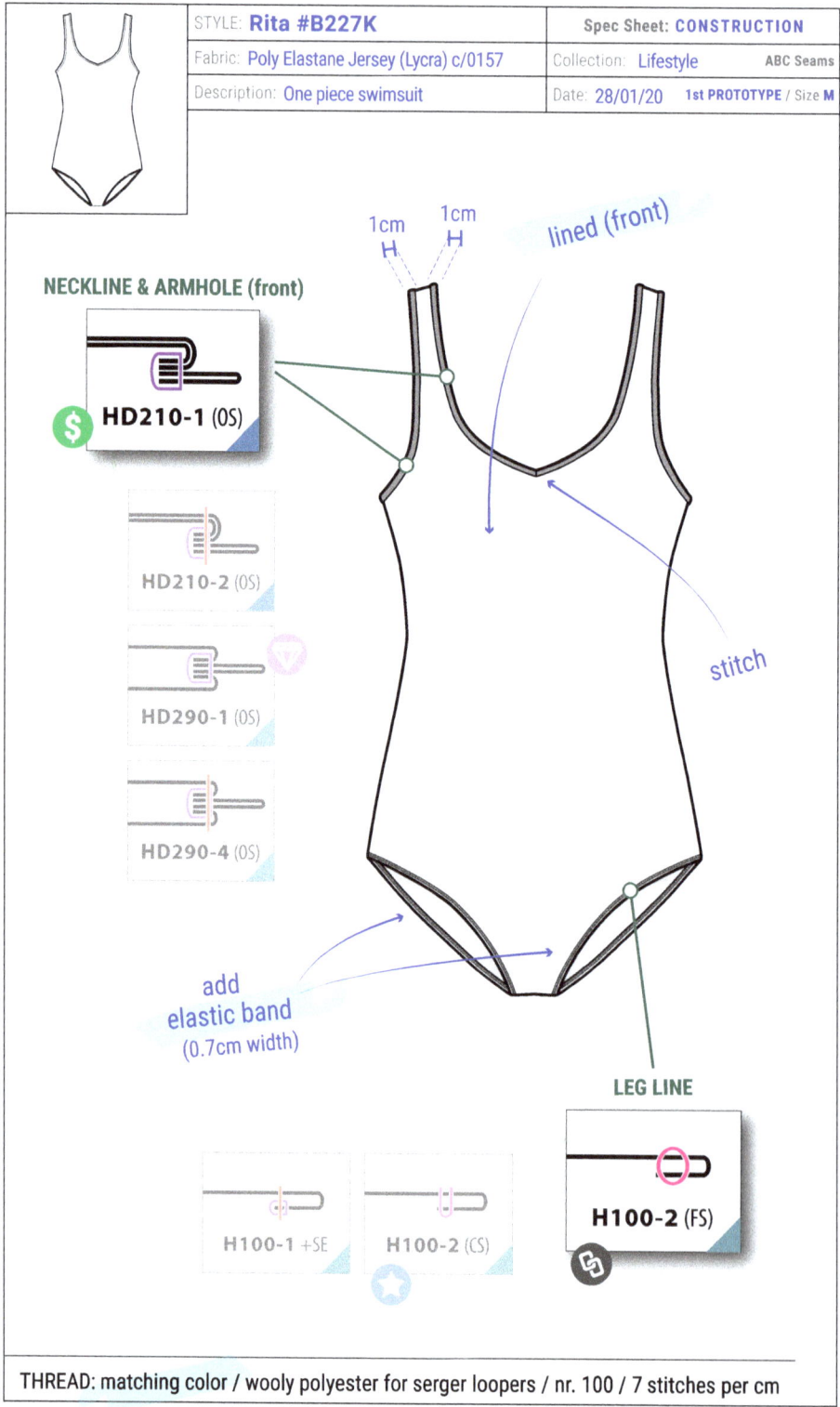

## Technical Specifications: One Piece Swimsuit

| | | |
|---|---|---|
| STYLE: **Rita #B227K** | Spec Sheet: **CONSTRUCTION** | |
| Fabric: **Poly Elastane Jersey (Lycra) c/0157** | Collection: **Lifestyle** — ABC Seams | |
| Description: **One piece swimsuit** | Date: **28/01/20** — 1st **PROTOTYPE** / Size **M** | |

**NECKLINE & ARMHOLE (back)**
H210-1 (OS)

**SIDE SEAM & SHOULDER**
C000-1 (OS)

stitch

**GUSSET SEAM**
CD190-1 +SE

CE100-1 (OS)

THREAD: matching color / wooly polyester for serger loopers / nr. 100 / 7 stitches per cm

## Part Three

# REFERENCE MATERIAL

# TECH PACK
## SHEET SAMPLES

MEASUREMENTS
FIT COMMENTS
PRINT
EMBROIDERY
COLORWAYS
TRIMMINGS
LABELLING
LAB DIPS
GRADING
BOM

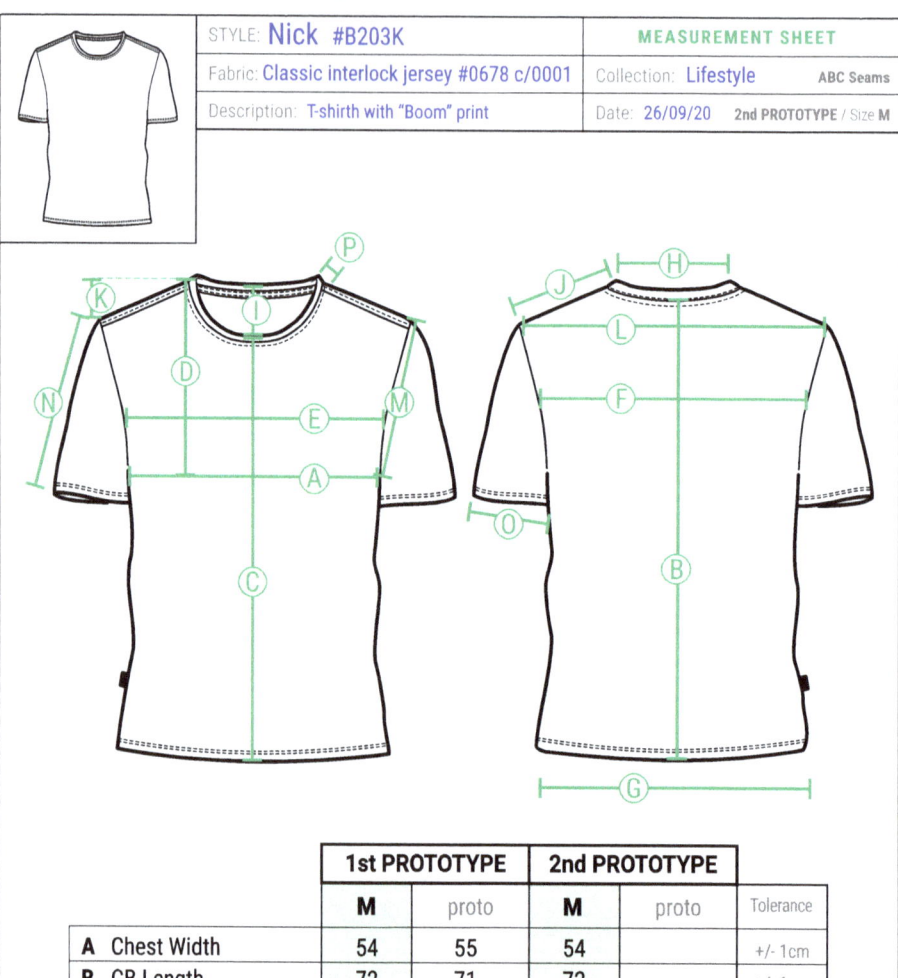

| | | 1st PROTOTYPE | | 2nd PROTOTYPE | | |
|---|---|---|---|---|---|---|
| | | M | proto | M | proto | Tolerance |
| A | Chest Width | 54 | 55 | 54 | | +/- 1cm |
| B | CB Length | 72 | 71 | 72 | | +/- 1cm |
| C | CF Length | 61 | 60 | 60 | | +/- 1cm |
| D | Chest Height | 25 | 25 | 25 | | +/- 1cm |
| E | Across Front | 38 | 38.5 | 38 | | +/- 1cm |
| F | Across Back | 40 | 40 | 40 | | +/- 1cm |
| G | Bottom Width | 54 | 56 | 54 | | +/- 1cm |
| H | Neckline Width | 22.5 | 22 | 22.5 | | +/- 1cm |
| I | CF Neckline Drop | 10 | 9.5 | 11 | | +/- 0,5cm |
| J | Shoulder Length | 12 | 11.5 | 12 | | +/- 0,5cm |
| K | Shoulder Slope | 4 | 4 | 4 | | +/- 0,5cm |
| L | Shoulder Width | 45 | 46.5 | 45 | | +/- 1cm |
| M | Armhole Straight | 26 | 26 | 26 | | +/- 1cm |
| N | Sleeve Length | 17 | 16 | 20 | | +/- 1cm |
| O | Bottom Sleeve Width | 17 | 17 | 17 | | +/- 0,5cm |
| P | Neckline Piping Width | 1.5 | 1.5 | 1.5 | | +/- 0,2cm |

● out of measure: adjust pattern     ● new measure: adjust pattern

| STYLE: **Nick** #B203K | **FIT COMMENTS** | |
|---|---|---|
| Fabric: Classic interlock jersey #0678 | Collection: Lifestyle | ABC Seams |
| Description: T-shirt with "Boom" print | Date: 26/09/20  1st PROTOTYPE / Size M | |

## COMMENTS

### PATTERN & FIT

Some measurements are out of tolerance (G and L) and some others need to be adjusted (I and N). Please, adjust the pattern by following the measurement chart.

### WORKMANSHIP

The workmanship overall is OK.

- Shoulder seam: please add the topstitch on the back as required. Follow the construction sheet / seam C100-3 (OS)

### MATERIALS

Back Neck Tape: the quality of the tape is too thick. Please send softer option/s to be approved for production.

### NEW REQUIREMENTS

Please follow the comments above and **send a 2nd prototype** in size M

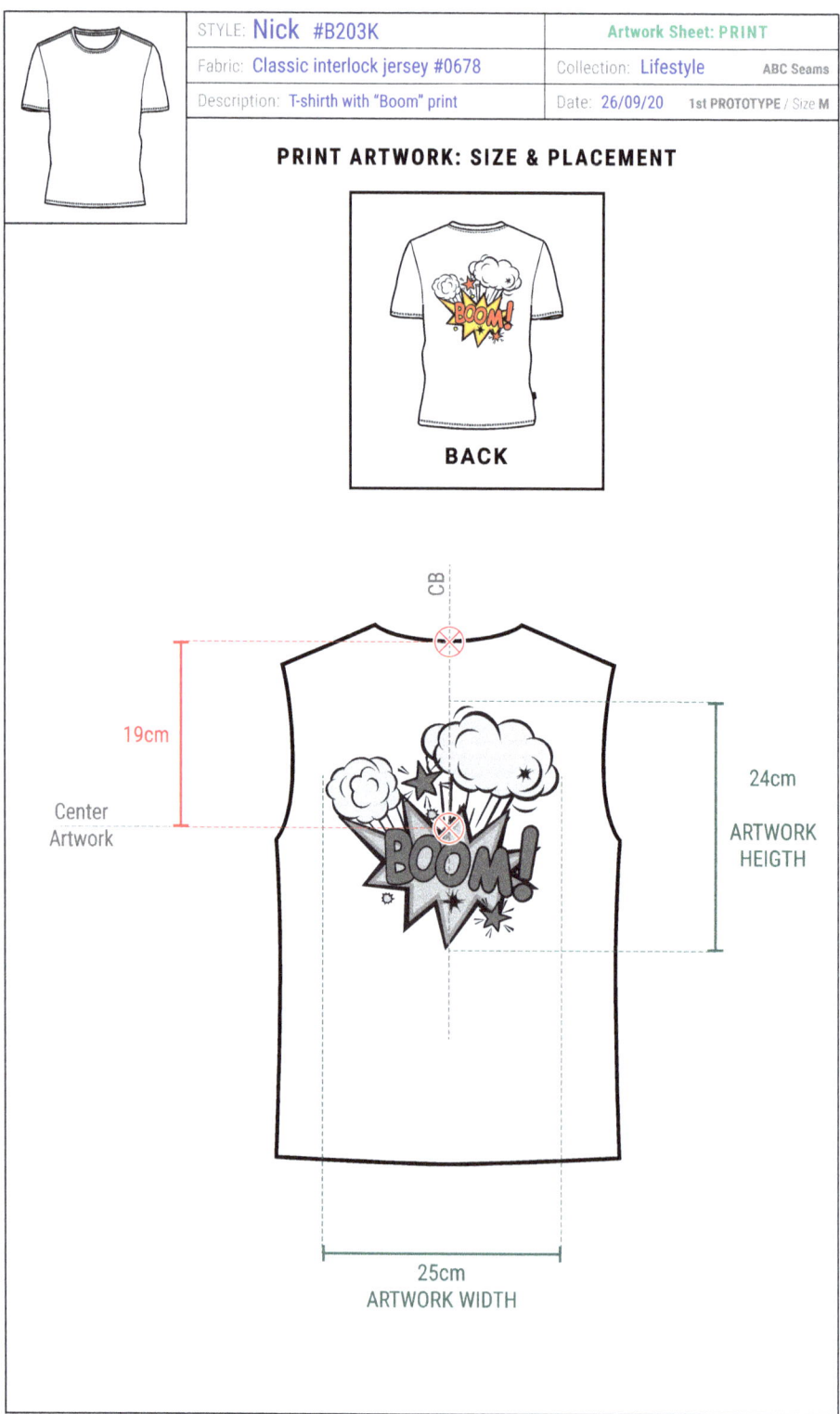

| STYLE: **Nick** #B203K | Artwork Sheet: **PRINT** |
|---|---|
| Fabric: **Classic interlock jersey #0678** | Collection: **Lifestyle**   ABC Seams |
| Description: **T-shirth with "Boom" print** | Date: **26/09/20**   **1st PROTOTYPE** / Size **M** |

## PRINT ARTWORK: COLORS & COMBINATIONS

- COLOR 1
- COLOR 2
- COLOR 3
- COLOR 4
- COLOR 5

|  |  | COMBO 1 | COMBO 2 | COMBO 3 | COMBO 4 |
|---|---|---|---|---|---|
| **FABRIC COLOR** | | WHITE: 001 | YELLOW: 237 | GREEN: 649 | BLACK: 999 |
| **PRINT COLOR** | COLOR 1 | black P 19-4004 | black P 19-4004 | black P 19-4004 | light grey P 13-4303 |
| | COLOR 2 | light grey P 13-4303 | light grey P 13-4303 | light grey P 13-4303 | dark grey P 17-3911 |
| | COLOR 3 | red P 17-1563 | purple P 18-3533 | red P 17-1563 | red P 17-1563 |
| | COLOR 4 | yellow P13-0758 | yellow P13-0758 | yellow P13-0758 | yellow P13-0758 |
| | COLOR 5 | orange P 14-1159 | orange P 14-1159 | purple P 18-3533 | orange P 14-1159 |

*Prototype*

| STYLE: Richard #B204K | Artwork Sheet: EMBROIDERY |
|---|---|
| Fabric: Cotton pike c/0001 | Collection: Lifestyle   ABC Seams |
| Description: Slim fit polo shirt | Date: 06/12/20   1st PROTOTYPE / Size M |

## EMBROIDERY ARTWORK SIZE & PLACEMENT

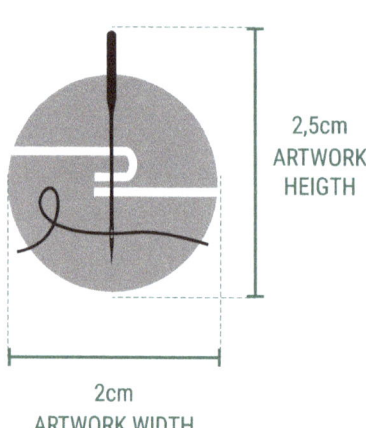

2,5cm ARTWORK HEIGTH

2cm ARTWORK WIDTH

FRONT

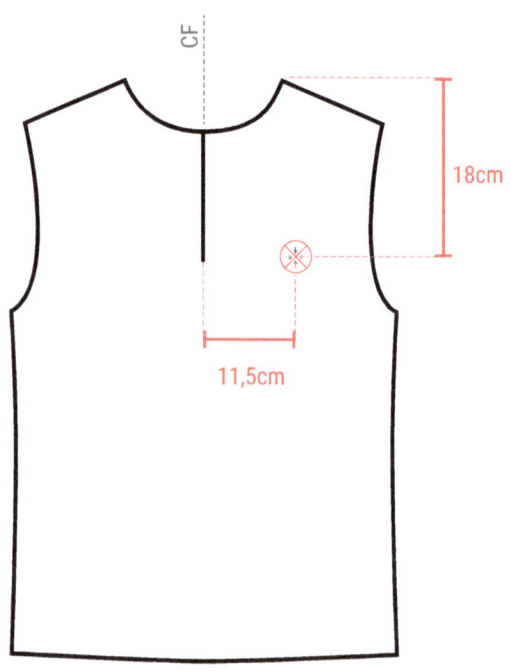

CF

18cm

11,5cm

| STYLE: **Richard** #B204K | Artwork Sheet: **EMBROIDERY** | |
|---|---|---|
| Fabric: **Cotton pike c/0001** | Collection: **Lifestyle** | ABC Seams |
| Description: **Slim fit polo shirt** | Date: **06/12/20** 1st PROTOTYPE / Size **M** | |

## EMBROIDERY ARTWORK: COLORS & COMBINATIONS

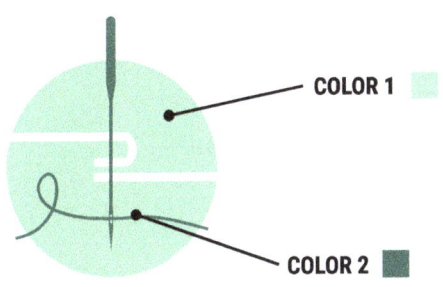

| FABRIC COLOR | | WHITE: 001 | YELLOW: 237 | GREEN: 649 | BLACK: 999 |
|---|---|---|---|---|---|
| **EMBROIDERY** | COLOR 1 | light green B5251 | light yellow B1181 | light green B5251 | green P 13-4303 |
| | COLOR 2 | dark green B5235 | dark yellow B1464 | dark green B5235 | dark green B5235 |

thread: **Coats Silko** / nr 100

Prototype

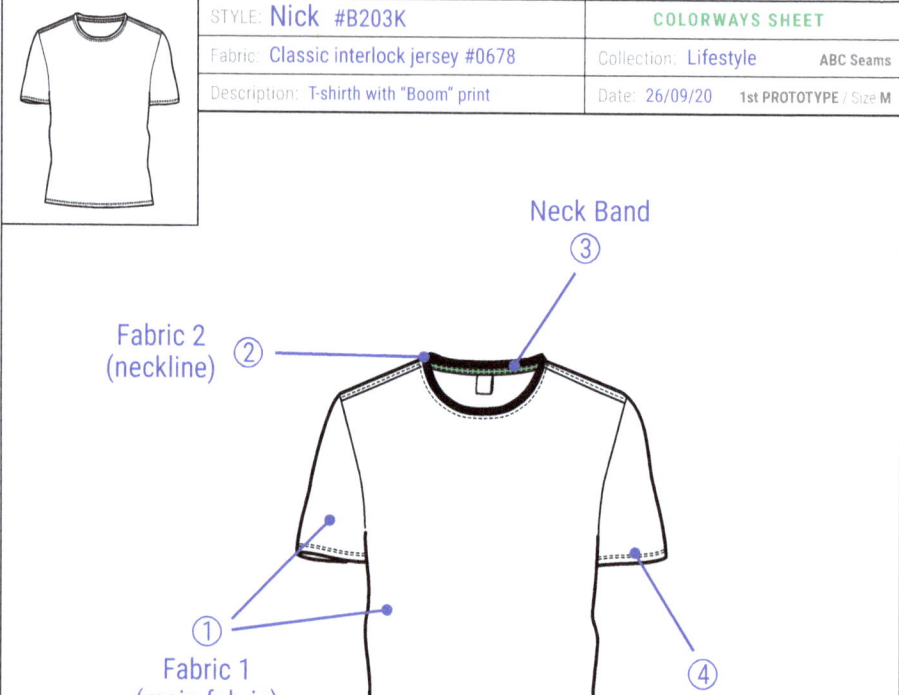

| STYLE: **Nick** #B203K | COLORWAYS SHEET | |
|---|---|---|
| Fabric: Classic interlock jersey #0678 | Collection: Lifestyle | ABC Seams |
| Description: T-shirt with "Boom" print | Date: 26/09/20 | 1st PROTOTYPE / Size M |

Neck Band ③

Fabric 2 (neckline) ②

Fabric 1 (main fabric) ①

④ Topstitching

| | | COMBO 1 | COMBO 2 | COMBO 3 | COMBO 4 |
|---|---|---|---|---|---|
| **FABRICS** | ① **MAIN FABRIC** | WHITE: 001 | YELLOW: 237 | GREEN: 649 | BLACK: 999 |
| | ② Fabric 2 | black c/ 999 | black c/ 999 | black c/ 999 | black c/ 999 |
| **TRIMMINGS** | ③ Neck Band | green P 16-5938 | green P 16-5938 | green P 16-5938 | green P 16-5938 |
| | ④ Topstitching | matching color | matching color | matching color | green P 16-5938 |

| STYLE: **Nick** #B203K | **COLORWAYS SHEET** | |
|---|---|---|
| Fabric: Classic interlock jersey #0678 | Collection: **Lifestyle** | **ABC Seams** |
| Description: T-shirth with "Boom" print | Date: 26/09/20 | **1st PROTOTYPE** / Size **M** |

**COMBO 1**

**COMBO 2**

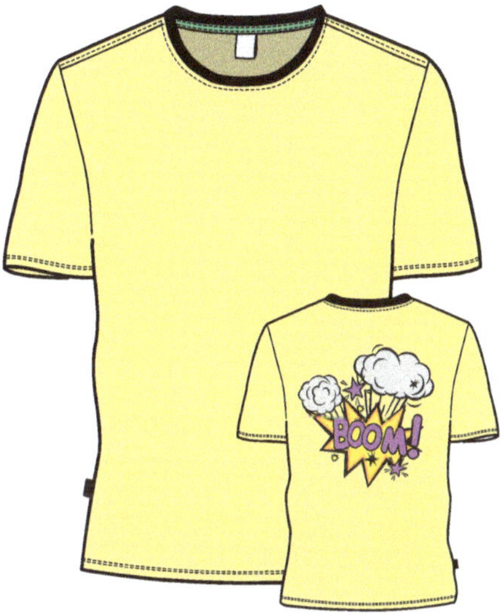

**COMBO 3**

**COMBO 4**

| STYLE: **Richard**  #B204K | TRIMMING SHEET | |
|---|---|---|
| Fabric: **Cotton pike** c/0001 | Collection: **Lifestyle** | **ABC Seams** |
| Description: **Slim fit polo shirt** | Date: 06/12/20 | **1st PROTOTYPE** / Size **M** |

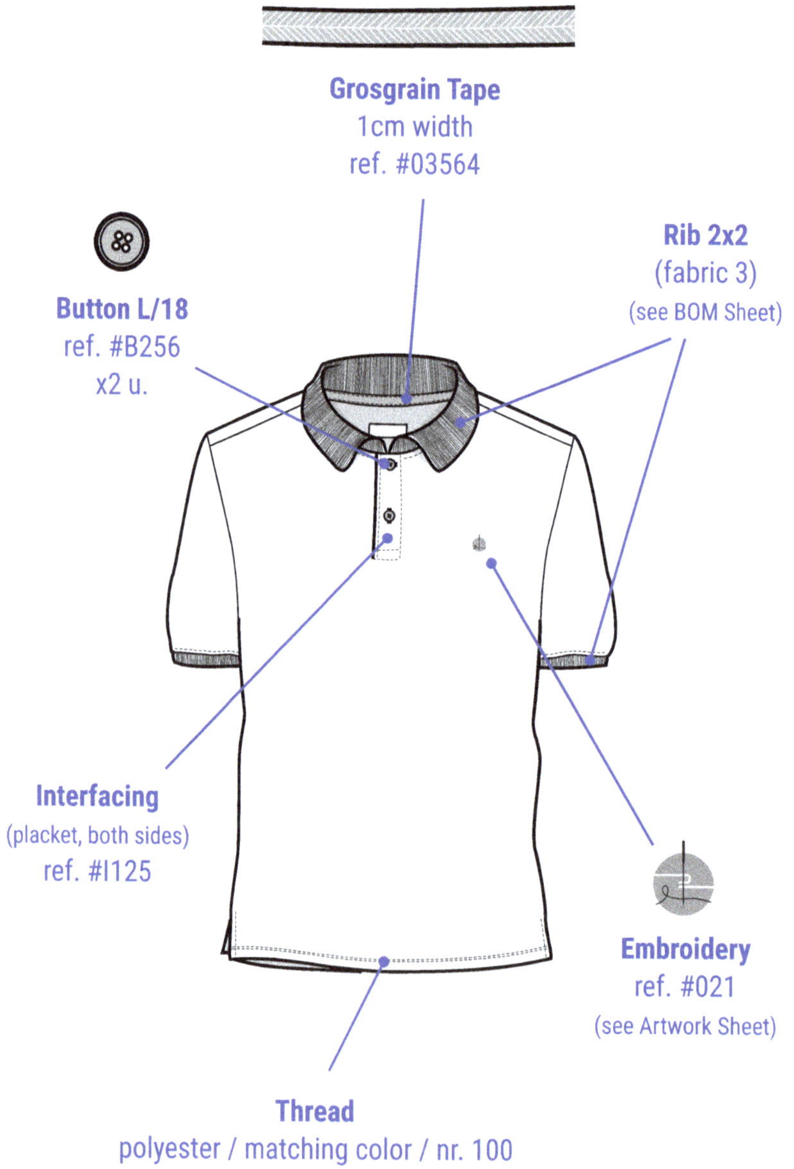

**Grosgrain Tape**
1cm width
ref. #03564

**Rib 2x2**
(fabric 3)
(see BOM Sheet)

**Button L/18**
ref. #B256
x2 u.

**Interfacing**
(placket, both sides)
ref. #I125

**Embroidery**
ref. #021
(see Artwork Sheet)

**Thread**
polyester / matching color / nr. 100

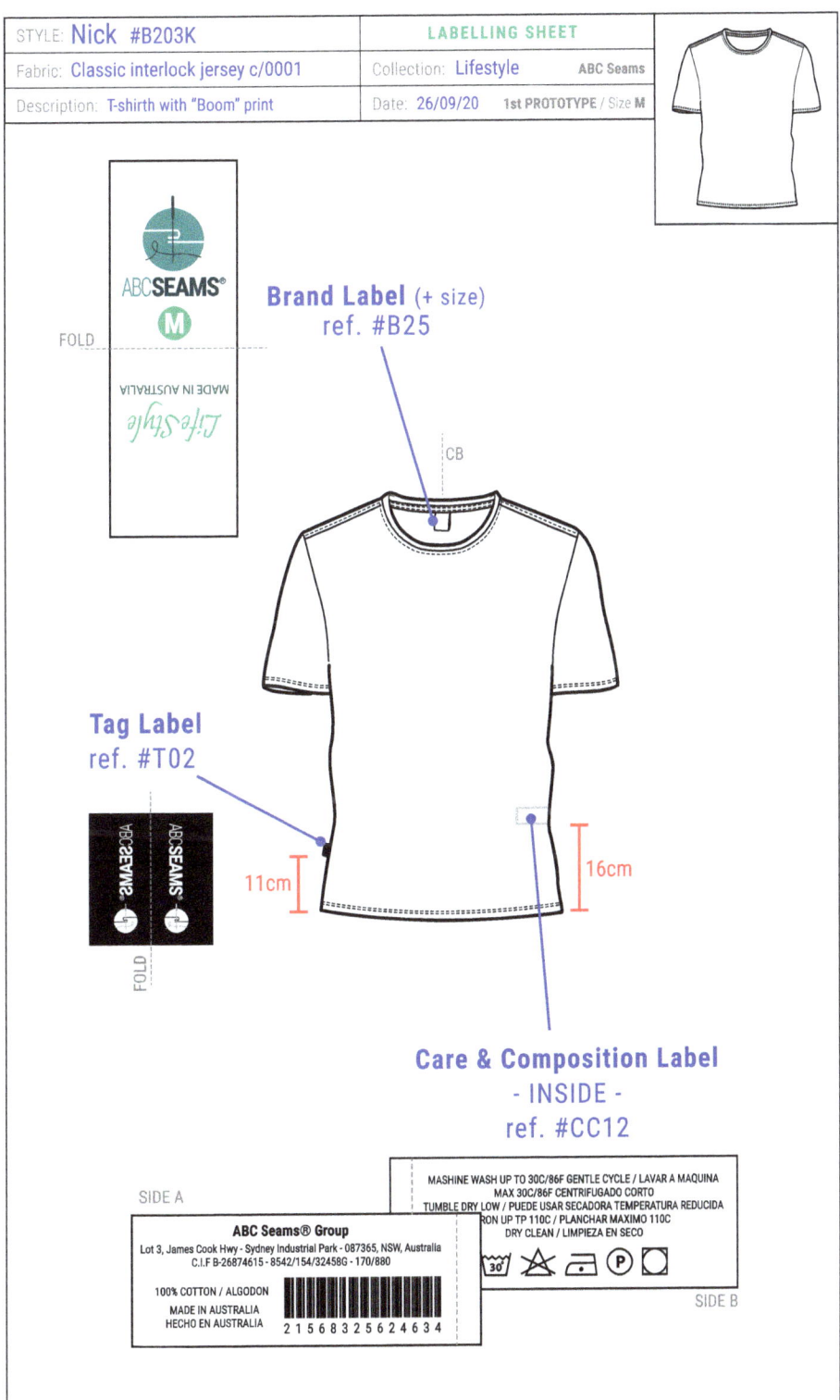

| STYLE: **Nick** #B203K | LAB DIPS APPROVAL | |
|---|---|---|
| Fabric: **Classic interlock jersey #0678 c/0001** | Collection: **Lifestyle** | ABC Seams |
| Description: **T-shirth with "Boom" print** | Date: **26/09/20** 2nd **PROTOTYPE** / Size **M** | |

**COLOR LAB DIPS**

We are herewith submitting color lab dips as per your request for approval.
Please advise your approval and/or comments as soon as possible. Thank you.

Date: *30-04-2020*

Fabric: *Classic Interlock Jersey*    Fabric Ref: *#0678*
Colour: *Wild Green 16-5422 TCX*    Color Code: *649*

Option A
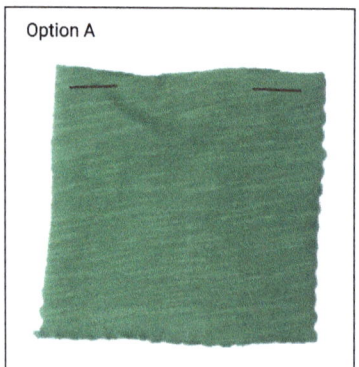

Option B

Option C

Option D

| STYLE: **Nick** #B203K | **GRADING SHEET** | |
|---|---|---|
| Fabric: Classic interlock jersey #0678 | Collection: Lifestyle | ABC Seams |
| Description: T-shirht with "Boom" print | Date: 26/09/20 | 1st PROTOTYPE / Size M |

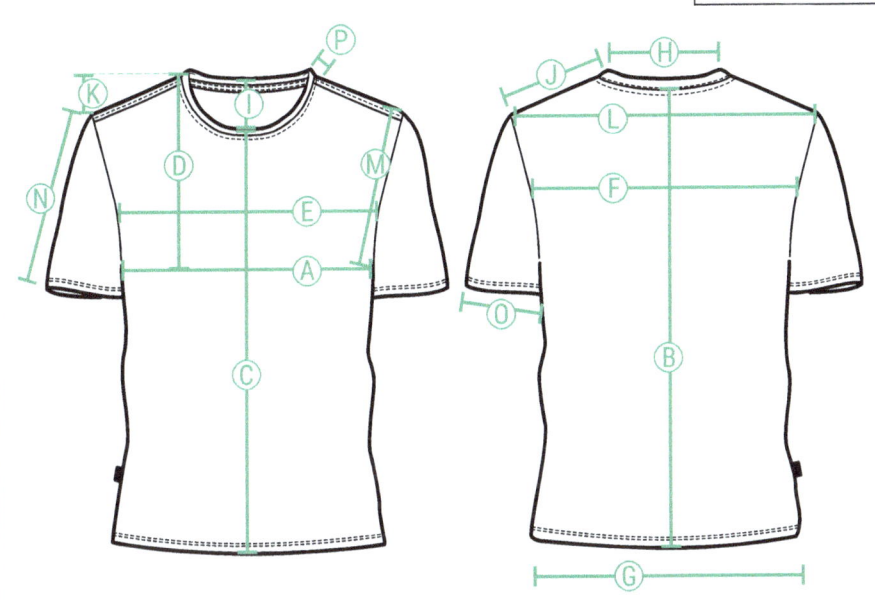

| | | XS | S | M | L | XL | Tolerance |
|---|---|---|---|---|---|---|---|
| A | Chest Width | 51 | 52.5 | 54 | 55.5 | 57 | +/- 1cm |
| B | CB Length | 71 | 71.5 | 72 | 72.5 | 73 | +/- 1cm |
| C | CF Length | 59 | 59.5 | 60 | 60.5 | 61 | +/- 1cm |
| D | Chest Height | 24.5 | 24.75 | 25 | 25.25 | 25.5 | +/- 1cm |
| E | Across Front | 35 | 36.5 | 38 | 39.5 | 41 | +/- 1cm |
| F | Across Back | 37 | 38.5 | 40 | 41.5 | 43 | +/- 1cm |
| G | Bottom Width | 51 | 52.5 | 54 | 55.5 | 57 | +/- 1cm |
| H | Neckline Width | 21.5 | 22 | 22.5 | 23 | 23.5 | +/- 0,5cm |
| I | CF Neckline Drop | 11 | 11 | 11 | 11 | 11 | +/- 0,5cm |
| J | Shoulder Length | 10.5 | 11.25 | 12 | 12.75 | 13.5 | +/- 0,5cm |
| K | Shoulder Slope | 3.5 | 3.75 | 4 | 4.25 | 4.5 | +/- 0,5cm |
| L | Shoulder Width | 42 | 43.5 | 45 | 46.5 | 48 | +/- 1cm |
| M | Armhole Straight | 25.5 | 25.75 | 26 | 26.25 | 26.5 | +/- 1cm |
| N | Sleeve Length | 20 | 20 | 20 | 20 | 20 | +/- 1cm |
| O | Bottom Sleeve Width | 15 | 16 | 17 | 18 | 19 | +/- 0,5cm |
| P | Neckline Piping Width | 1.5 | 1.5 | 1.5 | 1.5 | 1.5 | +/- 0,2cm |

| STYLE: **Nick** #B203K | BOM SHEET | |
|---|---|---|
| FABRIC: Classic interlock jersey #0678 | Collection: Lifestyle | ABC Seams |
| Description: T-shirt with "Boom" print | Date: 26/09/20 | 1st PROTOTYPE / Size M |

## BILL OF MATERIALS (BOM)

| | FABRIC / Reference Description / Weight Composition | Placement | Colors | Supplier |
|---|---|---|---|---|
| | Fabric 1 / #0678 Interlock jersey / 180gm. 45% polyester, 55% cotton | Body, sleeves | Follow Colorways Sheet | factory |
| | Fabric 2 / #1258 Cotton rib 1x1 / 180gm. 68% cotton, 32% lycra | Neckline | | |

| | TRIMS Description and comp. Reference / Qty. | Placement | Colors | Supplier |
|---|---|---|---|---|
| | Bias binding Cotton / 1.5cm width #f658 / 23cm | Follow Trimming Sheet | Follow Colorways Sheet | factory |
| | Thread Coats Astra Polyester nr.100 #36H / 70mts | | | |
| | Print Boom 5 colors #004 / 1u. | Follow Artwork Sheet | | |

| | LABELS | Ref. | Placement | Qty. | Colors | Supplier |
|---|---|---|---|---|---|---|
| | Main Label + Size | | Follow Labelling Sheet | 1 | 001 | Studio Lab |
| | Tab Label | | | 1 | 999 | |
| | Care Label | | | 1 | 001 | |
| | Poly Bag 20x18cm | #2018 | packing | 1 | 0063 | |

# SELECTION GUIDE

| FABRIC WEIGHT | LIGHT | | MEDIUM | | HEAVY | | |
|---|---|---|---|---|---|---|---|
| **THREAD** Tex size nr | 180 | 150 | 120 | 100 | 80 | 50 | 40 | 30 |
| | finest → thickest | | | | | | | |

### NEEDLE

| Metric | 65 to 80 | 80 to 90 | 90 to 100 |
|---|---|---|---|
| Singer Size | 9 to 12 | 12 to 14 | 14 to 18 |

### STITCH LENGHT

| stitches per cm | 5 to 8 | 3 to 5 | 2 to 3 |
|---|---|---|---|
| stitches per inch | 14 to 20 | 9 to 14 | 6 to 9 |

### COTTON THREAD

Wovens.

Basic sewing.

Cotton, linen, and rayon.

Garments that are going to be dyed after sewing.

Delicate fabrics.

Sheer fabrics.

Lingerie.

Embroidery.

### POLYESTER THREAD

Woven, knit and stretch fabrics.

Synthetic fabrics.

Multi-purpose: blouses, jeans, shirts, outwear and lingerie.

Embroidery.

### WOOLY NYLON and POLYESTER THREAD

Stretchable: ideal for garments using spandex and Lycra.

Active-wear, swimming wear.

### NYLON THREAD

Synthetic fabrics.

Good for heavy weight fabrics such as leather; vinyl, canvas, and suede.

Bags and shoes.

Upholstery.

### SILK THREAD

Embroidery.

Topstitching on delicate garments.

Reference Material: Seam Anatomy

# ANATOMY

Right Side
[ RS ]

Topstitch
Stitching Line
Seam Heading
Width
Depth
Seam Line
Structure
Stitch
Seam Allowance
(SA)

Wrong Side
[ WS ]

Page : 201

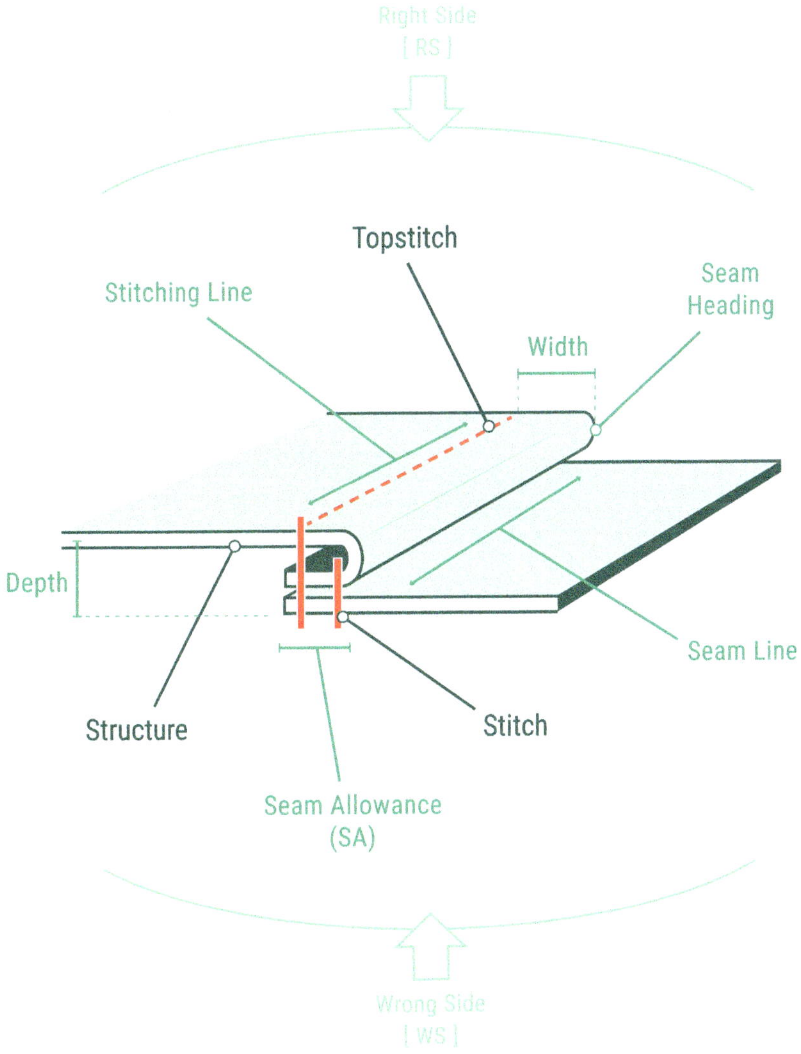

# TYPES

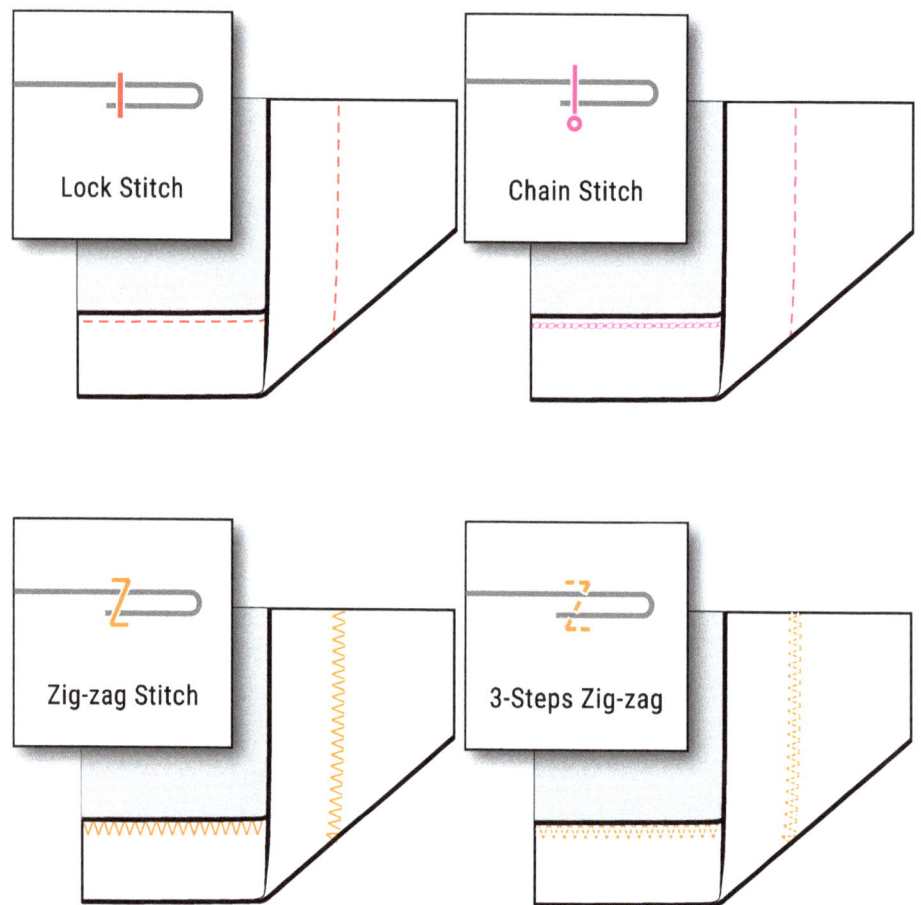

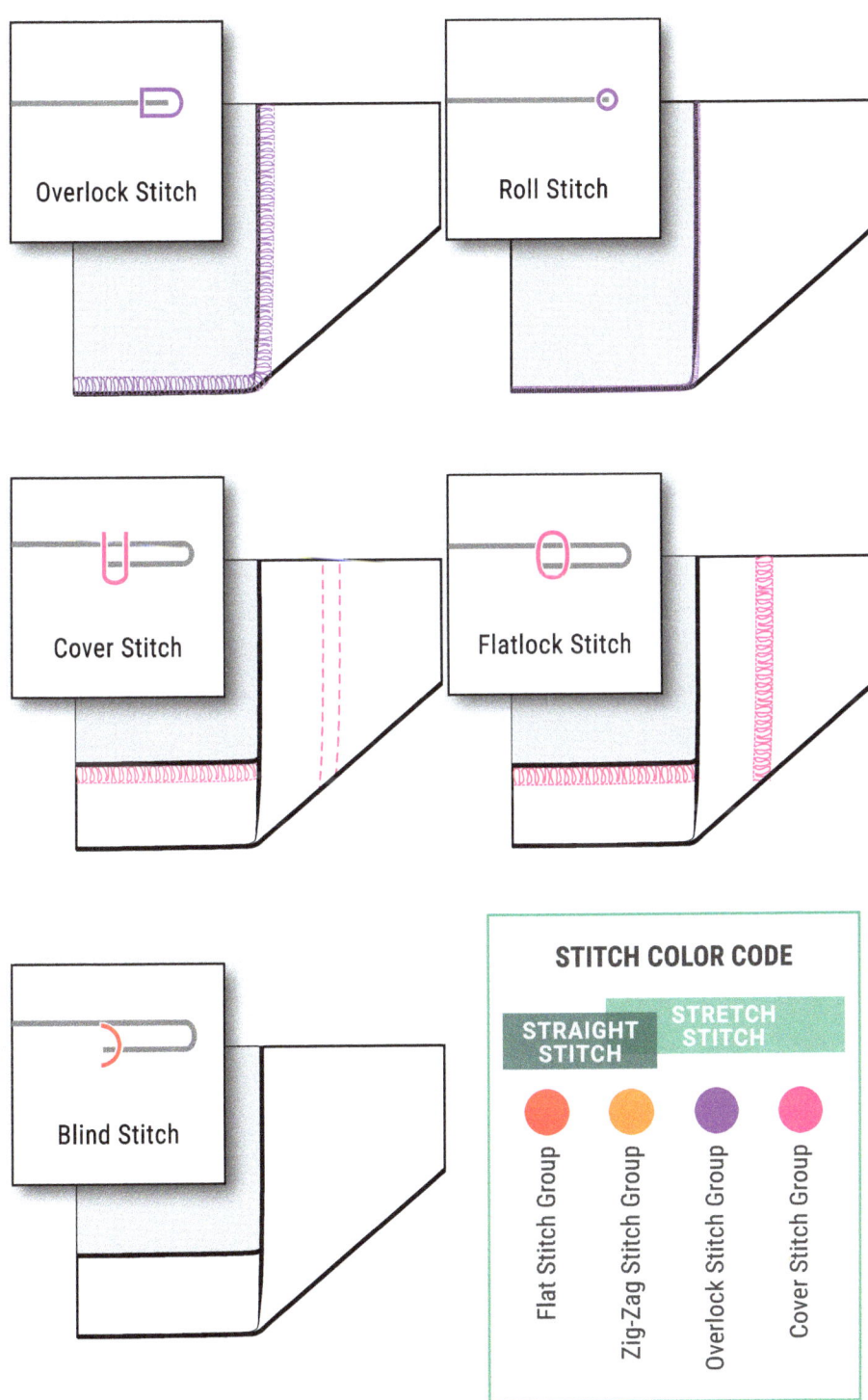

# TOP TYPES

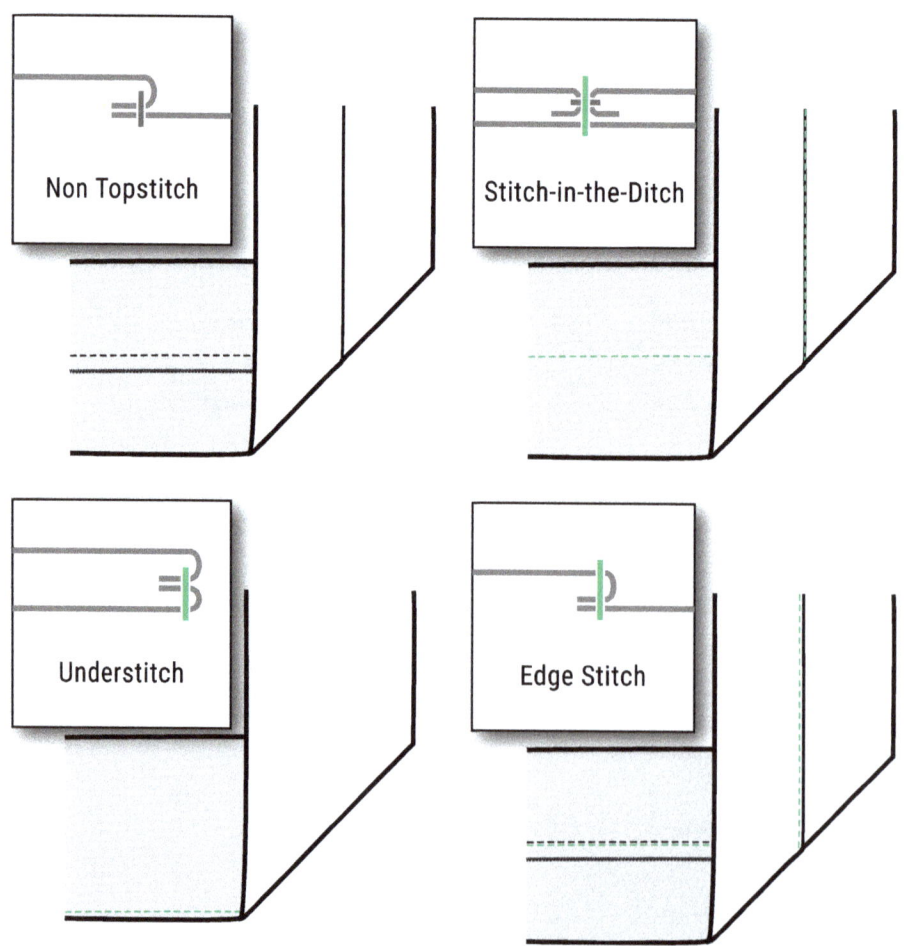

# Reference Material: Types of Topstitches

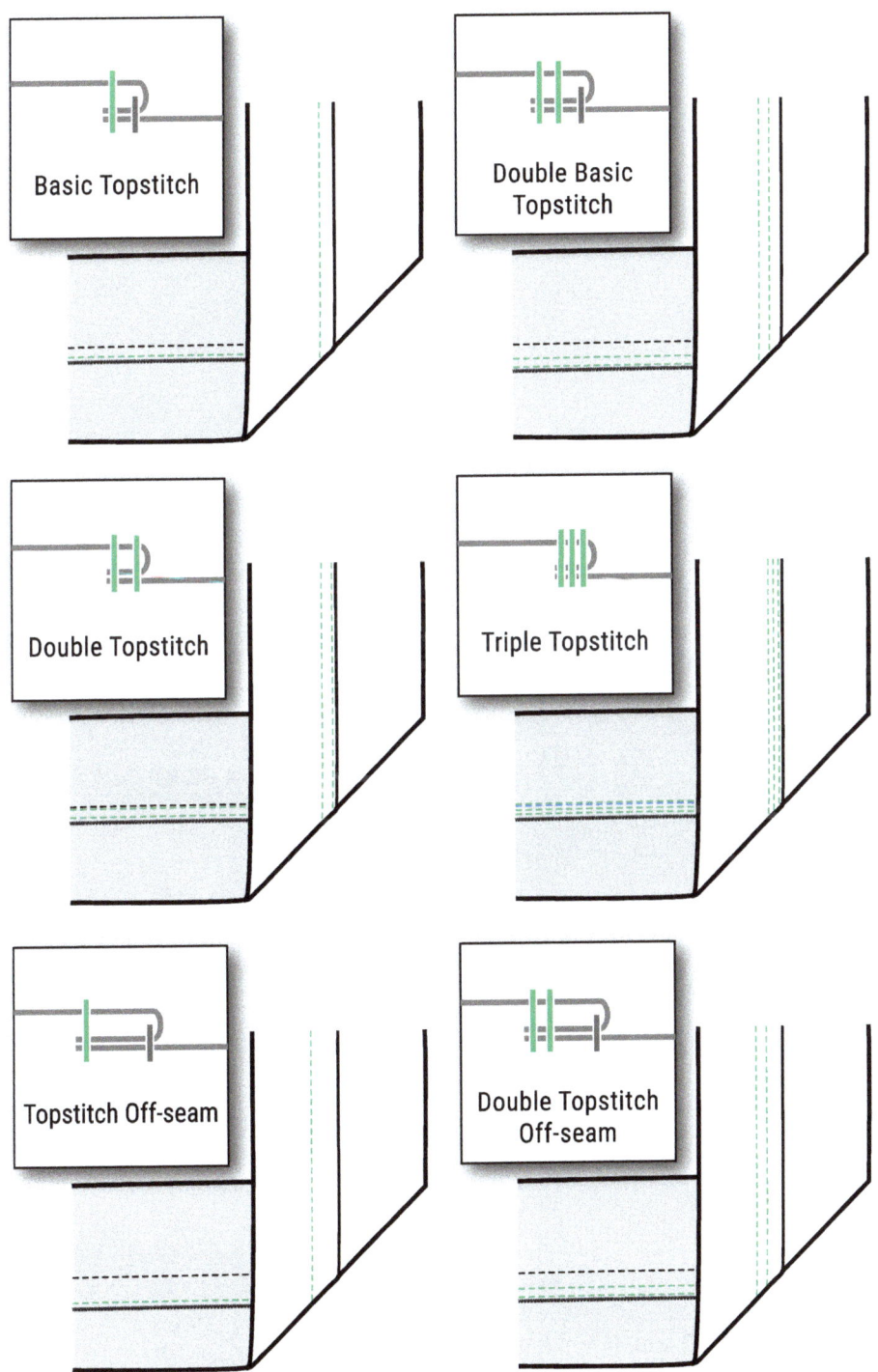

# INDEX

abbreviations, 23
armhole, 29, 33, 36, 40, 46, 55, 63, 70, 123, 131, 151, 173, 180, 181

belt loop, 115
belt, 159, 164
bottom, 28, 32, 36, 41, 47, 55, 63, 71, 75, 83, 93, 100, 104, 111, 123, 134, 140, 153, 161, 162, 173
box pleat, 55, 58, 59, 96
　inverted, 47, 59
button loop, 88

collar, 48, 56, 64, 142
　ribbed, 42, 152
　stand, 48
crotch, 75, 82, 83, 93, 95, 100, 104, 114, 115, 169
cuff, 51, 65, 143
　ribbed, 41, 127, 155

dart, 62, 63, 88, 100, 130

elbow seam, 131, 143
embroidery, 32, 40, 62, 68, 82, 108, 114, 122, 158
　sheet, 190, 191

facing, 70, 79, 87, 101, 125, 133, 154
fashion design, 12

garments production process, 14
gathers, 62, 63, 65, 169
gusset, 168, 169, 176, 181

icons, 23
inseam, 74, 82, 92

labels, 195
　back, 75
　main, 29, 36, 43, 48, 56, 64, 70, 130, 133, 142, size, 43, 48, 64
　tab, 28, 36
lapel, 132
leg line, 168, 169, 176, 180
lining, 70, 71, 79, 124, 130, 133, 152, 153, 154, 155, 176, 177, 180

neckline, 29, 33, 37, 42, 48, 56, 64, 70, 125, 132, 142, 160, 173, 180, 181

panel seam, 131, 140, 141, 150, 151
placket, 43, 49, 57, 64, 111, 142, 161
pleat, 82, 133, 162, 163
pocket, 50, 58, 59, 77, 78, 79, 86, 87, 88, 89, 92, 96, 97, 117, 118, 119, 126, 136, 137, 144, 145, 154, 164, 165
  false, 110
  flap, 58, 59, 96, 117, 136, 146, 147
princess seam, 68, 69, 70
print, 36
  artwork sheet, 188, 189

seam, index, 208, 209
  parts of a, 19, 201
  seams, options, 19
  types, 19, 208, 209
shoulder strap, 33, 172, 177,
shoulder, 28, 36, 40, 46, 54, 62, 122, 140, 152, 158,
side seam, 28, 32, 36, 40, 46, 54, 62, 68, 74, 78, 82, 86, 92, 100, 104, 108, 115, 122, 127, 141, 145, 151, 159, 168, 169, 173, 176, 181
sleeve, bottom, 36, 55, 135, 159
slit, 40, 54,
spec sheet, 16,
stitch, types, 202, 203

tech pack, 15, 185
  materials (BOM), 198
  colorways, 192, 193
  embroidery, 190, 191
  fit comments, 187
  grading, 197
  lab dips approval, 196
  labelling, 195
  measurement, 186
  print, 188, 189
  trimmings, 194
thread, types, 200
topstitch, types, 204, 205

vent, 51, 65, 71, 131, 134, 135, 143

waist line, 168, 176
waist tab, 141
waistband, 74, 83, 94, 101, 105, 110, 114, 169
  extension, 85

yoke, 47, 55, 62, 63, 75, 109, 115, 141, 147, 150, 151
  inner half-moon, 41, 123

ip guard, 76, 85, 116
zipper, 125, 152, 154
  invisible, 68

# INDEX

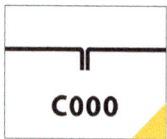

**BASIC SEAM**
Pg. 28, 32, 36, 40, 124, 127, 168, 169, 173, 176, 181

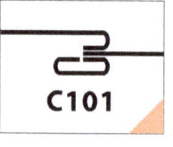

**BOUND SEAM**
Pg. 36, 42, 158, 160, 164

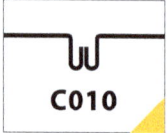

**FRENCH SEAM**
Pg. 62

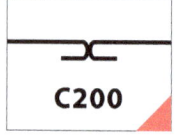

**OPEN SEAM**
Pg. 68, 69, 70, 82, 83, 86, 130, 131, 134, 135

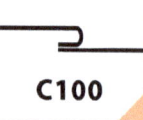

**FELLED SEAM**
Pg. 28, 36, 40, 46, 54, 62, 63, 69, 70, 74, 76, 78, 82, 92, 93, 95, 100, 104, 105, 108, 109, 110, 114, 115, 118, 122, 123, 124, 127, 130, 131, 133, 137, 141, 144, 147, 150, 151, 152, 172, 181

**HONG KONG SEAM**
Pg. 82, 159, 160

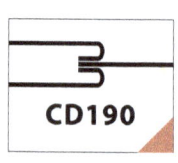

**SANDWICH SEAM**
Pg. 46, 48, 51, 54, 55, 56, 62, 63, 64, 65, 74, 94, 110, 114, 125, 132, 140, 142, 143, 152, 153, 155, 168, 172, 176, 181

**WELT SEAM**
Pg. 46, 54, 55, 74, 75, 92, 100, 108, 109, 115, 140, 141, 143, 145

## Reference Material: Seams Index

**H000** — UNHEMMED EDGE
Pg. 125, 137, 163

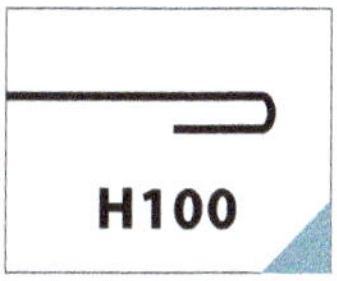

**H100** — SINGLE FOLD HEM
Pg. 28, 32, 36, 40, 41, 78, 104, 125, 169, 176, 177, 180

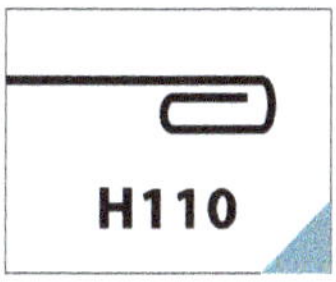

**H110** — DOUBLE FOLD HEM
Pg. 47, 51, 54, 63, 71, 75, 78, 116, 143, 162

**H130** — DOUBLE FOLD HEM - WIDE
Pg. 49, 50, 55, 57, 64, 75, 83, 93, 117, 142, 161

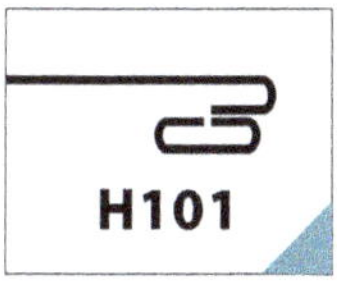

**H101** — BOUND HEM
Pg. 40, 47, 63

**H150** — FACED HEM
Pg. 43, 49, 50, 55, 57, 77, 86, 96, 101, 114, 160, 161

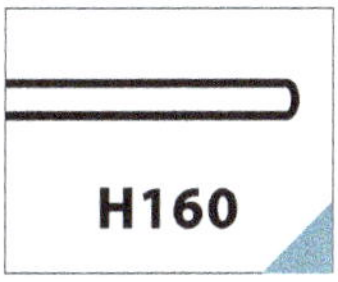

**H160** — TURNED EDGE
Pg. 51, 65, 76, 79, 85, 89, 94, 96, 104, 110, 116, 119, 123, 127, 140, 143, 152, 153, 155, 162, 164, 172

**HD190** — SANDWICH HEM
Pg. 48, 51, 56, 64, 70, 71, 74, 76, 78, 79, 83, 84, 85, 86, 89, 92, 95, 96, 101, 111, 114, 117, 119, 124, 132, 134, 135, 136, 141, 142, 145, 146, 164

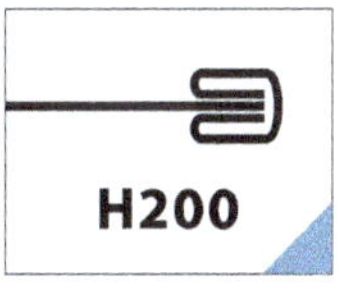

**H200** — BINDED EDGE
Pg. 29, 33, 65, 87, 89, 100, 119, 125, 163, 165, 173, 176, 177

**H210** — EXPOSED BAND
Pg. 37, 169, 173, 180, 181

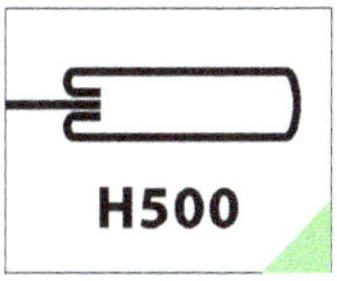

**H500** — BINDED EDGE - WIDE
Pg. 43, 51, 57, 111

 **D111** — BOX PLEAT
Pg. 47, 55, 58, 133

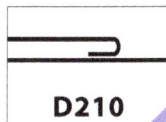 **D210** — PATCH SEAM
Pg. 41, 50, 58, 76, 77, 78, 79, 87, 96, 97, 101, 111, 117, 126, 147, 154

# INDEX

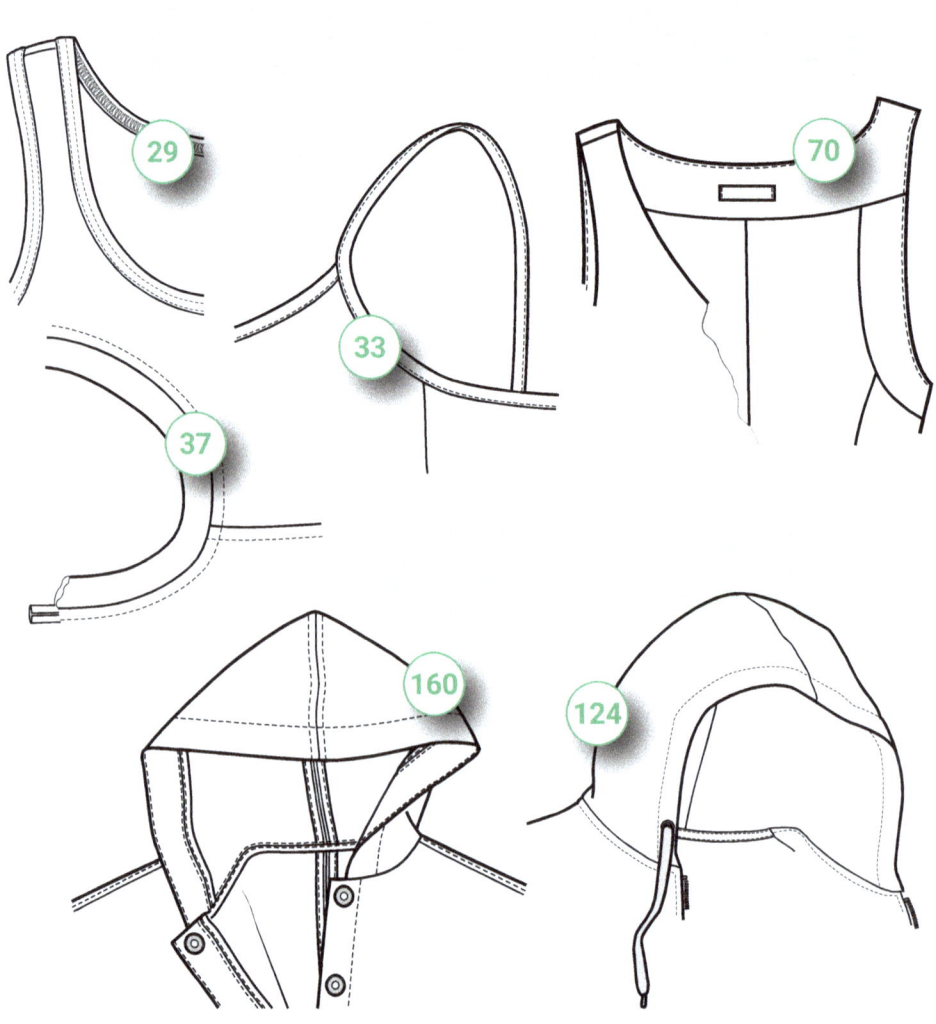

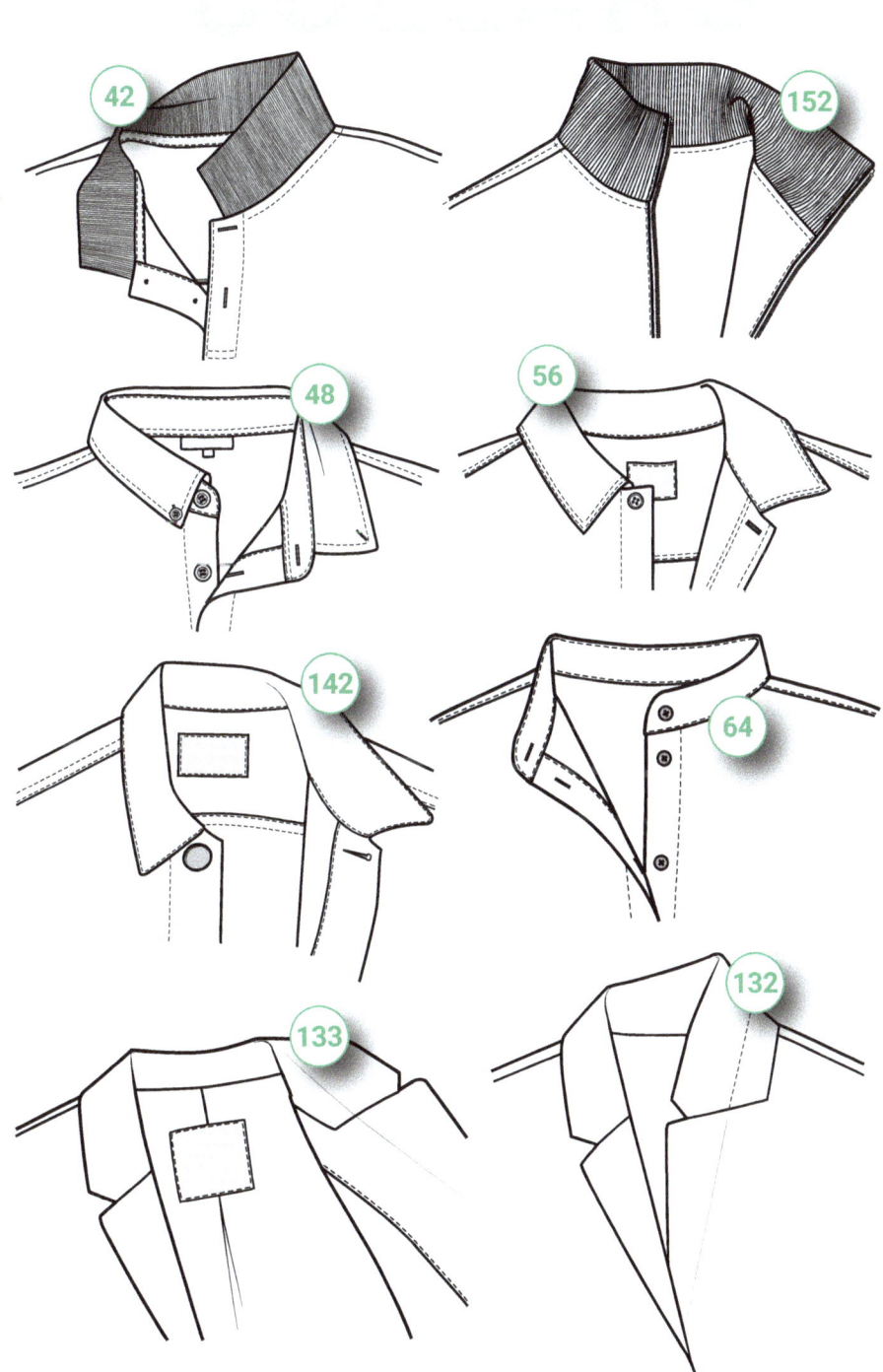

# Sewing Seams for Tech Packs

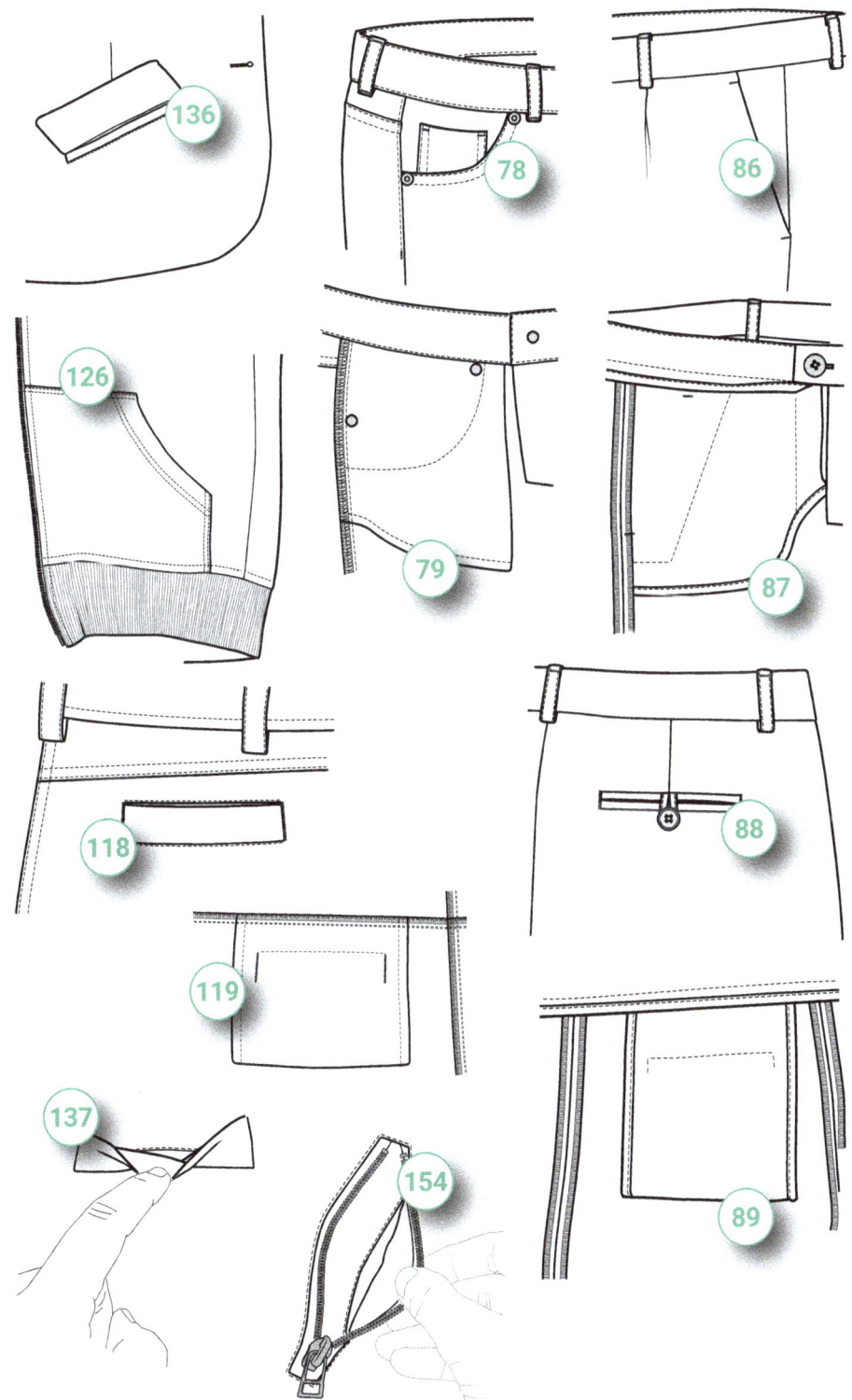

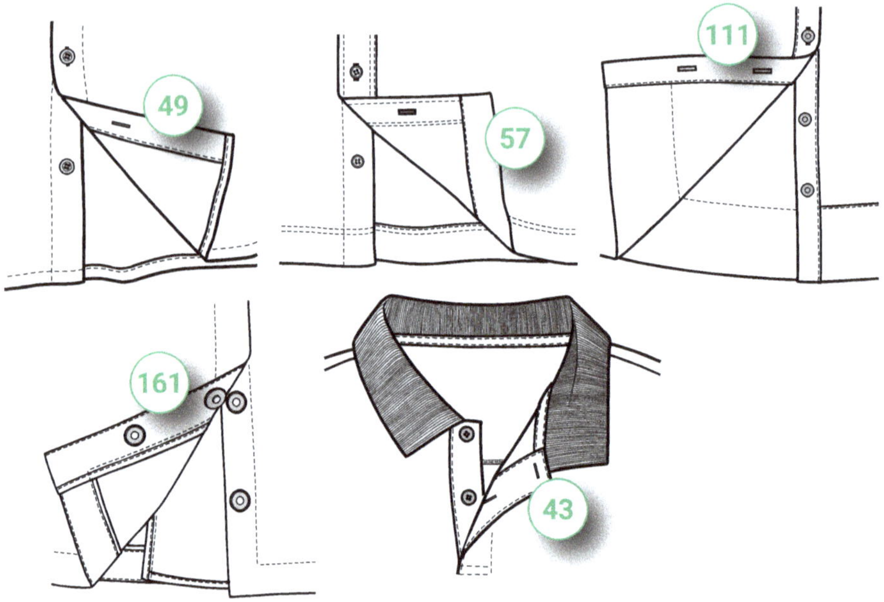

# Sewing Seams for Tech Packs

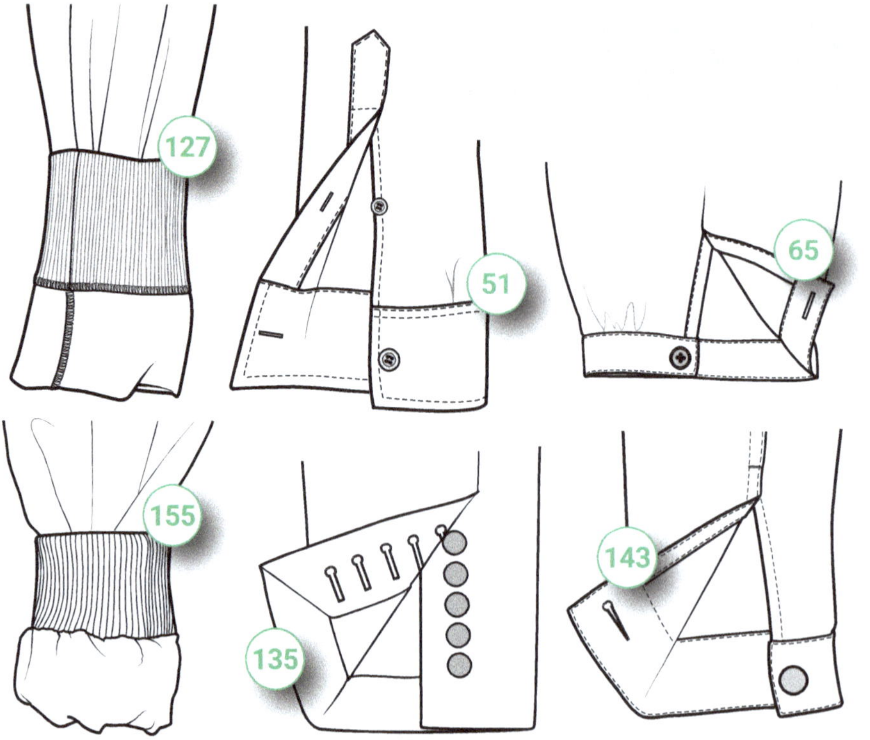

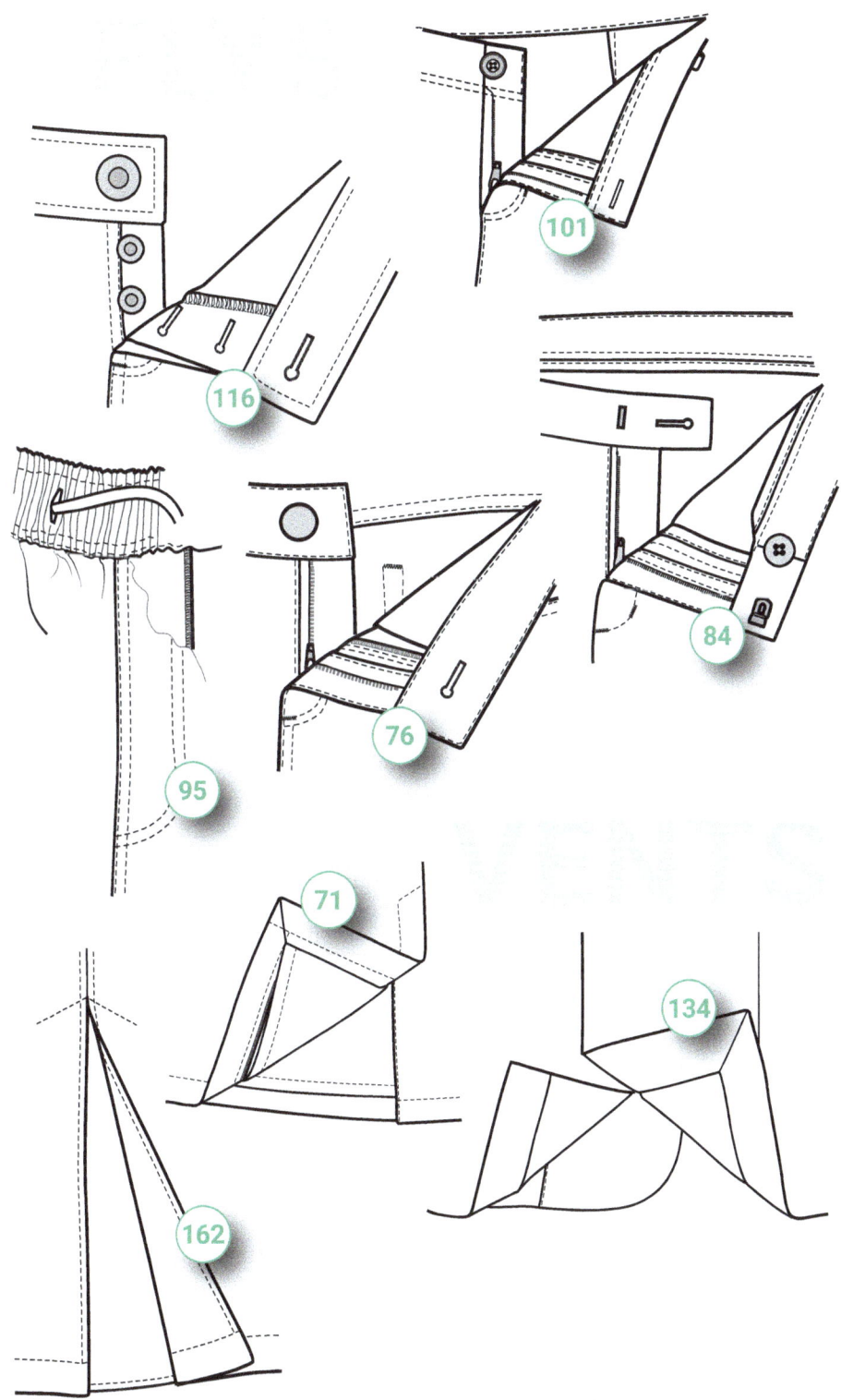

## MY NOTES

# BIBLIOGRAPHY

A&E Textiles. *Selecting Stitches Per Inch*. A&E Technical Bulletin. 2011. http://www.amefird.com/wp-content/uploads/2010/01/Selecting-the-right-SPI-2-5-10.pdf

ABC Seams® Pty. Ltd. *101 Sewing Seams. The Most Used Seams by Fashion Designers*. Australia: ABC Seams® Pty. Ltd., 2018. ISBN 978-0-6482734-0-0

Brown, Gali and Palmer, Pati. *Sewing with Sergers. The Complete Handbook for Overlock Sewing.* USA: Palmer/Pletsch Associates, 1996. ISBN 0-935278-25-7

Brown, Patty. and Rice, Jannett. *Ready to wear apparel analysis.* New Jersey, Prentice Hall, 2001. ISBN 0130254347

Cabrera, Roberto and Flaherty Meyers, Patricia. *Classic Tailoring Techniques: A Construction Guide for Women's Wear.* USA: Fairchild Books, 1991. ISBN 0-870054-35-8

Carr, H. and Latham. *Technology of Clothing Manufacture.* Blackwell Science; 4th edition, 2008. ISBN: 978-1-405-16198-5

Cole, Julie and Czachor, Sharon. *Professional Sewing Techniques for Designers.* USA: Fairchild Books, 2008. ISBN 978-1-56367-516-4

Eberle, Hannelore. *Clothing Technology: From Fibre to Fashion.* Verlag Europa-Lehrmittel Nourn; 5th edition edition, 2008. ISBN-10: 3808562250

Fashionary Ltd. *Fashionpedia. The Visual Dictionary of Fashion Design.* Hong Kong: Fashionary International Ltd, 2016. ISBN 978-988-13547-6-1

Friend, R.L. *Sewing Room Technical Handbook: Lock-stitch and Overlock Seams.* Nottingham: Hatra, 1977. ISBN-10: 0901056022

## Selected Bibliography

Gerry Cooklin. *Introduction to Clothing Manufacture.* Blackwell Science; 2nd Edition, 2006. ISBN: 978-0-632-05846-4

Ghani, Suzaini Abdul. *Seam Performance: Analysis and Modeling*. PhD diss., University of Manchester, 2011. https://www.research.manchester.ac.uk/portal/files/54512390/FULL_TEXT.PDF

Glock, Ruth and Kunz, Grace. *Apparel Manufacturing: Sewn Product Analysis.* USA: Pearson Higher Ed USA; 4th edition, 2004. ISBN: 9780131119826

ISO. Textile. *Seam Types: Classification and Terminology.* ISO 4916-1991. Genève: ISO, 1991.

ISO. Textiles. *Stitch Types: Classification and Terminology.* ISO 4915-1991. Genève: ISO, 1991

Kabir, Sultana, and Ali. *Impact of Stitch Type and Stitch Density on Seam Properties.* Journal of Science and Research, 2016. https://pdfs.semanticscholar.org/5e30/1434ea134b064b5fc481b3104f82b83ff38e.pdf

Kennett, Frances. *Secrets of the Couturiers.* England: Orbis, 1985. ISBN 978-0-85613-818-5

Laing, R.M. and Webster, J. *Stitches and Seams.* UK: The Textile Institute, 1998. ISBN: 978-1870812733

Manuel Estany; *Diccionario Textil y del Vestir - Textile and Clothing Dictionary.* Spain: Manuel Estany, 1987. ISBN 84-404-0611-8

Shaeffer, Claire B. *Couture Sewing Techniques.* USA: The Taunton Press, 2011. ISBN 978-1-60085-335-7

Wesen Bryant, Michele and DeMers, Diane. *The Spec Manual.* USA: Fairchild Publications, Inc; 2001. ISBN 1-56367-373-8

Wood, Dorothy. *The Practical Encyclopedia of Sewing*. London: Lorenz Books, 2001. ISBN 0-7548-0277-9

Zampar, Hermenegildo and Poratto, María Laura. *Corte y Confección. Curso Fácil.* Argentina: Editorial Atlantida, 1998. ISBN 950-08-1954-6

# ACKNOWLEDGEMENTS

Heartfelt thanks to all the colleagues and friends who contributed their experience and support. Their suggestions were an invaluable input to bring this book to life:

Belén Asensio

Camila Aguirre Moura

Carolina Ines Fay

Cristina Molina Villar

Danae Wilson

Elisenda Vidiella Esteban

Eva Basagaña Rusiñol

Eva Gines Martin

Gabby BR

Gabriela Bondancia

Jane Cruise

Julieta Bernadó

Luciana Cervini

Marcelo Santisi

Marianela Fernández

Mina Park

Robert M. Cooper

Sheila López Rubio

Sonia Sayago Rodríguez

Velia Tuppin

Verónica López Orce

www.ingramcontent.com/pod-product-compliance
Lightning Source LLC
Chambersburg PA
CBHW051536010526
44107CB00064B/2747